THIRD EDITION: READY FOR YOUR CLOSE UP? AFRICAN AMERICANS AND INTERNATIONALS IN CINEMA WHO ARE COLLEGE GRADUATES

EXPANDED HONORABLE MENTION EDITION

by G. SHIELDS

Profiles of professional actors, actresses, athletes who transitioned to film, early pioneers, independent filmmakers, directors, producers, screenplay writers and a wide spectrum of international contribution.

POSITIVE PROGRESSION PUBLISHER

Third Edition: Ready For Your Close Up?
Copyright © 2021
Copyright © 2018
by G. Shields. All rights reserved.

No part of this publication may be reproduced, stored in a retrieval system or transmitted in any way by any means, electronic, mechanical, photocopy, recording or otherwise without the prior permission of the author except as provided by USA copyright law.

This book is designed to provide accurate and authoritative information with regard to the subject matter covered. This information is given with the understanding that neither the author nor Positive Progression Publisher is engaged in rendering legal, professional advice. Since the details of your situation are fact dependent, you should additionally seek the services of a competent professional.

Book design copyright © 2021 by Author, G. Shields
Book design copyright © 2018 by Author, G. Shields
Cover design by G. Shields
Graphic Art & Logo Design: Sheryl Rhoades
Formatted by: Vision Novels
Published in the United States of America
ISBN: 978-0-578-92188-4

1. Performing Arts / Film & Video / Reference
2. Reference / Biographical Dictionaries

REMAIN

Fueled By Intelligence and

Motivated By Love

CONTENTS

Foreword.. viii
Introduction... ix
Actors..1
From Athlete to Cinema..................................109
Early Pioneers of Cinema................................115
International Talent Established in the United States
and Indigenous African Cinema (Folk Life)............121
Producers, Directors, Screenwriters,
and Cinematographers................................... 135
The Independent Filmmakers............................ 161
List of Honorable Mentions............................. 171
List of Honorable International Mentions................172
Bibliography... 174
Index..178
Review Questions...185

FOREWORD

This book will reward academics and aficionados of cinema with its scholarly but straightforward overview of the contribution of African Americans and others to cinema. It also provides support for the role of academe as a viable path to success, which is especially significant for a population of readers who may be unaware of the rigor that supports success in the field. It is an informative and engaging read.

—Dr. Barbara Rhodes,
Emeritus Professor of Africana Studies

INTRODUCTION

*"There is no barrier to success which diligence
and perseverance cannot hurdle."*
—Oscar Micheaux,
first African American best-selling author
and independent filmmaker

The perception that people with a career in film; actors, directors, writers, cinematographers, had to work a succession of unrelated jobs, be well connected, use nepotism, or possess extraordinary beauty on the path to success may be true in some instances. However, there is a growing number employed in the mercurial world of cinema who choose to secure their future and create options to ensure a certain quality of life by way of graduation from college. Many artists employed in film work from project to project. Though the income can be very lucrative, there can be gaps in employment that call for alternate means to generate funds to maintain a satisfactory lifestyle. In other words, until consistent maximum earning potential can be sustained by plan A, make sure plan B is firmly in place. Some of the graduates profiled in this compilation of actors, directors, screenwriters, and cinematographers completed their undergraduate degree (AA, AS, BA, BFA, or BS), graduate degree (MA, MS, MBA, and MFA), and/or a professional degree (PhD, JD, etc.) before venturing into the world of cinema professionally. Others took a hiatus from their lucrative career after they attained financial security and earned a degree for their own confidence-building and self-gratification.

In no way does pursuit of higher education minimize the value of internships, practical experience, and innate talent that contribute to a sustainable living in creative arts or mega success. College is not necessarily for everyone, yet exposure (attending) and completion can elevate confidence and provide reinforcement in extremely competitive fields of endeavor such as film. This topical reference book is intended for avid film enthusiasts, as well. The filmographies hold a treasure trove of cinematic works to be discovered. The various films listed in profile filmographies completely cover the genre spectrum: adventure, science fiction, drama, comedy, documentary. Armed with advanced education while trying to make it in the film industry can make the difference between working too many hours in limited option employment to working fewer hours in a desirable position, earning considerably more until a major career breakthrough. Another advantage of higher education is the enhanced understanding of how to maintain an enriched quality of life that sole possession of money can't buy. When you attend a four-year college or university there is a core of general education courses (English, life science, history, etc.) that most of these institutions require along with your major (theater, drama, mass communication, business, or whatever your area of interest).

Advanced education is not just about financial gain although money can matter when it comes to inevitable circumstances that are going to take place over the course of a lifetime. The knowledge gained can be indispensable in everyday maintenance and invaluable in social interaction. Broad-based knowledge is a vista to a vast array of constructive ways to enjoyably spend leisure and free time, enabling you to navigate, relate, articulate, and interact comfortably in a varied set of circumstances, be it formal or casual. No matter what an individual's background is, impoverished or privileged, education always has been and always will be the great equalizer. What about choosing a major course of study and the cost of going to college or university? An academic and financial aid counselor on a high school or college campus can suggest and guide you through the decision-making process of what path best suits your particular situation. Although you always want to do your best, don't be discouraged if there is a stumbling block with grades, or finances aren't quite where you think they should be. If you desire an advanced education, there is always a way to gain acceptance. The educational process, especially when it's your choice, should be and usually is enjoyable. The list of profiled graduates is composed of talents that range from Samuel Jackson, David Oyelowo, Oprah Winfrey, Denzel Washington, Thandie Newton, and Spike Lee to Taye Diggs, Morris Chestnut, Taraji P. Henson, Kerry Washington, Steve McQueen, and Lupita Nyong'o, to name a few, and others who succeeded before and after them in their chosen academic and cinematic field.

A list of cinematic occupations is represented in the field of acting, directing, screenwriting, and cinematography. Although some profiled have been awarded honorary degrees, all listed had to have "earned" at least one accredited college-level degree. For each, there is a brief description that includes where he or she went to school, their major, and a brief background summary that includes a partial list of awards and movie-and-television work. The profiles in this book are employed primarily in cinema and may have television credits listed in the filmography. Artists who primarily and exclusively work in television require another worthwhile book. Referenced is a brief summary of how those who inspire, inform, and entertain achieved their cinematic goal.

*The associate of arts and associate of science category (AA, AS) are two-year degree programs. The bachelor of arts, bachelor of fine arts, bachelor of science category (BA, BFA, BS) are three-to-four year degree programs. A bachelor's program is commonly referred to as undergraduate school. After graduation as an undergraduate, taking it to the next level is graduate school. Graduate school usually requires an additional two years to earn the master of arts, master of fine arts, master of business, or master of science (MA, MFA, MBA, MS). For professional degrees such as law, medical doctor, and doctorate (JD, MD, PhD and EdD), the added length
of time can vary.

Historical Spotlight On

James Edwards (1918-1970), actor, film, and television writer. Edwards' shoulders are the shoulders every post-racial nonstereotyped person of African origin in the film industry stands on. He broke barriers in role portrayal as a film actor, and as a writer for television. Edwards was born in Muncie, Indiana. He majored in psychology at Knoxville College in Tennessee and graduated from Northwestern University where he received a master's degree in drama. He financed his education, as so many Americans, after an honorable discharge from military service. During World War II, he was commissioned as a first lieutenant in the U.S. Army. After appearing on stage with the Federal Theatre Project and touring with the New York stage play, *Deep Are the Roots*, Edwards landed his first film acting role in 1949 as a prizefighter in the movie, The *Set-Up*. Of his many acting credits, he is most recognized for the lead role of soldier, Peter Moss in the movie *Home of the Brave* (1949), which deals with racial bigotry. In the 1950s and 1960s Edwards wrote television episodes for several popular series including Westinghouse Desilu Playhouse. John Drew Barrymore starred in his 1958 television play *Silent Thunder*. In 1980 Edwards was inducted into the Black Filmmakers Hall of Fame.

Movie (actor): *Legend of the Northwest* (1978), *Doomsday Voyage* (1972), *Patton* (1970), *Coogan's Bluff* (1968), T*he Young Runaways* (1968), *The Sandpiper* (1965), **The Manchurian Candidate** (1962), *Blood and Steel* (1959), *Pork Chop Hill* (1959), *Night of the Quarter Moon* (1959), *Anna Lucasta* (1958), *Tarzan's Fight for Life* (1958), *Fräulein* (1958), *Battle Hymn* (1957), *Men in War* (1957), *The Killing* (1956), *The Phenix City Story* (1955), *Seven Angry Men* (1955), *African Manhunt* (1955), *The Caine Mutiny* (1954, uncredited), *The Joe Louis Story* (1953), *The Member of the Wedding* (1952), *Bright Victory* (1951), *The Steel Helmet* (1951), *Manhandled* (1949, uncredited), *Home of the Brave* (1949), *The Set-Up* (1949)

Television (writer, credited): *Law of the Plainsmen* (1960, season 1, episode 26), *Westinghouse Desilu Playhouse* (1958, season 1, episode 6), *Fireside Theatre* (1954, season 7, episode 6)

Television (actor): A wide range of episodic appearances from 1953 to 1969

ACTORS

An actor is a person (performer) whose profession is acting on stage, in movies, or other forms of broadcast such as television, radio, Internet, etc.

Tatyana Ali (1979), actress, producer, vocalist. Ali has grown from child performer into adulthood only to get better with age. From her debut on *Sesame Street* at age four to the film role of Jessie in Hotel California in 2008, Ali has managed to maintain a wholesome consistency in the film industry. Her major breakthrough was as Ashley Banks in the television megahit The Fresh Prince of Bel-Air in 1990–96. While Ali's career was in high gear, she chose to take a break and pursue a BA in African American history and in government from Harvard University. Upon graduation, she returned to acting, also taking on the role of producer. Her talent for singing was recognized when she appeared twice on Star Search in 1983. She demonstrated her singing ability on The Fresh Prince of Bel-Air and had a certified gold single, "Daydreamin'." A cause Ali embraces is Black Girls Rock, a nonprofit youth empowerment and mentoring organization established to promote the arts for young women of color and the way they are portrayed in the media. Ali was born in Long Island, New York.

Awards: Image Award, 2014, 2013, 2012, 2011, 1996; Young Star Award, 1997; Young Artist Award, 1991.

Movies (actress): *Supermodel* (2016), *November Rule* (2015), *Locker 13* (2014), *Home Again* (2012), *Dysfunctional Friends* (2012), *Pete Smalls Is Dead* (2010), *Privileged* (2010), *Mother and Child* (2009), *Locker 13: Down and Out* (2009), *Hotel California* (2008), *Glory Road* (2006), *Back in the Day* (2005), *Domino One* (2005), *National Lampoon Presents Dorm Daze* (2003), *The Brothers* (2001), *Brother* (2000), *Jawbreaker* (1999), *Fakin' Da Funk* (1997), *Kiss the Girls* (1997), *Crocodile Dundee II* (1988) Television (producer and actress): Love That Girl! (2010–14), *Buppies* (2009–10)

Television movies (actress): *Wrapped up in Christmas* (2017), *The Divorce* (2014), *Fall Into Darkness* (1996), *Kidz in the Wood* (1996)

Television (actress): *Second Generation Wayans* (2013), *The Young and the Restless* (2007–13), *The Fresh Prince of Bel-Air* (1990–96), *Sesame Street* (1985–90)

Debbie Allen (1950), actress, dancer, choreographer, director, producer, and writer. Allen is the daughter of orthodontist Andrew Arthur Allen Sr. and mother, poet and Pulitzer Prize nominee, Vivian Allen. Born in Houston, Texas, Allen has two brothers, Andrew and Hugh, and a sister, actress Phylicia Rashad. After graduation from Howard University with a BFA in classical Greek literature, speech, and theater, Allen set her sights on the Broadway stage. Initially cast as a dancer in the New York stage production of *Purlie* in 1970, Allen continued performing as an actress, director, and choreographer for the stage while garnering awards in several Broadway productions, which include *Raisin, Ain't Misbehavin', West Side Story, Sweet Charity,* and *Cat on a Hot Tin Roof.* The multifaceted performer's extensive film and television credits as actress, director, producer, and choreographer include *Fame* (film and television series), *A Different World, Stompin' at the Savoy, Girlfriends,* and *The Game.* Films projects early in her career were *The Fish that Saved Pittsburgh, Jo Jo Dancer, Your Life Is Calling,* and *Amistad.* For her stage performances, Allen is the recipient of the Drama Desk Award and Tony Award. She owns and operates the Debbie Allen Dance Academy in Los Angeles for boys and girls, age four to eighteen in all the major dance techniques. Allen is married to former NBA player, businessman, and sports analyst Norm Nixon. They have three children, DeVaughn, Vivian, and Norm Jr.

Awards: Essence Black Women in Hollywood (2016), Nevada Ballet Theatre's Woman of the Year (2014), PGA (Producers Guild of America) Award (1998), Acapulco Black Film Festival Award (1998), Image Award (1995), Star on the Walk of Fame (1991), Emmy Award (1991, 1983, 1982), Golden Globe Award (1983), Golden Apple Award (1982)

Movies (producer): *The Painting* (2001), *Amistad* (1997)

Movie (director, actor): *Out-of-Sync* (1995)

Movies (actress): *Fame* (2009), *Next Day Air* (2009), *Tournament of Dreams* (2007), *The Painting* (2001), *All About You* (2001), *Everything's Jake* (2000), *Mona Must Die* (1994), *Blank Check* (1994), *Jo Jo Dancer, Your Life Is Calling* (1986), *Ragtime* (1981), *Fame* (1980), *The Fish that Saved Pittsburgh* (1979)

Television movie (producer, director, actress): *The Old Settler* (2001)

Television movies (producer): *Martin Luther King Special One Day* (1998), *The Boys* (1992)

Television (producer): *Grey's Anatomy* (2015-18), *My Parents, My Sister & Me* (2009–10), *Fame* (2003), *Cool Women* (documentary, 2002), *A Different World* (1988–1993), *Fame* (1983–85)

Television movie (director and actress): *Stompin' at the Savoy* (1992)

Television movies (director): *Life Is Not a Fairytale: the Fantasia Barrino Story* (2006), *Martin Luther King Special One Day* (1998), *The Boys* (1992), *Polly Comin' Home!* (1990), *Polly* (1989)

Television movies (actress): *Grace* (2011), *Michael Jordan: An American Hero* (1999)

Television (director): *Grey's Anatomy* (2010–18), *Hellcats* (2010–11), *My Parents, My Sister & Me* (2009–10), *Everybody Hates Chris* (2006–09), *Girlfriends* (2005–08), *All of Us* (2003–07), *I Was a Network Star* (TV documentary) (2006), *That's So Raven* (2004–06), *The Jamie Fox Show* (1997–98), *The Sinbad Show* (1993–94), *A Different World* (1998–99), *Sinbad: Afros and Bellbottoms* (TV Documentary) (1993), *Quantum Leap,* (1991–93), *The Fresh Prince of Bel-Air* (1990), *Family Ties* (1987–88), *Fame* (1984–87)

Television (actress): *Grey's Anatomy* (2011–18), *In the House* (1995–96), *A Different World* (1988–93), *Fame* (1982–87)

John Amos (1939), actor. After attending Long Beach City College, Long Beach, California, Amos graduated from Colorado State University with a degree in sociology. The Emmy-nominated actor is recognized mostly for acting in several popular television series. In the 1974–76 runaway success *Good Times*, he was head of the household,

James Evans Jr., along with appearances in the groundbreaking miniseries *Roots* in 1977 and *Mary Tyler Moore* in 1970–77. Numerous big-screen roles followed, which include the 1970s African American film renaissance era's *Sweet Sweetback's Baadasssss Song and Let's Do It Again*. *Die Hard 2* and *Ricochet* were released in the early '90s and *Madea's Witness Protection* in 2012. Like many actors, he honed his craft appearing on stage. Unlike many actors, he held positions that could have sufficed as fully sustainable careers to build upon before he decided to act. After college, Amos was at one time a social worker and an advertising copywriter. He also played semiprofessional football and was a Golden Gloves boxing champion. Predominantly credited as an actor, early in his career, circa 1969, Amos was a writer for *The Leslie Uggams Show*. In 2014 he executive produced a television documentary titled *Althea* based on the life of tennis great Althea Gibson.

Awards: TV Land Award (2007), Impact Award (2006), Groundbreaking Show Award (2004)

Movies: *Act of Faith* (2014), *Madea's Witness Protection* (2012), *Perfect Sunday* (2010), *The Players Club* (1998), *Ricochet* (1991), *Die Hard 2* (1990), *Coming to America* (1988), *Let's Do It Again* (1975), *Sweet Sweetback's Baadasssss Song* (1971)

Television movies: *Untitled Martin Lawrence Project* (2012), *Voodoo Moon* (2006), *Disappearing Acts* (2000), *The Rockford Files: Shootout at the Old Pagoda* (1997), *Alcatraz: The Whole Shocking Story* (1980), *Willa* (1979), *Cops and Robin* (1978), *Keeping Up with the Joneses* (1972)

Television: *The Ranch* (2016-17), *Two and Half Men* (2010), *Men in Trees* (2006–08), *The West Wing* (1999–2004), *All About the Andersons* (2003–04), *The District* (2000–01), *In the House* (1995–97), *The Fresh Prince of Bel-Air* (1994–95), *704 Hauser* (1994), *Hunter* (1984–89), *Future Cop* (1976–77), *Mary Tyler Moore* (1970–1977), *Roots* (1977), *Good Times* (1974–76), *Maude* (1973–74), *Love, American Style* (1971–72)

Margaret Avery (1944), actress. Methodical and practical Avery earned a BA in Education at San Francisco State University prior to full time pursuance of an acting career. She was born in Mangum, Oklahoma. Immediately recognized as the character Shug in the 1985 classic, *The Color Purple,* Avery taught in the Los Angeles Unified School District before her commitment to acting full time. Along with being nominated for an Oscar for best supporting actress in *The Color Purple* she won The Los Angeles Drama Critics Circle Award for the stage play "*Does A Tiger Wear A Necktie?*" in 1973. Since 2013 she has majestically filled the role of matriarch on the television series *Being Mary Jane.* In 2017 she won the Massachusetts Film Festival Award for best actress in a film short titled *Symposium.* Avery is acknowledged for her work with at risk teenagers and women.

Movies: *Proud Mary* (2018), *Welcome Home, Roscoe Jenkins* (2008), *White Man's Burden* (1995), *Lightning in a Bottle* (1993), *The Return of Superfly* (1990), *Riverbend* (1989), *Blueberry Hill* (1988), *The Color Purple* (1985), *The Fish That Saved Pittsburgh* (1979), *Which Way Is Up?* (1977), *Hell Up in Harlem* (1973), *Cool Breeze* (1972)

Television Movies: *The Jacksons: An American Dream* (1992), *Heat Wave* (1990), *The Sky Is Gray* (1980), *Scott Joplin* (1977), *Louis Armstrong-Chicago Style* (1976)

Television: *Being Mary Jane* (2013–18), *Harry O* (1974–76)

Rochelle Aytes (1976), actress. Raised in Harlem and born in New York City, Aytes achieved leading-lady status in the 2013 television drama *Mistresses*, and as a major cast member the same year in the biographic television movie *CrazySexyCool: The TLC Story.* Having graduated as a dance major with a BA in fine arts from State University of New York in Purchase, Aytes first gained major attention in *White Chicks* in 2004 and as Lisa in *Madea's Family Reunion* in 2006.

Movies: *The Inheritance* (2011), *Trick 'r Treat* (2007), *Madea's Family Reunion* (2006), *White Chicks* (2004)

Television movies: *Doomsday* (2017), *CrazySexyCool: The TLC Story* (2013), *Mistresses* (2009), *13 Graves* (2006)

Television: *Designated Survivor* (2017-18), *Mistresses* (2013–16), *Desperate Housewives* (2011), *Detroit 1-8-7* (2010–11), *The Forgotten* (2009–10), *Drive* (miniseries) (2007)

Angela Bassett (1958), actress, producer. Bassett was born in Harlem, New York, and reared in St. Petersburg, Florida. Bassett was exceedingly active in Boca Ciega High School extracurricular activities. A member of the student government, debate team, drama club, and choir, Bassett was cheerleading when she wasn't studying. Upon high school graduation, Bassett attended Yale University on a scholarship and graduated with a BA in African American studies. She went on to earn an MFA from the Yale School of Drama. Privy to some of the more substantial roles offered in Hollywood blockbusters such as *What's Love Got to Do with It, Waiting to Exhale*, and *How Stella Got Her Groove Back,* were catalyst for her stratospheric rise to the A list. Bassett possesses a strong work ethic. She honed her craft on stage with the Yale Repertory Theatre and the Pasadena Playhouse in California.

Awards (select): Gracie Allen Award (2016), Win Award (2013), LA Femme Film Festival (2010), TV Land Award (2009), Image Award (2009, 2003, 2002, 2000, 1999, 1996,1995), Star on the Walk of Fame (2008), Black Movie Award (2006), Black Reel Award (2003, 2002), Women in Film Crystal Award (1996), Golden Globe Award (1994), Golden Apple Award (1994)

Movies (actress): *Black Panther* (2018), *London Has Fallen* (2015), *Survivor* (2015), *Sea Isle* (2014), *Black Nativity* (2013), *Olympus Has Fallen* (2013), *This Means War* (2012), *Green Lantern* (2011), *Jumping the Broom* (2011), *Notorious* (2009), *Meet the Browns* (2008), *Akeelah and the Bee* (2006), *The Lazarus Child* (2005), *Mr. 3000* (2004), *Masked and Anonymous* (2003), *Sunshine State* (2002), *The Score* (2001), *Boesman and Lena* (2000), *Whispers: An Elephant's Tale* (2000), *Supernova* (2000), *Music of the Heart* (1999), *How Stella Got Her Groove Back* (1998), *Contact* (1997), *Waiting to Exhale* (1995), *Strange Days* (1995), *Panther* (1995), *Vampire in Brooklyn* (1995), *What's Love Got to Do with It* (1993), *Malcolm X* (1992), *Innocent Blood* (1992), *Passion Fish* (1992), *Critters 4* (1992), *City of Hope* (1991), *Boyz n the Hood* (1991), *Kindergarten Cop* (1990)

Television movies (producer and actress): *The Rosa Parks Story* (2002), *Ruby's Bucket of Blood* (2001)

Television documentary (director): *Breakthrough* (2015)

Television movies (actress): *Betty and Coretta* (2013), *Identity*

(2011), *Time Bomb* (2006), *The Jacksons: An American Dream* (1992)
   Television (producer and actress): *9-1-1* (2018)
   Television movie (director): *Whitney* (2015)
   Television (actress) *American Horror Story* (2013–16).
   Independent Lens: *"Daisy Bates: First Lady of Little Rock"* (documentary) (2012), *The Simpsons* (2010), *ER* (2008–09), *Alias* (2005), *Freedom: A History of Us* (documentary) (2003)

Michael Beach (1963), actor, producer. Beach graduated from the Juilliard School. While attending Juilliard, performing arts conservatory located in the Lincoln Center for the Performing Arts in New York City, he won the Drama Award for Outstanding Achievement in 1984 and the New York Shakespeare Festival Award. Born in Boston, Massachusetts, his ambition prior to acting was to be a professional football player. Beach continually worked in film and television throughout the 1980s and 90s. He entered the ranks of the recognizable actor in *Waiting to Exhale* in 1995. With reoccurring roles in television series *ER* and *Third Watch*, his screen presence was established.
   Awards: Image Award (2003), Golden Globe Award (1994)
   Movies (producer): *Scrapper* (also actor) (2013), *America the Beautiful* (documentary) (2007)
   Movies (actor): *Insidious: Chapter 2* (2013), *Things Never Said* (2013) *Red Dawn* (2012), *Sparkle* (2012), *Pastor Brown* (2009), *Hell Ride* (2008), *First Sunday* (2008), *Soul Food* (1997), *Casualties* (1997), *A Family Thing* (1996), *Waiting to Exhale* (1995), *Bad Company* (1995), *True Romance* (1993), *Short Cuts* (1993), *Lean on Me* (1989)
   Television movie (actor): *Playing Father* (2012), *Justice for Natalee Holloway* (2011), *Gimme Shelter* (2010), *Night and Day* (2010), *Relative Stranger* (2009), *Critical Assembly* (2009), *Ruby Ridges* (1998), *Ms. Scrooge* (1997), *Rebound: The Legend of Earl 'The Goat' Manigault* (1996), *Midnight Run for Our Life* (1994), *Final Appeal* (1993), *Fire: Trapped on the 37th Floor* (1991), *Dangerous Passion* (1990), *Open Admissions* (1998), *Weekend War* (1988), *Vengeance: The Story of Tony Cimo* (1986)
   Television (actor): *The 100* (2016), *The Client List* (2013), *The Game* (2011–15), *Sons of Anarchy* (2010–14), *League* (2004–06), *Third Watch*

(1999–2005), *Spawn* (1999), *Stargate Atlantis* (2007–09), *Brothers & Sisters* (2006), *Sweet Justice, ER* (1994–97), *NYPD Blue* (1994)

Jennifer Beals (1963), actress. In 1983, Beals set precedence as a woman of color taking the lead in the "general audience" motion picture *Flashdance*. Beals is a graduate of Yale University with a BA in American literature. She was born in Chicago. The role in *Flashdance* came after an unaccredited role in the 1980 film My Bodyguard while still in high school. She was inspired by stage plays. During Beals' freshman year in college, she auditioned for *Flashdance*. After the film wrapped, she returned to Yale immediately and completed her studies before continuing to pursue her film career. The actress later broke barriers in the lead role of Bette Porter in the television series *The L Word* (2004–09). Beals is also an accomplished photographer with a book of her work entitled *The L Word*. All proceeds from the book go to charities Matthew Shepard Foundation, advocating the eradication of gay hate crimes; the Pablove Foundation, seeking cures for childhood cancer; and the I Live Here Projects, empowering those who live in extreme poverty. Beals is also an advocate for environmental and lesbian, gay, bisexual, transgender issues.

Awards: GLAAD Media Award (2005), Cinequest San Jose Film Festival Award (1999), Satellite Award (1998), Image Award (1984)

Movies: *The Book of Eli* (2010), *Runaway Jury* (2003), *Fear of Flying* (1999), *Devil in a Blue Dress* (1995), *In the Soup* (1992), *Split Decision* (1988), *Vampire's Kiss* (1988), *Flashdance* (1983)

Television movies: *Proof* (2014), *A Wife's Nightmare* (2014), *Westside* (2013), *Widow Detective* (2012), *The Night Before the Night Before Christmas* (2010), *My Name Is Sarah* (2007), *They Shoot Divas, Don't They?* (2002), *Feast of All Saints* (2001), *After the Storm* (2001), *The Big House* (2001), *A House Divided* (2000), *Without Malice* (2000), *The Spree* (1998), *Night Owl* (1993), *Indecency* (1992), *Terror Stalks the Class Reunion* (1992), *The Madonna and the Dragon* (1990)
Television: *Taken* (2017-18) *Proof* (2015), *Lauren* (2012-13), *The Mob Doctor* (2012–13), *Castle* (2012), *The Chicago Code* (2012), *Lie to Me* (2009–10), *The L Word* (2004–09)

Darryl Bell (1963), actor. Bell personified comedic college fraternity roles in the movie *School Daze* in 1988 and television series *A Different World* in 1987–1993. A graduate of Syracuse University and born in Chicago, Illinois, Bell's father, Travers J. Bell, founded the first African American firm on the New York Stock Exchange.

Movies (actor): *Brother* (2001), New Jersey Turnpikes (1999), *Mr. Wright* (1994), *School Daze* (1988)

Television movie (producer): *Bill Cosby: Far from Finished* (2013)

Television movie (actor): *Beverley Hills S.U.V.* (2004), *Black Scorpion* (1995)

Television (actor): Househusbands of Hollywood (2009), For Your Love (1999), Cosby (1997), Homeboys in Outer Space (1996–97), Living Single (1996), A Different World (1987–1992)

Bill Bellamy (1965), actor, producer, writer, comedian. While attending Rutgers University studying for his BA in economics, Bellamy, at the urging of friends, entered a male beauty pageant and created a comedic stand-up routine for the talent category. The routine met with so much success he knew after graduation he would pursue a career as a comedian. He has quoted his mother telling him, "Make sure you get your education because they can never take that away from you." The Newark, New Jersey–native gained national screen attention on Russel Simon's Def Comedy Jam. Television success led to film. In 1997, Love Jones and How to Be a Player, along with Any Given Sunday in 1999, showcased his appeal as an actor.

Movies (actor): *Kindergarten Cop 2* (2016), *Lottery Ticket* (2010), *Neverwas* (2005), *Buying the Cow* (2002), *The Brothers* (2001), *Any Given Sunday* (1999), *Love Stinks* (1999), *How to Be a Player* (1997), *Love Jones* (1997), *Fled* (1996), *Who's the Man?* (1993), *Joey Breaker* (1993)

Television (producer): *Mr. Box Office* (2012–13), *Bill Bellamy: Crazy Sexy Dirty* (2012), *Who's Got Jokes?* (2006)

Television (writer): *Def Comedy Jam* (2006), *Back to My Roots* (TV movie) (2005), *Bill Bellamy: Booty Call* (documentary) (1996)

Television movies (actor): *Getting Played* (2006), *Amy Coyne* (2006)

Television (actor): *Hot in Cleveland* (2014), *Mr. Box Office* (2012–13), *October Road* (2007–08), *Fastlane* (2002–03), *Men, Women & Dogs* (2001–02), *Cousin Skeeter* (1998–2001), *The Bill Bellamy Show* (1996), *MTV Beach House* (1993)

Tempest Bledsoe (1973), actress. Bledsoe's primary medium is television although she has made forays onto the big screen. Born in Chicago, Illinois, Bledsoe is a graduate of New York University Stern School of Business with a BA in finance. She started out as a child actor on the iconic *The Cosby Show* (1984–1992) as daughter Vanessa Huxtable and made a graceful transition to adult actress starring in the television series Guys with Kids.
Awards: TV Land Award (2011), Black Filmmakers Hall of Fame Award (1992), Young Artist Award (1989)
Movies: *ParaNorman* (voice) (2012), *N-Secure* (2010), *BachelorMan* (2003), *Johnny B Good* (1998)
Television movies: *Husband for Hire* (2008), *Fire & Ice* (2001), *The Expendables* (2000), *Santa and Pete* (1999), *Dream Date* (1989), *Dance Till Dawn* (1988)
Television: *Guys with Kids* (2012–13), *Vietnam in HD* (2011, voice), *The Replacements* (2008–09), *South of Nowhere* (2006), *The Practice* (1998), *The Cosby Show* (1984–1992)

Chadwick Boseman (1977), actor. Not one to be trifled with, Boseman is quick to inform he is a proactive "artist" who does not sit and wait for an opportunity to present itself. The Howard University, fine arts major, born in Anderson, South Carolina, is also an award-winning producer, writer, director and editor. Boseman also studied at the British American Drama Academy in London, England. His stage experiences extend from acting in Shakespeare to collaboration with the Hip-Hop Theater Festival. He won the Hollywood Black Film Festival Award in 2008 for a short film, *Blood Over Broken Pawn*. His breakout film was *42,* with *Draft Day,* and *Get On Up* following very close behind. Between 2008 and 2010 he was a familiar face on the television series *Persons Unknown* and *Lincoln Heights*. In 2014 he won the CinemaCon, USA award for Male Star of Tomorrow. In 2018 he achieved stratospheric success in his portrayal of T'Challa in the movie, *Black Panther*.

Awards: BET Award (2018), MTV Movie + TV Award (2018), Santa Barbara International Film Festival (2015), CinemaCon, USA (2014), Hollywood Black Film Festival (2008)

Movies: *Avengers: Infinity War* (2018), *Black Panther* (2018), *Marshall* (2017), *Captain America: Civil War* (2016), *Gods of Egypt* (2016), *Get on Up* (2014), *Draft Day* (2014), *42* (2013)

Television: *Persons Unknown* (2010) and *Lincoln Heights* (2008–09).

Andre Braugher (1962), actor, producer. Braugher was a seasoned stage performer before embarking on a film career. He won an Obie Award for the title role in *Henry V* at New York City's Shakespeare in the Park. Braugher graduated with a BA in theatre from Stanford University and a master of fine arts from the Juilliard School. He was born in Chicago, Illinois. His irrepressibly intelligent demeanor, for the most part, has him cast as cerebral characters. He first impressed film audiences in 1989 with his portrayal of Corporal Thomas Searles in the movie classic *Glory*. His career gained momentum in 1993–98 on the television series *Homicide: Life on the Street*. Since then, numerous popular television series and film roles have followed including the movie *Salt* in 2010 and television series *Brooklyn Nine-Nine* in 2013.

Awards: Critics Choice Award (2016, 2014), Online Film & Television (2014), NAMIC Vision Award (2012), Black Reel Award (2007), Emmy Award (2006, 1998), Blockbuster Entertainment Award (2001), Television Critics Association Award (1998,1997), Viewers for Quality Television Award (1995)

Movies (actor): *The Gambler* (2014), *Salt* (2010), *Passengers* (2008), *The Mist* (2007), *Live* (2007), *Poseidon* (2006), *Duets* (2000), *Frequency* (2000), *All the Rage* (1999), *Thick as Thieves* (1999), *City of Angels* (1998), *Get on the Bus* (1996), *Striking Distance* (1993), *Glory* (1989)

Television (producer and actor): *10,000 Black Men Named George* (2002)

Television movies (actor): *Love Songs* (1999), *Murder in Mississippi*

(1990), *Kojak* (five separate tv movie sagas 1989-1990)
Television (actor): *Brooklyn Nine-Nine* (2013–19), *Last Resort* (2012–13), *House M.D.* (2009–12), *Law and Order: Special Victims Unit* (2011–15), *Men of a Certain Age* (2009–11), *The Andromeda Strain* (2008), *Thief* (2006), *Hack* (2002–04), *Gideon's Crossing* (2000–01), *Homicide: Life on the Street* (1993–98)

Golden Brooks (1970), actress. Brooks didn't leave a stone unturned before pursuing an acting career. The San Francisco, California born academician first earned a BA in sociology from University of California, Berkeley with a focus on media representation of minorities. She went on to obtain a master's in creative writing from Sarah Lawrence College. At UCB, she appeared in classic stage productions such as *Romeo and Juliet* and *For Colored Girls*. While attending Sarah Lawrence, she also studied and taught African ballet and modern dance. Brooks set fashion and upwardly mobile social trends along with the stellar ensemble cast on the groundbreaking television series *Girlfriends* from 2000–08. She also wrote one *Girlfriends* episode and directed another. Brooks lit up the big screen in *Beauty Shop* in 2005 and *Something New* in 2006. In 2012–13, she appeared in a reoccurring role on the television series *Hart of Dixie*.
Awards: American Black Film Festival Award (2011), BET Comedy Award (2004)
Movies (actress): *The Great Divide* (2012), *The Perfect Gift* (2011), *The Inheritance* (2011), *Polish Bar* (2010), *Something New* (2006), *Beauty Shop* (2005), *Imposter* (2001), *Timecode* (2000), *Hell's Kitchen* (1998), *Zero Stress* (1998)
Television movie (actress): *Second Chance Christmas* (2014), *In Sickness and in Health* (2012)
Television (actress): *Blunt Talk* (2015-16), *Hart of Dixie* (2012–13), *Girlfriends* (2000–08)

Roscoe Lee Browne (1925–2007), actor. Browne earned a BA in 1946 from Lincoln University in Pennsylvania. He continued post-graduate study in Middlebury College, Columbia University and at the University of Florence in Italy. Before he pursued an acting career, he taught comparative literature, French, and English. Widely recognized for his rich masterful command of language, Browne won an Obie Award and two Los Angeles Drama Circle Critics Awards for his stage performances. Browne was born in Woodbury, New Jersey, one of four sons to Baptist minister, Sylvanus S. Browne, and his wife, Lovie. He was one of the first African American actors to take on roles that were traditionally written for Euro American actors. Alternately, he appeared in one of the first race-conscious incendiary movies *Uptight* in 1968. Always in demand for stage, film, or television, his resonant baritone voice was often called upon for narrations in albums, tapes, CDs, and films.

Awards: Image Award (1988), Primetime Emmy Award (1986), Western Heritage Award (1972)

Movies: *Behind the Broken Words* (2003), *Treasure Planet* (2002), *Morgan's Ferry* (2001), *Dear God* (1996), *Babe* (1995), *The Mambo Kings* (1992), *Oliver & Company* (1988), *Nothing Personal* (1980), *Twilight's Last Gleaming* (1977), *Logan's Run* (1976), *Uptown Saturday Night* (1974), *Super Fly T.N.T.* (1973), *Cisco Pike* (1972). *The Cowboys* (1972), *The Liberation of L.B. Jones* (1970), **Topaz** (1969), *Me and My Brother* (1969), *Uptight* (1968), *The Comedians* (1967), *Black Like Me* (1964), *Terror in the City* (1964), *The Connection* (1962)

Television movies: *Hamlet* (2000), *Hard Time: The Premonition* (1999), *The Notorious 7* (1997), *You Must Remember This* (1992), *Lady in the Corner* (1989), *Stuck with Each Other* (1989), *John Grin's Christmas* (1986), *Dr. Scorpion* (1978), *The Big Rip-Off* (1975), *Rex Harrison Presents Stories of Love* (1974), *Swing Out, Sweet Land* (1970)

Television: *Spider-Man: The Animated Series* (1995–98), *Cosby* (1996), *SeaQuest 2032* (1993–94), *A Different World* (1988–92), *Ring Raiders* (1989), *Falcon Crest* (1988), *Visionaries: Knights of the Magical Light* (1987), *The Cosby Show* (1986–87), *Soap* (1980–81), *Miss Winslow and Son* (1979), *King* (TV miniseries) (1978), *All in the Family* (1972–73), *Mannix* (1968), *East Side/West Side* (1963)

Vanessa Bell Calloway (1957), actress, dancer. Calloway danced with Alvin Ailey, George Faison, and Otis Salid. Her career launch was as a dancer in the Broadway production of Dreamgirls. Calloway's birthplace is Cleveland, Ohio. She received a BFA degree with a concentration in dance from Ohio University. Her breakout film role was as Imani Izzi in *Coming to America* (1988). Calloway's career continues to thrive in film and television with reoccurring roles on a variety of series including *Shameless* and *Rizzoli & Isles*. The mother of two daughters, she and her husband, Dr. Anthony Calloway, are steadfast advocates for the homeless.

Movies (actress): *The Obama Effect* (2012), *A Beautiful Soul* (2012), *The Last Fall* (2012), *The Undershepherd* (2012), *The Killing of Wendy* (2009), *Truly Blessed* (2009), *Lakeview Terrace* (2008), *Stompin'* (2007), *Cheaper by the Dozen* (2003), *Love Don't Cost a Thing* (2003), *Biker Boyz* (2003), *Bad Boy* (2002), *All About You* (2001), *The Brothers* (2001), *Crimson Tide* (1995), *The Inkwell* (1994), *What's Love Got to Do with It* (1993), *Bebe's Kids* (1992), *Death Spa* (1989), *Coming to America* (1988), *Number One with a Bullet* (1987)

Television movie (producer, writer, and host): *In the Company of Friends* (2013)

Television movies (actress): *Love Once and Always* (2018), *Between Sisters* (2013), *Pryor Offences* (2004), *The Red Sneakers* (2002), *Love Song* (2000), *The Temptations* (1998), *The Cherokee Kid* (1996), *America's Dream* (1996), *Stompin'at the Savoy* (1992), *Memphis* (1992), *Polly: Comin' Home!* (1990), *Polly* (1989), *The Return of Desperado* (1988)

Television (actress): *Saints & Sinners* (2016-18), *Shameless* (2011–15), *Rizzoli & Isles* (2012–13), *Hawthorne* (2010–11), *All of Us* (2006), *The District* (2003–04), *10-8: Officers on Duty* (2003–04), *Boston Public* (2001), *Under One Roof* (1995), *Rhythm & Blues* (1992-93), *Equal Justice* (1990), *All My Children* (1985)

Cedric The Entertainer aka **Cedric Antonio Kyles** (1964), actor, comedian, writer and producer. Living up to his show business name, Cedric is the consummate entertainer. Born in Johnson City, Missouri, Cedric graduated from Southeast Missouri State University with a BA in Mass Communication. Prior to performing as a stand-up comic he was at one time a substitute high school teacher, and at another, an insurance agent. Comic television appearances on shows such as BET's Comicview and Def Comedy Jam paved the way to a successful television serial, hosting and cinematic career. The Steve Harvey Show, 1996-2002 and the movie Barbershop in 2002 were pivotal to the start of Cedric's television and film pursuit. His talent as actor, creator, writer, producer is evident in the television show, The Soul Man, 2012-15. Cedric is active in community outreach through his "Cedric the Entertainer Charitable Foundation" where the focus is college scholarships.

Awards: Gotham Award (2007), St. Louis International Film Festival (2005), BET Comedy Award (2004), Image Award, (2003, 2002, 2001, 2000, 1999), Washington, DC Area Film Critics Association Award (2002) Movies (actor and producer): The Honeymooners (2005), Johnson Family Vacation (2004)

Movies (actor): *Barbershop: The Next Cut* (2016), *Top Five* (2014), *Planes: Fire & Rescue* (2014), *A Haunted House 2* (2014), *Planes* (2013), *A Haunted House* (2013), *Larry Crowne* (2011), *Cadillac Records* (2008), *Welcome Home, Roscoe Jenkins* (2008), *Talk to Me* (2007), *Barbershop 2: Back in Business* (2004), *Barbershop* (2002), *Big Mama's House* (2000)

Television (actor): *The Last O.G.* (2018), *The Soul Man* (2012-16), *The Proud Family* (2001-05), *The Steve Harvey Show* (1996-2002)

Gaius Charles (1983), actor. Deeply religious, Charles took a break from acting soon after his career took off to pursue a master's in theology from Drew University. He was born in New York, New York. Charles' major career break occurred with the network television hit *Friday Night Lights*, almost immediately after graduation from Carnegie Mellon University with a BA in drama. His stage preparation took place while in junior high school, high school, and college. Charles' film credits include *The Messenger* in 2009 followed by *Salt* and *Takers* in 2010. The medium of television has been great for Charles stepping into the reoccurring role of Dr. Shane Ross in *Grey's Anatomy* starting in 2012–13.

Movies: *Takers* (2010), Salt (2010), *Toe to Toe* (2009). *The Messenger* (2009),

Television: *Taken* (2017), *Aquarius* (2015-16, *Grey's Anatomy* (2012–14), *Necessary Roughness* (2012), *Friday Night Lights* (2006–08)

Don Cheadle (1964), actor, producer, author, philanthropist. Cheadle majored in acting and graduated with a BA in fine arts from California Institute of the Arts. He is a native of Kansas City, Missouri. Cheadle combines A-list actor success with social consciousness. He has used his celebrity status to champion causes from humanitarian to environmental. Cheadle initially drew attention on the big screen for his portrayal as Mouse Alexander in *Devil in a Blue Dress* and won best supporting actor awards from the Los Angeles Film Critics Association and the National Society of Film Critics. He combined his acting and producing skills in societal-issue films *Hotel Rwanda*, for which he was nominated for the Academy Award for Best Actor, and *Crash*, which won the Academy Award for Best Picture in 2005. In 2007, along with actor George Clooney, Cheadle was presented the Summit Peace Award by the Nobel Peace Prize Laureates for their labor to halt genocide and alleviate the suffering in Darfur, Africa. In 2007, Cheadle coauthored a book with John Prendergast, *Not on Our Watch: The Mission to End Genocide in Darfur and Beyond*. Cheadle teamed up with Prendergast again in 2010 to publish *The Enough Moment: Fighting to End Africa's Worst Human Rights Crimes*.

Awards (select): Grammy Award (2017), Image Award (2016, 2013), Golden Globes Award (2013, 1999) Black Reel Award (2012, 2006, 2001, 2000), BAFTA/LA Britannia Award (2008), Broadcast Film Critic Association Award (2008, 2006), BET Award (2007), Gotham Award (2007, 2004), ShoWest Convention, USA Award (2007), Independent Spirit Award (2006), Screen Actors Guild Award (2006, 2001), Black Movie Award (2005), Satellite Award (2005), San Diego Film Critics Society (2004), Florida Film Critics Circle Award (1998), National Society of Film Critics Award (1996), Los Angeles Film Critics Award (1995) Movie (producer, director, writer, actor): Miles Ahead (2015)

Movies (producer and actor): *The Guard* (2011), *Talk to Me* (2007), *Crash* (2004)

Movies (producer): *St. Vincent de Van Nuys* (2014), *Traitor* (2008), *Darfur Now* (documentary) (2007)

Movies (actor): *Avengers: Infinity War* (2018), *Captain America: Civil War* (2016), *Avengers: Age of Ultron* (2015), *Iron Man 3* (2013),

Flight (2012), *Iron Man 2* (2010), *Brooklyn's Finest* (2009), *Hotel for Dogs* (2009), *Traitor* (2008), *Ocean's Thirteen* (2007), *Reign Over Me* (2007), *The Dog Problem* (2006), *Ocean's Twelve* (2004), *After the Sunset* (2004), *Hotel Rwanda* (2004), *The Assassination of Richard Nixon* (2004), *The United States of Leland* (2003), *Ocean's Eleven* (2001), *Rush Hour 2* (2001), *Swordfish* (2001), *Manic* (2001), *Thing Behind the Sun* (2001), *Traffic* (2000), *The Family Man* (2000), *Mission to Mars* (2000), *Out of Sight* (1998), *Bulworth* (1998), *Boogie Nights* (1997), *Volcano* (1997), *Rosewood* (1997), *Devil in a Blue Dress* (1995), *The Meteor Man* (1993), *Roadside Prophets* (1992), *Colors* (1988), *Hamburger Hill* (1987), *Moving Violations* (1985)

Television movies (actor): *Make Your Own Superbowl Ad* (2006), *Fail Safe* (2000), *A Lesson Before Dying* (1999), *The Rat Pack* (1998), *Rebound: The Legend of Earl 'The Goat' Manigault* (1996), *Lush Life* (1993)

Television (producer, director, actor): *House of Lies* (2012–16)

Television (producer): *Crash* (2008–2009)

Television (Actor): *Independent Lens: Death of a Shaman* (2003), *ER* (2002), *Picket Fences*, (1993–95), *The Golden Palace* (1992–93), *Fame* (1986)

Morris Chestnut (1969), actor, producer. Self-described as being very private, Chestnut was born in Cerritos, California. He majored in finance with a minor in drama, earning a BA from California State University, Northridge. He made an enduring impression as Rickey Baker in his freshman 1991 film *Boyz in the Hood*. In the '90s, Chestnut kept afloat as a working actor in projects that include the lead in the 1993 television movie *The Ernest Green Story*. With his 1999 appearance in *The Best Man*, he crossed over into the comfortable position of being consistently cast as a lead in substantial projects. Chestnut has stated that his heroes are his mother and father.

Award: Acapulco Black Film Festival (2014), Image Award (2014)

Movies (producer and actor): *When the Bough Breaks* (2016), *Not Easily Broken* (2009)

Movies (actor): *The Best Man Wedding* (2016), *The Perfect Guy* (2015), *The Best Man Holiday* (2013), *Kick-Ass 2* (2013), *The Call*

(2013), *Identity Thief* (2013), *Think Like a Man* (2012), *The Perfect Holiday* (2007), *The Game Plan* (2007), *Ladder 49* (2004), *Breakin' All the Rules* (2004), *Confidence* (2003), *Half Past Dead* (2002), *Like Mike* (2002), *Two Can Play That Game* (2001), *The Brothers* (2001), *The Best Man* (1999), *G.I. Jane* (1997), *Under Siege 2: Dark Territory* (1995), The Inkwell (1994), *The Last Boy Scout* (1991), *Boyz n the Hood* (1991)

Television movies (actor): *The Prince of Motor City* (2008), *Dante* (2005), *The Killing Yard* (2001), *Firehouse* (1997), *The Ernest Green Story* (1993), In the Line of Duty: Street War (1992)

Television (actor): *Goliath* (2018), *Rosewood* (2015-17), *Legends* (2014-15), *Nurse Jackie* (2013–2014), *American Horror Story* (2011), *V* (2009–11), *ER* (2000), *C-16: FBI* (1997–98), *Living Single* (1994), *Out All Night* (1992–93)

Ji-Tu Cumbuka (1940-2017), actor. A native of Helena, Alabama, Cumbuka, one of seven children born to Reverend Cleveland and Mrs. Mary Holifield, is a veteran of the renaissance African American/Blaxploitation film era of the late 1960s and all of the 1970s. One of the busiest actors in Hollywood well into the '90s, Cumbuka graduated with a BA in telecommunications and an MA in cinematography from Columbia College, Tarzana, California. He transitioned into film as a result of his working every aspect of the stage from designing and building sets to acting with the Performing Arts Society of Los Angeles (PASLA). He earned his degrees while supporting a family as a husband and father, working for the United States Postal Service between film roles until his acting career stabilized. His reputation in the African American film community was as an advocate for fair treatment and equality. On the set of the television miniseries *Roots* (1977), he stopped production until real chains, which could have sunk actors on ship had one fallen overboard, were replaced with plastic replicas. He worked tirelessly with the Black Stuntmen's Association for equity in film and television. Drawing from service as a former All Army athlete, he formed the Hollywood Sharpshooters, a celebrity basketball team with players that included Jim Brown, Fred Williamson, Roger Mosley, and Tony King to play for charitable causes. His first movie role was as Rick in the vanguard revolutionary film *Uptight* (1968). His dashing six-foot-five frame made quite an impact as the wise wrestler in *Roots*. In the 1976 Academy Award winner *Bound for Glory*, his character, Slim Snedeger, Complimented actor David Carradine's portrayal of Woody Guthrie. Cumbuka was also a fine-arts painter and screenwriter.

Movies: *Caged in Paradiso* (1990), *Harlem Nights* (1989), *Glitch* (1988), *Moving* (1988), *Outrageous Fortune* (1987), *Out of Bounds* (1986), *Volunteers* (1985), *Brewster's Millions* (1985), *Bachelor Party* (1984), *Walk Proud* (1979), *Angela* (1978), *Fun with Dick and Jane* (1977), *Bound for Glory* (1976), *Dr. Black and Mr. Hyde* (1976), *Mandingo* (1975), *Lost in the Stars* (1974), *Maurie* (1973), *Trader Horn* (1973), *Up the Sandbox* (1973), *Blacula* (1972), *Top of the Heap* (1972), *Change of Habit* (1969), *Uptight* (1968) Television movies: *Sister Margaret and the Saturday Night Ladies* (1987), *Death Ray 2000* (1981), *Flesh & Blood* (1979), *Ebony, Ivory and Jade* (1979), *The Jericho Mile* (1979), *Mandrake* (1979)

Television: *Knot's Landing* (1990), *Matlock* (1989), *Hunter* (1986–87), *The A-Team* (1985), *A Man Called Sloane* (1979), *Young Dan'l Boone* (1977), *Roots* (1977), *Kojak* (1973–74), *Ironside* (1974)

Viola Davis (1965), actress. Davis majored in theater and a little over a decade later, received an honorary doctorate from Rhode Island College in fine arts. After receiving her BA from Rhode Island College and relocation to New York, Davis attended the Juilliard School of Performing Arts. Davis took her classical training to the stage, performing at the Lincoln Center in New York City, the New York Shakespeare Festival, and on Broadway. For her stage work, she has won a Tony Award, Drama Desk Award, and Outer Critics Circle Award. Davis, the second of six children, is candid in regard to her being raised in an impoverished environment. Her father, Dan Davis, was a horse trainer, and mother, Mary Alice, was a factory worker, maid, and homemaker. Davis is quick to acknowledge the benefits of affirmative action programs and the people who took an interest, mentored, and nurtured her desire early on to act. While a teenager, she was awarded a scholarship to go to Africa and study cultural arts. Before Davis was recognized for her Academy Award-nominated performances in The Help in 2011 and Doubt in 2008, her so-called overnight success had been years in the making. Married to fellow actor Julius Tennon, they are the parents of three children.

Awards: Academy Award (2017), Golden Globes, USA Award (2017), Black Reel Award (2017, 2012, 2008), Black Film Critic Circle Award (2016), People's ChoiceAwards, USA(2015), ScreenActors Guild Award (2015), National Board of Review, USA (2013), Image Award (2013, 2012), BET Award (2012), Broadcast Film Critics Association Award (2012), Chicago International Film Festival Award (2012), Santa Barbara International Film Festival Award (2012, 2009), Screen Actors Guild Award (2012), Women in Film Crystal Award (2012), Hollywood Film Festival Award (2011), National Board of Review, USA (2011, 2008), Satellite Award (2011), Southeastern Film Critics Association Award (2011), Dallas-Fort Worth Film Critics Association Award (2008), Washington DC Area Film Critics Association Awards (2008)

Movies (actress): Widows (2018), Fences (2016), Suicide Squad (2016), Lila & Eve (2015), Get on Up (2014), Ender's Game (2013), Prisoners (2013), Won't Back Down (2012), Extremely Loud & Incredibly Close (2011), The Help (2011), Eat Pray Love (2010), Madea Goes to Jail 2009), Doubt (2008), Nights in Rodanthe (2008), Disturbia (2007), Get Rich or Die Tryin' (2005), Solaris (2002), Antwone Fisher (2002), Kate & Leopold (2001), Traffic (2000), Out of Sight (1998)

Television movies (actress): *Life Is Not a Fairytale: The Fantasia Barrino Story* (2006), *Amy & Isabelle* (2001), *Grace & Glorie* (1998), *The Pentagon Wars* (1998)

Television series documentary (producer): The Last Defense (2018)

Television (producer and actress): How to Get Away with Murder 2014–18)

Television (actress): United States of Tara (2010), The Andromeda Strain (2008), Traveler (2007), Century City (2004), City of Angels (2000)

Ruby Dee (1922–2014), actress, screenwriter, producer, playwright, poet, author, and activist. There is no medium Dee has not conquered. She was a consummate artist. In high school, she knew she wanted to be an actress. From there she set about a course of being able to methodically build a career that started in college while simultaneously appearing on stage with the American Negro Theatre. Dee graduated with a BA in French and Spanish from Hunter College, New York City. She was raised in Harlem. Her work in radio developed from a college course. Award-winning success followed in film, television, and written works. Not long after graduation, she met her soul mate, Ossie Davis, a renowned actor, director, producer, writer, and activist—a dynamic force in his own right. They met working in the Broadway play, *Jeb*. Although Davis attended Howard University for three years, he left without graduating to pursue his acting career on stage with the Rose McClendon Players. The husband-and-wife team worked together in a variety of mediums on numerous occasions. They also amassed a number of awards for their joint endeavors. Although Davis passed away in 2005 at age eighty-seven, Dee continued to work in her chosen profession. With a film career that spans over six decades, Dee again peaked when she was nominated for an Academy Award for her role in *American Gangster* (2008). She won an Image Award for *Do the Right Thing* in 1991. Davis cowrote, produced, and acted in one of the first films to launch the African American film renaissance of the 1960s and 70s; *Uptight*, in 1968. Over the course of her unparalleled career, Dee made stellar contributions to cinematic progression and mass communication.

Awards: Image Award (2008, 1999, 1991, 1989), Spingarn Medal, NAACP (2008), the Eleanor Roosevelt Val-Kill Medal Award (2008), Screen Actors Guild Award (2008), Atlanta Film Festival Award (2006), Method Fest Award (2006), New Zealand Screen Award (2006), Primetime Emmy Award (1991), Women in Film Crystal Award (1991), CableACE Award (1983), Drama Desk Award (1973, 1971), Obie Award (1971), National Board of Review, USA (1961) Shared awards with husband, Ossie Davis: Grammy Award (audiobook) (2007), Marian Anderson Award (2005), Kennedy Center Honors (2004), Screen Actors Guild Lifetime Achievement Award (2001), St. Louis International Film Festival (1998), National Medal of Art from President Clinton (1995), the Actors' Equity Paul Robeson Citation Award "for outstanding creative contributions both in the performing arts and in society at large" (1975)

Movie (producer, writer, actress): *Uptight* (1968)

Movies (actress): *1982* (2013), *A Thousand Words* (2012), *Video*

Girl (2011), *Dream Street* (2010), *American Gangster* (2007), *The Way Back Home* (2006), *Naming Number Two* (2006), *Baby of the Family* (2002), *Cop and ½* (1993), *Jungle Fever* (1991), *Love at Large* (1990), *Do the Right Thing* (1989), *Go Tell It on the Mountain* (1984), *Cat People* (1982), *The Torture of Mothers* (1980), *Cool Red* (1976), *Black Girl* (1972), *Buck and the Preacher* (1972), *The Incident* (1967), *Gone Are the Days* (1963), *The Balcony* (1963), *A Raisin in the Sun* (1961), *Take a Giant Step* (1959), *Our Virgin Island* (1959), *St. Louis Blues* (1958), *Edge of the City* (1957), *The Great American Pastime* (1956), *Go Man Go* (1954), *The Tall Target* (1951), *No Way Out* (1950), *The Jackie Robinson Story* (1950), **The Fight Never Ends** (1947), *What a Guy* (1947), *That Man of Mine* (1946), *Love in Syncopation* (1946)

Television movies (actress): *Betty and Coretta* (2013), *America* (2009), *Their Eyes Were Watching God* (2005), *Taking Back Our Town* (2001), *Feast of All Saints* (2001), *Finding Buck McHenry* (2000), *A Storm in Summer* (2000), *Shelly Fisher* (1999), *Having Our Say: The Delany Sisters' First 100 Years* (1999), *Passing Glory* (1999), *The Wall* (1998), *Stories from the Edge* (1996), *Captive Heart: The James Mink Story* (1996), *Mr. and Mrs. Loving* (1996), *The Ernest Green Story* (1993), *The Poetry Hall of Fame* (1993), *Jazztime Tale* (1991), *Decoration Day* (1990), *The Court-Martial of Jackie Robinson* (1990), *Windmills of the Gods* (1988), *Crown Dick* (1987), *Long Day's Journey into Night* (1982), *All God's Children* (1980), *I Know Why the Caged Bird Sings* (1979), *Wedding Band* (1974), *It's Good to Be Alive* (1974), *Chelsea D.H.O.* (1973), *To Be Young, Gifted, and Black* (1972), *Seven Times Monday* (1962), *The First Year* (1946)

Television (actress): *Street Gear* (1994–95), *American Masters* (1995), *The Stand* (1994), *American Playhouse* (1985–90), *Ossie and Ruby!* (1980–81), *Roots: The Next Generation* (1979), *Peyton Place* (1968–69), *Play of the Week* (1960–61)

Loretta Devine (1949), actress, songstress. Beneath the soft, smooth demeanor lies a highly evolved intellectual. Born and bred in Houston, Texas, Divine holds a bachelor of arts in speech and drama from the University of Houston and a master's of fine arts in theater from Brandeis University. Love for the stage and a tenacious work ethic earned her a coveted role in the original Broadway run of *Dreamgirls* from 1981 to 1985. Being cast as Lorell Robinson enabled her to showcase her singing talent. Although her appearance in film and television started in 1981, *Waiting to Exhale* in 1995 and numerous award-winning television portrayals solidified her placement as a welcome presence in film.

Awards: Image Award (2015, 2013, 2004, 2003, 2001, 1997, 1996), Gracie Allen Award (2012), Primetime Emmy Award (2011), Black Reel Award (2011, 2006)

Movies: *Back to School Mom* (2015), *Teachers* (2013), *Jumping the Broom* (2011), *Madea's Big Happy Family* (2011), *For Colored Girls* (2010), *Lottery Ticket* (2010), *Death at a Funeral* (2010), *Spring Breakdown* (2009), *First Sunday* (2008), *Dreamgirls* (2006), *Dirty Laundry* (2006), *King's Ransom* (2005), *Crash* (2004), *Woman Thou Art Loosed* (2004), *Baby of the Family* (2002), *I Am Sam* (2001), *Kingdom Come* (2001), *What Women Want* (2000), *Urban Legends: Final Cut* (2000), *Urban Legend* (1998), *Down in the Delta* (1998), *Hoodlum* (1997), *The Preacher's Wife* (1996), *Waiting to Exhale* (1995)

Television movie (producer and actress): *Teachers* (2013)

Television movies (actress): *Life Is Not a Fairytale: The Fantasia Barrino Story* (2006), *Freedom Song* (2000), *Introducing Dorothy Dandridge* (1999), *Don King: Only in America* (1997)

Television (actress): *Love Is_* (2018), *The Carmichael Show* (2015-17), *Being Mary Jane* (2015), *The Doc Files* (2013), *The Client List (2012–13)*, *Grey's Anatomy* (2005–13), *The Soul Man* (2012), *Doc McStuffins* (2012–17), *State of Georgia* (2011), *Eli Stone* (2008–09), *The PJs* (1999–2008), *Boston Legal* (2006–07), *Everybody Hates Chris* (2006–07), *Girlfriends* (2005–06), *Wild Card* (2004–05), *Boston Public* (2000–04), *Half & Half* (2003), *Touched by an Angel* (1997), *Roc* (1992–93), *Sugar and Spice* (1990), *A Different World* (1987–88)

Taye Diggs (1971), actor, dancer. Diggs was born in Newark, New Jersey. He graduated with a Bachelor of Fine Arts in Musical Theater from Syracuse University. Performances in a number of stage productions led to his originating the role of Benny in the award-winning play *Rent*. Stage led to television's *Guiding Light*. Diggs's movie debut and ascent was in *How Stella Got Her Groove Back*. Diggs personifies smooth, cool, and charismatic.

Awards: Acapulco Film Festival (2014), Image Award (2009, 2005), Broadcast Film Critics Association Award (2003), Chicago International Film Festival Award (2003), Screen Actors Guild Award (2003), Blockbuster Entertainment Award (2000)

Movies (actor): *River Runs Red* (2018), *The Best Man Wedding* (2016), *The Best Man Holiday* (2013), *Baggage Claim* (2013), *Between Us* (2012), *Dylan Dog: Dead of Night* (2010), *Our Family Wedding* (2010), *Days of Wrath* (2008), *Rent* (2005), *Slow Burn* (2005), *Drum* (2004), *Malibu's Most Wanted* (2003), *Basic* (2003), *Chicago* (2002), *Equilibrium* (2002), *Brown Sugar* (2002), *House on Haunted Hill* (1999), *The Best Man* (1999), *The Wood* (1999), *Go* (1999), *How Stella Got Her Groove Back* (1998)

Television (producer and actor): *Day Break* (2006–07), *Kevin Hill* (2004–05)

Television (actor): *Empire* (2016-17), *Murder in the First* (2014–16), *Private Practice* (2007–13), *Grey's Anatomy* (2007–09), *Will & Grace* (2006), *The West Wing* (2003), *Ally McBeal* (2001)

Ivan Dixon (1931– 2008), actor, producer, director. Dixon, highly esteemed in the film industry, contributed greatly to creating a road map on how to navigate the industry and be sustained by it. Dixon was born in New York's Harlem; his dad, a grocery store owner, moved the family to North Carolina. Dixon graduated from North Carolina Central University where he majored in drama and minored in political science. While at NCCU, he established a theater troupe known as the Ivan Dixon Players and was a member of Omega Psi Phi fraternity. After appearing on Broadway in *Cave Dwellers* in 1957, he stunt-doubled for and formed a solid friendship with Sidney Poitier in the film *The Defiant Ones* in 1958. Costarring in the original film version *A Raisin in the Sun* in 1961, he was unstoppable and wore many hats in the course of his varied career, including that of a radio station owner in Hawaii. Some of his motivation for becoming a director was a fierce determination never to accept acting roles he felt were demeaning. A member of the Black Filmmakers Hall of Fame, Dixon won numerous honors including four NAACP Image Awards, The National Black Theatre Award and the Paul

Robeson Pioneer Award from the Black American Cinema Society.

Movie (producer and director): *The Spook Who Sat by the Door* (1973)

Movies (director): *Trouble Man* (1972)

Movies (actor): *Car Wash* (1976), *Claudine* (1974), *Suppose They Gave a War and Nobody Came* (1970), *Where's Jack?* (1969), *A Patch of Blue* (1965), *Nothing But a Man* (1964), *Battle at Bloody Beach* (1961), *Porgy and Bess* (1959), *Something of Value* (1957)

Television movies (director): *Percy & Thunder* (1993), *The Sty of a Blind Pig* (1974)

Television (director): *Brewster Place* (1990), *Magnum, P.I.* (1982–86), *The Greatest American Hero* (1981–83), *Counterattack: Crime in America* (documentary) (1982), *Bret Maverick* (1981–82), *Palmerstown, U.S.A.* (1981), *The Rockford Files* (1975–79), *The Waltons* (1974–75), *Nichols* (1971–72), *Room 222* (1970–71), *Monty Nash* (1971), *The Bill Cosby Show* (1970–71)

Television (actor): *Amerika* (1987), *Hogan's Heroes* (1965–70), *The Name of the Game* (1968–69), *The Fugitive* (1964–67), *CBS Playhouse* (1967), *The Outer Limits* (1963–64), *The Defenders* (1963–64), *Dr. Kildare* (1962–64), *Twilight Zone* (1960–64), *Perry Mason* (1962–63), *Cain's Hundred* (1961–62), *The New Breed* (1962), *Armstrong Circle Theatre* (1957)

Tamara Dobson (1947–2006), actress, fashion model. A statuesque, absolutely stunning, six-foot-two explosion of dynamite, Dobson possessed extraordinary presence on the big screen. As leading lady in action films *Cleopatra Jones* in 1973 and *Cleopatra Jones and the Casino of Gold* in 1975, Dobson's film career was brief yet a hallmark of the Blaxploitation film era. Born in Baltimore, Maryland, she earned her degree in illustration from the Maryland Institute College of Art while working as a licensed beautician. Once in New York, she was targeted for work in numerous high-fashion magazines and television commercials, which segued into a film acting career.

Movies (actress): *Chained Heat* (1983), *Norman...Is That You?* (1976), *Cleopatra Jones and the Casino of Gold* (1975), *Cleopatra Jones* (1973), *Fuzz* (1972), *Come Back Charleston Blue* (1972)

Movie (makeup artist): *Cleopatra Jones and the Casino of Gold* (1975)

Television movies (actress): *Amazons* (1984), *Murder at the World Series* (1977)

Television (actress): *Jason of Star Command* (1979–81)

Bill Duke (1943), actor, director, producer. A film veteran in front and behind the camera, Duke is committed to community enlightenment and influencing youth to pursue their dreams. The Poughkeepsie, New York–native started out a premed major. He discovered theater while in college and graduated with a BA in theater from Boston University then earned an MFA from New York University and studied directing at the American Film Institute. Highly regarded for his directing skill and acting ability, Duke has built his career on firm foundation. During the 1970s, he was involved in numerous Off-Broadway and Broadway stage productions as an actor and director including writer Melvin Van Peebles's musical Ain't Supposed to Die a Natural Death. The mid-'70s ushered in guest-starring roles on various television series when recognition came on the silver screen in the comedy *Carwash* in 1976. With an appearance in the 1980 drama *American Gigolo*, audiences and the film industry knew this was one to watch. He broke through the glass ceiling of consistently directing popular television series starting with *Flamingo Road* in 1982 and *Falcon Crest*. Major film directing would follow with *A Rage in Harlem, Deep Cover, The Cemetery Club*, and *Sister Act 2: Back in the Habit*. The recipient of the Lifetime Achievement Tribute from the Directors Guild of America, Duke has established Duke Media, which is committed to viewers who seek entertainment that educates. He also received the American Film Institute's Lifetime Achievement Award and the NAACP Special Award for Outstanding Achievement. In 2004 Governor Arnold Schwarzenegger appointed Dukes to the California Film Commission. President Bill Clinton appointed him to the National Endowment for the Humanities.

Awards: Sunscreen Film Festival, US (2017), Black Reel Award (2004), Acapulco Black Film Festival Award (1997), Sundance Film Festival Award (1985)

Movies (producer and director): *Dark Girls* (documentary) (2011),

Not Easily Broken (2009), *Cover* (2007), *Hoodlum* (1997)

Movies (producer): *Brooklyn Gangster: The Story of Jose Lucas* (2012), *The Pact* (documentary) (2009)

Movies (director): *Light Girls* (documentary) (2015), *Prince Among Slaves* (documentary) (2007), *Sister Act 2: Back in the Habit* (also actor) (1993), *The Cemetery Club* (1993), *Deep Cover* (1992), *A Rage in Harlem* (1991)

Movies (actor): *Mandy* (2018), *Bad Country* (2014), *Freaky Deaky* (2012), *Henry's Crime* (2010), *The Big Bang* (2010), *Get Rich or Die Tryin'* (2005), *Red Dragon* (2002), *Exit Wounds* (2001), *Never Again* (2001), *Fever* (1999), *Foolish* (1999), *Payback* (1999), *Susan's Plan* (1998), *Menace II Society* (1993), *Bird on a Wire* (1990), *Action Jackson* (1988), *No Man's Land* (1987), *Predator* (1987), *Commando* (1985), *American Gigolo* (1980), *Car Wash* (1976)

Television movie (director): *Created Equal* (2018)

Television movies (actor): *R.U.S.H.* (2002), *Who Killed Atlanta's Children?* (2000), *Always Outnumbered* (1998), *Dallas: The Early Years* (1986), *Sergeant Matlovich vs. the U.S. Air Force* (1978)

Television documentary (director): *The American Experience: Partners of the Heart* (2002)

Television movie (producer, director, writer): *Preying for Mercy* (2014)

Television movies (director): *Deacons for Defense* (2003), *The Golden Spiders: A Nero Wolfe Mystery* (2000), *America's Dream* (1996), *Johnnie Mae Gibson: FBI* (1986)

Television (director): *The Outsiders* (1990), *American Playhouse* (1984–89), *Knots Landing* (1982–84), *Falcon Crest* (1982)

Television (actor): *Karen Sisko* (2003–04), *Fastlane* (2002–03), *Palmerstown, U.S.A.* (1980–81), *ABC Afterschool Specials* (1972, 1975)

Starletta DuPois (1941), actress. In constant demand, the character actress was initially a premedical major graduating with a BS in biology from Maryland State College. She received a Master's of Fine Art in theater from University of California, Los Angeles. DuPois pursued the master's degree after having won the Audelco Award for Best Actress in her stage performance of Mary Goldstein and the Author. Appearing in numerous films including *South Central* (1992), *Waiting to Exhale* (1995), *Big Momma's House* (2000), *Friday After Next* (2002), and *First Sunday* (2008), DuPois still managed to stay true to her love of the theatrical stage and win the Woodie King, Jr. Best Actress Award for her role in August Wilson's King Hedly II in 2006. DuPois is a philanthropist and has taught as a professor in the theater arts department at University of Southern California.

Awards: Eternity Award (2013), NAACP Image Award (1989), Tony Award (1978)

Movies: *A Beautiful Soul* (2012), *The Least Among You* (2009), *First Sunday* (2008), *The Notebook* (2004), *Friday After Next* (2002), *Big Momma's House* (2000), *3 Strikes* (2000), *The Maker* (1997), *Waiting to Exhale* (1995), *Wolf* (1994), *The Thing Called Love* (1993), *South Central* (1992), *The Waterdance* (1992), *Convicts* (1991), *Ricochet* (1991), *Hollywood Shuffle* (1987), *Odd Jobs* (1986), *Pee Wee's Big Adventure* (1985), *The Torture of Mothers* (1980), *The Gambler* (1974)

Television movies: *Alone* (1997), *Full Circle* (1996), *The Road to Galveston* (1996), *A Passion for Justice: The Hazel Brannon Smith Story* (1994), *Strapped* (1993), *Runaway Father* (1991), *Frogs* (1991), *Chiller* (1985), *Deadly Intentions* (1985), *The Kid with the 200 I.Q.* (1983), *Games Mother Never Taught You* (1982), *Uptown Saturday Night* (1979)

Television: *The Rich & the Ruthless* (2017-18), *Lost* (2008), *The District* (2003), *Knots Landing* (1983 and 1992), *American Playhouse* (presents *"A Raisin in the Sun"* 1989), *St. Elsewhere* (1984), *Falcon Crest* (1983), *Hill Street Blues* (1981)

Charles Dutton (1951), actor, director, producer, writer. Life for Dutton began in a housing project in Baltimore, Maryland. Dutton dropped out of the seventh grade. With a dozen or so troublesome years of intermittent incarceration, he obtained his GED and AA degree from a junior college. From there he graduated from Towson State University with a BA in theater and a master's from Yale Drama School. By the time Dutton graduated from Yale, he had begun a collaborative relationship with playwright August Wilson, performing to rave reviews in Wilson's *Ma Rainey's Black Bottom*, which he took to Broadway along with

Joe Turner's Come and Gone. Dutton's acting career was destined for longevity with his stage performance in Wilson's *The Piano Lesson*. Success on stage quickly led to television and films that include *Mississippi Masala* in 1991 and *Menace II Society* in 1993. A three-year run with television show Roc from 1991–94 was pivotal in taking his career to the next level. He took his turn at directing, starting with a television movie, First Time Felon, in 1991 and was bona fide by the time he took the reins with the television miniseries *The Corner*.

Awards: Image Award (2004, 2003,1994), Black Reel Award (2003, 2001), Primetime Emmy Awards (2003, 2002, 2000)

Movie (producer): *Peeples* (2013)

Movie (writer, director, and actor): *The Obama Effect* (2012), *Against the Ropes* (director, actor) (2004)

Movies (actor): *The Perfect Guy* (2015), LUV (2012), *The Gift* (2010), *Fame* (2009), *Legion* (2009), *The Express* (2008), *American Violet* 2008), *Honeydripper* (2007), *Secret Window* (2004), *Gothika* (2003), *Eye See You* (2002), *Random Hearts* (1999), *Cookie's Fortune* (1999), *Black Dog* (1998), *Blind Faith* (1998), *Mimic* (1997), *Get on the Bus* (1996), *A Time to Kill* (1996), *Nick of Time* (1995), *Cry, The Beloved Country* (1995), *A Low Down Dirty Shame* (1994), *Foreign Student* (1994), *Surviving the Game* (1994), *Rudy* (1993), *Menace II Society* (1993), *The Distinguished Gentleman* (1992), *Alien* (1992), *Mississippi Masala* (1991), *Pretty Hattie's Baby* (1991), *Q&A* (1990), *An Unremarkable Life* (1989), *Jacknife* (1989), *Crocodile Dundee II* (1988), *No Mercy* (1986), *Cat's Eye* (1985),

Television (producer): *Roc* (1993), *Laurel Avenue* (TV movie) (1993)

Television movies (director): *Racing for Time* (2008), *Under* (2008), *First Time Felon* (1997)

Television movies (actor): *Bessie* (2015), *40 Minutes of Hell* (2012), *Racing for Time* (2008), *Suspect* (2007), *Something the Lord Made* (2004), *D.C. Sniper: 23 Days of Fear* (2003), *Conviction* (2002), *10,000 Black Men Named George* (2002), *For Love or Country: The Arturo Sandoval Story* (2000), *Aftershock: Earthquake in New York* (1999), *The '60s* (1999), *Jack Reed: Death and Vengeance* (1996), *Night Visitors* (1996), *Jack Reed: A Killer Among Us* (1996), *Jack Reed: One of our Own* (1995), *Zooman* (1995), *The Piano Lesson* (1995), *Jack Reed: A*

Search for Justice (1994), *A Matter of Justice* (1993), *Runaway* (1989), *Apology* (1986)

Television (director): Sleeper Cell (2006), The Corner (2000)

Television (actor): Longmire (2012–14), Zero Hour (2013), Threshold (2005–06), A History of Us (TV documentary 2003), Roc (1991–94)

Michael Ealy (1973), actor. Recognized for his range and ability to take on complex roles, Ealy graduated from the University of Maryland an English major. He was born in Washington, DC. After college, he decided to pursue a suppressed passion and headed to New York for acting classes, supporting himself as a waiter and acting in Off-Broadway productions. Following a succession of television appearances in 2002, in the role of Ricky Nash in *Barbershop*, his career as an actor excelled.

Awards: African-American Film Critics Association (AAFCA) (2010), Black Reel (2006), Washington DC Area Film Critics Association Award (2002)

Movie (producer and actor) *The Perfect Guy* (2015)

Movies (actor): *Think Like a Man Too* (2014), *About Last Night* (2014), *Unconditional* (2012), *Think Like a Man* (2012), *Underworld: Awakening* (2012), *Margaret* (2011), *For Colored Girls* (2010), *Takers* (2010), *Seven Pounds* (2008), *Miracle at St. Anna* (2008), *Jellysmoke* (2005), *Barbershop 2: Back in Business* (2004), *Never Die Alone* (2004), *November* (2004), *2 Fast 2 Furious* (2003), *Justice* (2003), *Barbershop* (2002), *Bad Company* (2002), *Kissing Jessica Stein* (2001)

Television movies (actor): *Suspect* (2007), *Their Eyes Are Watching God* (2005), *Metropolis* (2000)

Television (actor): *Being Mary Jane* (2017-18), *Secrets and Lies* (2016), *Almost Human* (2013–14), *Common Law* (2012), *Californication* (2011), *The Good Wife* (2010–11), *Flashforward* (2009–10), *Sleeper Cell* (2005–06), *ER* (2005–06)

Kimberly Elise (1967), actress. Elise is the embodiment of the complex, emotionally driven character. Elise's BA is in liberal arts and communication from University of Minnesota. She is also a graduate of the American Film Institute. Choosing to focus on marriage and motherhood immediately after college, Elise's film career gained considerable momentum once she decided it was time to take the plunge. Audiences got a good idea in 1996 of what she could do as the character Tisean in *Set It Off*. In *Beloved* and *John Q*, there was no doubt Elise would be a familiar face in film.

Awards: Black Reel Award (2011, 2006, 2005, 2002), Image Award (2011, 2010, 2007, 2006), MovieGuide Award (2010), BET Comedy Award (2005), Black Movie Award (2005), Chicago Film Critics Association Award (1999), Satellite Award (1999), CableACE Award (1997)

Movies: *Death Wish* (2018), *Almost Christmas* (2016), *Back to School Mom* (2015), *Dope* (2015), *Highland Park* (2013), *Ties That Bind* (2011), *For Colored Girls* (2010), *The Great Debaters* (2007), *Pride* (2007), *Diary of a Mad Black Woman* (2005), *The Manchurian Candidate* (2004), *Woman Thou Art Loosed* (2004), *John Q* (2002), *Bait* (2000), *Beloved* (1998), *Set It Off* (1996)

Television movies: *Confirmation* (2016), *Hannah's Law* (2012), *Gifted Hands: The Ben Carson Story* (2009), *Bojangles* (2001), *The Loretta Claiborne Story* (2000), *The Ditchdigger's Daughters* (1997)

Television: *Hit the Floor* (2013–16), *Grey's Anatomy* (2009), *Close to Home* (2005–07), *Soul Food* (2002–03), *Girlfriends* (2003)

Vivica A. Fox (1964), actress, producer. Fox's goal in her senior year in high school was to attain high-profile status in the entertainment industry. Her mother agreed to her trek to Los Angeles at seventeen years old on one condition, that she attend college and graduate. The South Bend, Indiana native graduated with an associate's arts degree in social science from Golden Coast College in Huntington Beach, California. Fox has never been one to bemoan the lack of opportunity for actresses in Hollywood. When the right blockbuster opportunity such as *Kill Bill: Vol. 1* and *Kill Bill: Vol. 2* is not available, she creates lucrative projects like television's *Glam God with Vivica A. Fox* or reinvents herself without compromise. She exemplifies the vivacious, confident woman with a flair for comedy.

Awards: CinemaCon, USA (2016), Image Award (2006), Acapulco

Black Film Festival Award (1998), MTV Movie Award (1997), Sci-Fi Universe Magazine, USA Award (1996)

Movies (producer and actress): *Three Can Play That Game* (2007), *The Salon* (2005), *Motives* (2004), *Ride or Die* (2003)

Movies (actress): *Independence Day: Resurgence* (2016), *Terms and Conditions* (2014), *Q* (2014), *Mission Park* (2013), *In the Hive* (2012), *Black November* (2012), *The Cookout 2* (2011), *1 Out of 7* (2011), *Kickin' It Old Skool* (2007), *Blast* (2004), *Kill Bill: Vol. 2* (2004), *Ella Enchanted* (2004), *Kill Bill: Vol. 1* (2003), *Juwanna Mann* (2002), *Little Secrets* (2001), *Two Can Play That Game* (2001), *Kingdom Come* (2001), *Idle Hands* (1999), *Why Do Fools Fall in Love* (1998), *Soul Food* (1997), *Batman & Robin* (1997), *Booty Call* (1997), *Set It Off* (1996), *Independence Day* (1996), *Don't Be a Menace to South Central While Drinking Your Juice in the Hood* (1996), *Born on the Fourth of July* (1989)

Television movie (producer and actress): *Getting Played* (2006)

Television movies (actress): *Bobbi Kristina* (2017), *Sharknado 2: The Second One* (2014), *Annie Claus Is Coming to Town* (2011), *Farewell Mr. Kringle* (2010), *Kim Possible: A Stitch in Time* (2003), *Hendrix* (2000), *Solomon* (1997), *The Tuskegee Airmen* (1995)

Television (produce, host, actress): *Glam God with Vivica A. Fox* (2008), *1-800-Missing* (2004–06), *Getting Personal* (1998)

Television (actress): *Empire* (2015-18), *Mr. Box Office* (2012–13), *Scooby-Doo! Mystery Incorporated* (2010–12), *Curb Your Enthusiasm* (2007–09), *Ozzy & Drix* (2002–03), *City of Angels* (2000), *The Hughleys* (1999), *A Saintly Switch* (TV movie) (1999), *Arsenio* (1997), *Out All Night* (1992–93), *China Beach* (1998)

Carl Franklin (1949), actor, director, writer. Born and raised in the extremely rough environs of Richmond, California, Franklin made his way into University of California, Berkeley as the first ever in his family to attend college. Armed with a scholarship, he graduated UCB with a BA in Theater Arts after switching over from history. Unfulfilled with his career as an actor, Franklin enrolled into the directing program at the American Film Institute where he received his Master's of Fine Arts. He directed *One False Move* in 1992 then wrote the screenplay and directed

Devil in a Blue Dress in 1995.

Awards: Image Award (2018, 2015), Online Film & Television Award (2010), American Film Institute, USA Award (1996), Cognac Festival du Film Policier Award (1993), Independent Spirit Award (1993), MTV Movie Award (1993), Los Angeles Film Critics Association Award (1992), Mystfest Award (1992)

Movies (writer): *Bless Me, Ultima* (2013), *Devil in a Blue Dress* (1995), *Last Stand at Lang Mei* (1989), *Eye of the Eagle 2: Inside the Enemy* (1989), *Punk* (short film) (1986)

Movies (director): *Bless Me, Ultima* (2013), *Out of Time* (2003), *High Crimes* (2002), *One True Thing* (1998), *Devil in a Blue Dress* (1995), *One False Move* (1992), *Full Fathom Five* (1990), *Eye of the Eagle 2: Inside the Enemy* (1989), *Nowhere to Run* (1989), *Punk* (1986)

Movies (actor): *In the Heat of Passion* (1992), *Full Fathom Five* (1990), *Last Stand at Lang Mei* (1989), *Eye of the Eagle: Inside the Enemy* (1989), *Five on the Black Hand Side* (1973)

Television movies (actor): *Too Good to Be True* (1988), *A Smokey Mountain Christmas* (1986)

Television movies (director): *Last of the Ninth* (2009), *Laurel Avenue* (1993)

Television (director): *Mindhunter* (2018), *House of Cards* (2013–14), *Magic City* (2012), *Falling Skies* (2011), *The Pacific* (2010), *The Riches* (2007), *Rome* (2007), *Partners* (1999)

Television (actor): *Roseanne* (1991–92), *The A-Team* (1983–85), *The Devlin Connection* (1982) *McClain's Law* (1981–82), *The Fantastic Journey* (1977), *Good Times* (1975–76), *Cannon* (1974–75)

Al Freeman Jr. (1934–2012), actor, director, writer, educator. Freeman Jr. was about to leave acting behind for a life rich in academia as chairman/artistic director and professor in the theater arts department at Howard University when a role he just couldn't say no to came along. The role being his portrayal of Elijah Muhammad in the 1992 movie *Malcolm X*. Freeman Jr.'s long and varied acting career ranged from the avant-garde 1967 film *The Dutchman* to his 1979 Daytime Emmy Award–winning character, Captain Ed Hall, on the long running soap opera *One Life to Live*. Freeman Jr. first became interested in acting at

Los Angeles City College. After he served in the Air Force, he began to appear on stage and television in New York. Later he received his master's degree in education from the University of Massachusetts. Born in San Antonio, Texas, Freeman Jr.'s father, Albert Cornelius Freeman, was a jazz pianist.

Awards: Image Award (1995), Daytime Emmy Award (1979)

Movie (writer): *Cool Red* (1976) *Movie* (director): *A Fable* (1971)

Movies (actor): *Down in the Delta* (1998), *Once Upon a Time... When We Were Colored* (1995), *Malcolm X* (1992), *Seven Hours to Judgment* (1988), *Castle Keep* (1969), *The Lost Man* (1969), *Finian's Rainbow* (1968), *The Detective* (1968), *The Dutchman* (1967), *For Pete's Sake* (1966), *Ensign Pulver* (1964), *Black Like Me* (1964), *Sniper's Ridge* (1961), *This Rebel Breed* (1960), *Torpedo Run* (1958)

Television movies (actor): *Boy Meets Girl* (1993), *Perry Mason Returns* (1985), *To Be Young, Gifted, and Black* (1972), *My Sweet Charlie* (1970)

Television (director): *One Life to Live* (1968)

Television (actor): *Law & Order* (2004 and 1990), *Homicide: Life on the Street* (1995–96) *One Life to Live* (1978–88), *King* (TV miniseries) (1978), *Hot L Baltimore* (1975)

Robin Givens (1964), actress, producer. A most capable performer, Givens was born in New York City. She entered Sarah Lawrence College at age fifteen, a premed major and graduated with a BA. Though Givens has appeared in numerous movie and television roles, her portrayal of Darlene Merriman in the television series *Head of the Class* led to prominence in the film industry. Her acting career transgressed well from teenager to adult.

Award: Wind International Film Festival (2017) ShoWest Convention, USA Award (1991)

Movie (producer, actress): *Dreams I Never Had* (2018)

Movies (actress): *The Perfect Match* (2016), *Church Girl* (2011), *Queen of Media* (2011), *The Family That Preys* (2008), *Flip the Script* (2005), *Love Chronicles* (2003), **A Good Night to Die** (2003), *Head of State* (2003), *The Elite* (2001), *Everything's Jake* (2000), *Blankman* (1994), *Foreign Student* (1994), *Boomerang* (1992), *A Rage in Harlem* (1991)

Television movies (actress): *The Love You Save* (2011), *Tagged* (2011), *The Verdict* (2008), *Take 3* (2006), *Captive Hearts* (2005), *Hollywood Wives: The New Generation* (2003), *Spinning Out of Control* (2001), *The Expendables* (2000), *Michael Jordan: AN American Hero* (1999), *A Face to Die For* (1996), *Angel Street* (1992), *The Women of Brewster Place* (1989), *The Penthouse* (1989), *Beverly Hills Madam* (1986)

Television (actress): *The Bold and the Beautiful* (2018), *90210* (2013), *Chuck* (2011), *My Parents, My Sister & Me* (2010), *House of Payne* (2007–08), *Sparks* (1996–98), *In the House* (1996), *Courthouse* (1995), *Head of the Class* (1986–91)

Louis Gossett Jr. (1936), actor, producer. Gossett was an award winner way before he won the Academy Award for best supporting actor in 1983 for An Officer and a Gentleman. He took home an Emmy in 1977 for the television miniseries Roots. In 1953, at age seventeen, he won the Donaldson Award for best new actor in the Broadway production of Take a Giant Step. The recipient of a basketball and drama scholarship, he attended and graduated from New York University with a BA. Upon graduation, the six-foot-four Gossett had two lucrative opportunities beckoning. One was continuing on as a draft pick with the New York Knickerbockers or go with a role he had just won for the Broadway stage production of A Raisin in the Sun. He decided he was better suited for acting. He was born in New York City. Gossett was entrenched in his work and love for theater prior to his lucrative career in television and movies.

Awards: TV Land Award (2007), Temecula Valley International Film Festival Award (2004), Black Reel Award (2000), Daytime Emmy Award (1998), Image Award (1998, 1982), Taos Talking Pictures Festival Award (1997), Golden Globes Award (1992, 1983), Walk of Fame Award (1992), Academy Award (1983), ShoWest Convention, USA Award (1983), Primetime Emmy Award (1977)

Movie (producer and actor): *Managua* (1996)

Movies (actor): *Why Did I Get Married Too?* (2010), *Daddy's Little Girls* (2007), *Left Behind: World at War* (2005), *Iron Eagle IV* (1995), *Curse of the Staving Class* (1994), *A Good Man in Africa* (1994),

Diggstown (1992), *Aces: Iron Eagle III* (1992), *Toy Soldiers* (1991), *The Punisher* (1989), *Iron Eagle II* (1988), *The Principal* (1987), *Firewalker* (1986), *Iron Eagle* (1986), *Enemy Mine* (1985), *An Officer and a Gentleman* (1982), *It Rained All Night the Day I Left* (1980), *The Choirboys* (1977), *The Deep* (1977), *J.D.'s Revenge* (1976), *The River Niger* (1976), *The White Dawn* (1974), *The Laughing Policeman* (1973), *Travels with My Aunt* (1972), *The Landlord* (1970), *The Bushbaby* (1969), *A Raisin in the Sun* (1961)

Television documentary (producer): *For Love of Liberty: The Story of America's Black Patriots* (2010), *Renew Orleans* (2007)

Television movies (producer and actor): *For Love of Olivia* (2001), *The Color of Love: Jacey's Story* (2000), *The Inspectors 2: A Shred of Evidence* (2000), *The Inspectors* (1998), *In His Father's Shoes* (1997), *To Dance with Olivia* (1997), *Inside* (1996), *Run for the Dream: The Gail Devers Story* (1996), *A Father for Charlie* (1995), *Ray Alexander: A Taste for Justice* (1994), *Father & Son: Dangerous Relations* (1993)

Television movies (actor): *Solar Attack* (2006), *Lackawanna Blues* (2005), *Momentum* (2003), *Jasper, Texas* (2003), *What About Your Friends: Weekend Getaway* (2002), *Dr. Lucille* (2001), *Strange Justice* (1999), *Love Songs* (1999), *Captive Heart: The James Mink Story* (1996), *Zooman* (1995), *The Josephine Baker Story* (1991), *Roots: The Gift* (1988), *Sam Found Out: A Triple Play* (1988), *The Father Clements Story* (1987), *The Gathering of Old Men* (1987), *Sadat* (1983), *Benny's Place* (1982), *Don't Look Back: The Story of Leroy 'Satchel' Paige* (1981), *Lawman Without a Gun* (1979), *The Lazarus Syndrome* (1978), *Freeman* (1977), *Sidekicks* (1974), *It's Good to Be Alive* (1974), *The Living End* (1972)

Television (actor): *Hap and Leonard* (2018), *The Book of Negroes* (2015), *The Batman* (2007), *Stargate SG-1* (2005–06), *Gideon Oliver* (1989), *The Powers of Matthew Star* (1982–83), *The Lazarus Syndrome* (1979), *Roots* (TV miniseries, 1977), *The Young Rebels* (1970–71), *The Big Story* (1957–58)

David Alan Grier (1955), actor, comedian, writer, producer. Grier received his BA in Radio, Film, and Television from the University of Michigan and his master's from the Yale School of Drama. He fast-tracked to the New York stage and appeared in the original production of Dreamgirls and A Soldier's Play (later adapted for the screen as A Soldier's Story in 1984). He is the son of psychiatrist and writer Dr. William Henry Grier and Aretas Ruth Grier. When Grier focused on doing comedy, he became a familiar face to a wide audience. His calling to do comedy took off with the megahit television show In Living Color that aired 143 episodes from 1990–94. Just as cerebral as he is lighthearted, Grier took time out to author a book, Barack Like Me: The Chocolate-Covered Truth, published in 2009.

Awards: Image Award (2016), TV Land Award (2012), Western Heritage Award (2003), Venice Film Festival Award (1983)

Movie (producer, writer, actor): *The Poker House* (2008)

Movies (actor): *Road Hard* (2015), *Peeples* (2013), *Hoodwinked Too! Hood vs. Evil* (2011), *Astro Boy* (2009), *Dance Flick* (2009), *The Hustle* (2008), *Little Man* (2006), *Bewitched* (2005), *The Woodsman* (2004), *Tiptoes* (2003), *Baadasssss!* (2003), *15 Minutes* (2001), *The Adventures of Rocky & Bullwinkle* (2000), **Return to Me** (2000), *East of A* (2000), *3 Strikes* (2000), *Stuart Little* (1999), *McHale's Navy* (1997), *Jumanji* (1995), *Tales from the Hood* (1995), *Goldilocks and the Three Bears* (1995), *Blankman* (1994), *In the Army Now* (1994), *Boomerang* (1992), *Loose Cannons* (1990), *I'm Gonna Git You Sucka* (1988), *Off Limits* (1988), *Amazon Women on the Moon* (1987), *From the Hip* (1987), *Beer* (1985), *A Soldier's Story* (1984), *Streamers* (1983)

Television (producer, writer, actor): *David Alan Grier: Comedy You Can Believe In* (documentary, 2009), *Chocolate News* (2008), *Thank God You're Here* (2007), *The Davey Gee Show* (TV movie) (2005)

Television movies (actor): *A Christmas Story Live!* (2017), *The Wiz Live!* (2015), *En Vogue Christmas* (2014), *Gym Teacher: The Movie* (2008), *Thugaboo: A Miracle on D-Roc's Street* (2006), *Thugaboo: Sneaker Madness* (2006), *The Muppets' Wizard of Oz* (2005), *Rock Stars Do the Dumbest Things* (2003), *King of Texas* (2002), *Angels in the Infield* (2000), *The '60s* (1999)

Television (producer and actor): *The Preston Episodes* (1995)

Television (writer): *Jamie Foxx Presents Laffapalooza* (2003), *Premium Blend* (2001–02), *Soul Train Comedy Awards* (TV movie) (1993), *In Living Color* (special material, 1992–93)

Television (actor): *The Carmichael Show* (2015-17), *My Wife and Kids* (2003–05), *Crank Yankers* (2002–05), *Life with Bonnie* (2002–04), *DAG* (2000–01), *In Living Color* (1990–94, 2001), *Happily Ever After: Fairy Tales for Every Child* (1995–2000), *Damon* (1998), *Martin* (1993–97), *Tanner '88* (1988), *All Is Forgiven* (1986)

Moses Gunn (1929–1993), actor. A commanding presence, Gunn carried his New York stage success over to film. Known for his Shakespearean performances, he won an Obie Award for his Off-Broadway role in *The First Breeze of Summer* in 1975. He cofounded the Negro Ensemble Company in the 1960s. The oldest of seven children, Gunn graduated from Tennessee State University. After the army, he completed his master's degree at Kansas University. He taught speech and drama at Grambling College prior to pursuance of an acting career. He was born in St. Louis, Missouri, the son of Mary and George Gunn, a laborer. At age twelve, his mother died, and he went into the foster care of his English teacher, Jewel Richie. In 1971, after a few initial film roles, his audience appeal grew when he was cast as Bumpy Jonas in *Shaft* and reprised the same role in *Shaft's Big Score!* (1972). No stranger to television, he had many notable appearances that include reoccurring roles on the series *Good Times, Roots,* and *A Man Called Hawk.*

Awards: Image Award (1982), Obie Award (1975, 1968)

Movies: *Leonard Part 6* (1987), *Heartbreak Ridge* (1986), *Certain Fury* (1985), *Firestarter* (1984), *The NeverEnding Story* (1984), **Amityville II: The Possession** (1982), *Ragtime* (1981), *The Ninth Configuration* (1980), *Remember My Name* (1978), *Aaron Loves Angela* (1975), *Rollerball* (1975), *Cornbread, Earl and Me* (1975), *Amazing Grace* (1974), *The Iceman Cometh* (1973), *Shaft's Big Score!* (1972), *The Hot Rock* (1972), *Shaft* (1971), *The Great White Hope* (1970), *WUSA* (1970), *Nothing But a Man* (1964)

Television movies: *No Room for Opal* (1993), *Memphis* (1992), *Perfect Harmony* (1991), *Brother Future* (1991), *Murder Times Seven* (1990), *The Women of Brewster Place* (1989), *Bates Motel* (1987), *The House of Dies Drear* (1984), *Law of the Land* (1976), *If You Give a Dance, You Gotta Pay the Band* (1972), *Haunts of the Very Rich* (1972), *The Sheriff* (1971), *Carter's Army* (1970), *Of Mice and Men* (1968)

Television: *The Cosby Show* (1989), *A Man Called Hawk* (1989), *American Playhouse* (1984–85), *Father Murphy* (1981–83), *Little House on the Prairie* (1977–81), *Good Times* (1977), *Roots* (1977), *Great Performances: The First Breeze of Summer* (1976), *The Cowboys* (1974), *The Wide World of Mystery* (1973–74)

Arsenio Hall (1956), actor, comedian, talk-show host, writer, producer. Hall chooses which facet of his talent he wants to focus on at any given time. Acting was his major entrée into the world of entertainment with a number of television appearances and the movies Coming to America in 1988 and Harlem Nights in 1989. Born in Cleveland, Ohio, to parents, Fred Hall, a Baptist minister, and wife, Anne, Hall has stated his father's position from the pulpit influenced his desire to be center stage. Hall graduated from Kent State University with a degree in communications.

Awards: Image Award (1990), People's Choice Award (1990), American Comedy Award (1989), Star on the Walk of Fame (1990)

Movie (producer): *Bopha!* (1993)

Movies (actor): *Black Dynamite* (2009), *Igor* (voice) (2008), *Harlem Nights* (1989), *Coming to America* (1988), *Amazon Women on the Moon* (1987)

Television (producer): *The Arsenio Hall Show* (2013)

Television (host): *The Arsenio Hall Show* (2013–14)

Television specials (writer): *A Party for Richard Pryor* (1991), *MTV Video Music Awards* (1990), *Uptown Comedy Express* (1987)

Television (host, writer, producer): The Arsenio Hall Show (1989–94)

Television movie (actor): *The Proud Family Movie* (voice) (2005)

Television (actor): *The Mayor* (2017-18), *Martial Law* (1998–2000), *Arsenio* (1997), *The Real Ghost Busters* (1986–87)

Regina Hall (1970), actress. Before recognition in four *Scary Movie* sequels, Hall earned a Master's in Journalism from New York University. After graduation, her future assured; she appeared in commercials and quickly moved on to the big screen. Hall was born in Washington, DC. After television appearances, Hall made an impression on film audiences in 1999 as Candy in *The Best Man and* as Lena Wright in

Love & Basketball in 2000.

Award: Acapulco Black Film Festival (2014), San Diego Film Festival Award (2006)

Movies: *Shaft* (2019), *Girls Trip* (2017), *Barbershop: The Next Cut* (2016), *The Best Man Wedding* (2016), *Vacation* (2015), *People Places, Things* (2015), *Think Like a Man Too* (2014), *About Last Night* (2014), *The Best Man Holiday* (2013), *Think Like a Man* (2012), *Mardi Gras: Spring Break* (2011), *Death at a Funeral* (2010), *Law Abiding Citizen* (2009), *First Sunday* (2008), *Danika* (2006), *Scary Movie 4* (2006), *The Honeymooners* (2005), *King's Ransom* (2005), *Scary Movie 3* (2003), *Malibu's Most Wanted* (2003), *Paid in Full* (2002), *Scary Movie 2* (2001), *Scary Movie* (2000), *Love & Basketball* (2000), *The Best Man* (1999)

Television movie: **With This Ring** (2015)

Television: *Black-ish* (2016-17), *Real Husbands of Hollywood* (2014), *Second Generation Wayans* (2013), *Law & Order: LA* (2010–11), *Ally McBeal* (2001–02), *Disappearing Acts* (TV movie) (2000)

Lisa Gay Hamilton (1964), actress, director, producer. Hamilton knew at an early age she wanted to act. She saw her dream through to fruition. Hamilton was born in Los Angeles, California. She graduated from New York University with a BA in Theater and earned a master's from Juilliard School of Drama. Though best known for her television role of Rebecca Washington in *The Practic*e from 1997 to 2003, Hamilton has garnered two Obie Awards for phenomenal stage performances in *Valley Song* and *The Ohio State Murders*. She produced and directed a documentary on the life of the inspirational and profound actress Beah Richards entitled *Beah: A Black Woman Speaks*. Hamilton was introduced to the big screen in the youth-driven *Krush Groove* in 1985. She received critical acclaim for her stirring performance as young Sethe in *Beloved* in 1998.

Awards: Locarno International Film Festival Award (2005), AFI Fest Award (2003)

Movie documentary (producer and director): *Beah: A Black Woman Speaks* (2003)

Movies (actress): *Life of a King* (2013), *Go for Sisters* (2013),

The Soloist (2009), *Honeydripper* (2007), *Nine Lives* (2005), *Ten Tiny Love Stories* (2002), *True Crime* (1999), *Beloved* (1998), *Jackie Brown* (1997), *Drunks* (1995), *Naked in New York* (1993), *Reversal of Fortune* (1990), *Krush Groove* (1985)

Television movies (actress): *Conviction* (2005), *Hamlet* (2000), *A House Divided* (2000), *Swing Vote* (1999)

Television (director): *The Practice* (2003)

Television (actress): *Chance* (2016), *House of Cards* (2016), *Grey's Anatomy* (2013), *Men of a Certain Age* (2009–2011), *The Practice* (1997–2003), *One Life to Live* (1996)

Omari Hardwick (1974), actor, poet. Born in Savannah, Georgia, and raised in Decatur, Hardwick's career path was football before he was sidetracked by a knee injury while with the San Diego Chargers. Raised in a household of four boys and a girl by his attorney father and stay-at-home mom, Hardwick is the middle child in his close-knit family. He is a graduate of University of Georgia where he reveled in sports and theater. A featured actor in *Miracle at St. Anna* in 2008 and *Middle of Nowhere* in 2012, Hardwick has maintained a passion for writing his award winning poetry since a young teen. Just as comfortable applying his skills to television as well as film, his fan base grew with the television series *Saved* in 2006 and *Dark Blue* in 2009–10. He is highly praised for his award-winning performances in the television series, *Power*.

Awards: Image Award (2018), NAMIC Vision Award (2016), Black Reel Award (2014)

Movie (producer, actor): *A Boy. A Girl. A Dream: Love on Election Night* (2018)

Movies (actor): *Reach Me* (2014), *Things Never Said* (2013), *Sparkle* (2012), *Middle of Nowhere* (2012), *I Will Follow* (2011), *For Colored Girls* (2010), *Kick-Ass* (2010), *Everyday Black Man* (2010), *Next Day Air* (2009), *Linewatch* (2008), *Miracle at St. Anna* (2008), *The Guardian* (2006), *Gridiron Gang* (2006), *Speechless* (2006), *Beauty Shop* (2005), *Circles* (2001)

Television (actor): *Power* (2014–18), *Being Mary Jane* (2013–14), *Dark Blue* (2009–10), *Saved* (2006), *Sucker Free City* (TV movie) (2004)

Dorian Harewood (1950), actor. Harewood ushered in an era that demonstrated the multifaceted roles African Americans can play. Appearing in nearly two hundred television and film productions since 1975, the actor has nearly worked continuously without interruption. After graduation from the University of Cincinnati, Harewood got an auspicious start in stage productions including *Jesus Christ Superstar*. After a couple of television appearances in 1975, by 1976 his career was on solid ground with the role of Levi in the 1976 movie *Sparkle*. He received critical acclaim for his aging role of Simon Haley in *Roots: The Next Generations* television miniseries in 1979. The movie *Full Metal Jacket* bought another boost to Harewood's career in 1987. He has been featured in many voiceovers for video games and animated television series such as *The Batman* in 2007–08. Harewood was born in Dayton, Ohio.

Award: Image Award (1994)

Movies: *Mayor Cupcake* (2011), *Assault on Precinct 13* (2005), *Gothika* (2003), *Levity* (2003), *Glitter* (2001), *Archibald the Rainbow Painter* (1998), *Sudden Death* (1995), *Pacific Heights* (1990), *Full Metal Jacket* (1987), *The Falcon and the Snowman* (1985), *Sparkle* (1976)

Television movies: *The Right Girl* (2015), *Grave Misconduct* (2008), *Framed* (2002), *Walter and Henry* (2001), *Hendrix* (2000), *12 Angry Men* (1997), *Polly: Comin' Home!* (1990), *Polly* (1989), *God Bless the Child* (1988), *Guilty of Innocence: The Lenell Geter Story* (1987), *The Jesse Owens Story* (1984)

Television: *Handy Manny* (2007–12), *House of Payne* (2007–2009), *7th Heaven* (1996–2003), *The Hoop Life* (1999–2000), *Viper* (1994), *I'll Fly Away* (1992), *The Trials of Rosie O'Neill* (1990–92), *Glitter* (1984–85), *Trauma Center* (1983), *Strike Force* (1981–82), *Roots: The Next Generations* (1979)

Hill Harper (1966), actor, producer, writer. Harper created many life-path options as a result of his substantial educational background. He graduated at the very top of his class throughout his college academic career. Harper holds a BA from Brown University and a JD (law degree) and Master's in Public Administration from Harvard. He hails from Iowa City, Iowa, and is the son of Harry Harper, a psychiatrist, and Marilyn Hill (Harper), the first African American practicing anesthesiologist in the United States. While in law school, he met and became associated with President Barack Obama. He became a familiar face as Aaron in 1993 on the television situation comedy *Married with Children*. Although he has had quite a few turns on the cinematic screen, television has been extremely good for Harper's exposure as evidenced in his portrayal of Dr. Sheldon Hawkes on *CSI: NY*. His first theatrical film appearance was in the thought-provoking *Get on the Bus* in 1996. Harper demonstrates a tendency toward involvement with independent film projects. In 2000, he portrayed a prisoner dying of AIDS in *The Visit*. Whether he is awash in accolades, such as being voted one of the Sexiest Men Alive in 2004 by *People* magazine, or winning his personal challenge of beating thyroid cancer, Harper remains in complete control of his destiny. Harper has written several motivational books.

Awards: Santa Barbara International Film Festival Award (2014), Image Award (2010, 2009, 2008), Urbanworld Film Festival Award (2008), Method Fest Award (2000)

Author (books): *Letters to an Incarcerated Brother* (2013), *The Wealth Cure: Putting Money in Its Place* (2011), *The Conversation: How Men and Women Can Build Loving, Trusting Relationships* (2010), *Letters to a Young Sister: DeFINE Your Destiny* (2008), *Letters to a Young Brother: Manifest Your Destiny* (2006)

Movies (producer and actor): *1982* (2013), *This Is Not a Test* (2008)

Movies (actor): *All Eyez On Me* (2017), *Concussion* (2015), *The Boy Next Door* (2015), *For Colored Girls* (2010), *Premium* (2006), *Love, Sex and Eating the Bones* (2003), *The Badge* (2002), *The Visit* (2000), *Box Marley* (2000), *In Too Deep* (1999), *Loving Jezebel* (1999), *Slaves of Hollywood* (1999), *Beloved* (1998), *Park Day* (1998), *He Got Game* (1998), *Get on the Bus* (1996)

Television documentaries (producer): *Alpha Man: The Brotherhood of MLK* (2011), *Lessons from Little Rock: A National Report Card* (2008)

Television movies (actor): *Stonehenge Apocalypse* (2010), *Lackawanna Blues* (2005), *Mama Flora's Family* (1998), *The Dave Chappelle Project* (1998), *Zooman* (1995)

Television (actor): *The Good Doctor* (2017-18), *Homeland* (2016-17), *Limitless* (2015-16), *Covert Affairs* (2013–14), *CSI: NY* (2004–13), *Soul Food* (2004), *The Handler* (2003–04), *City of Angels* (2000), *Live Shot* (1995), *Married with Children* (1993–94)

Steve Harris (1965), actor. Harris was able to turn adversity into an advantage when a torn ligament during a college football game shifted his focus to acting. He was already a theater major at Northern Illinois University where he earned a BA when the injury took place. Education was a high priority for him and his brother, actor Wood Harris, emphasized by their parents. He was born in Chicago, Illinois. Harris became known for his award winning performance as Eugene Young on the television series *The Practice*. He earned an MFA in Fine Arts from the Professional Theater Training Program at the University of Delaware. His career took off after his appearance in *Sugar Hill* in 1993. The science-fiction-themed film *Minority Report* in 2002 and television series *Awake* in 2012 were prime showcasing for Harris's talent.

Awards: Image Award (2004), Viewers for Quality Television Award (1999, 1998)

Movies: *Chi-Raq* (2015), *In Your Eyes* (2014), *Takers* (2010), *The Unseen* (2005), *Diary of a Mad Black Woman* (2005), *Bringing Down the House* (2003), *The Skulls* (2000), *The Mod Squad* (1999), *The Rock* (1996), *Sugar Hill* (1993)

Television movies: *Protect and Serve* (2007), *King of the World* (2000), *George Wallace* (1997), *Against the Wall* (1994)

Television: *The Crossing* (2018), *Legends* (2014), *Justified* (2014), *Awake* (2012), *Friday Night Lights* (2009–10), *The Batman* (voice) (2004–06), *Heist* (2006), *The Practice* (1997–2004)

Wood Harris (1969), actor, producer. Harris, the younger brother of actor Steve Harris, holds his own. Born in Chicago, Illinois, Harris was working on his Master of Fine Arts from New York University, which he completed when he made his screen debut in *Above the Rim* in 1994. He earned his BA in theater arts from Northern Illinois University. It wasn't long before he was cast in the first of several legendary roles starting with Jimi Hendrix in the television movie *Hendrix* in 2000. In the role of Julius Campbell in *Remember the Titans*, Harris received critical acclaim. The role of Avon Barksdale in *The Wire* from 2002–08 brought constant exposure. In 2009, he produced *Just Another Day*, a film that explores the world of rap music.

Award: Black Reel Award for Television (2017)

Movie (producer and actor): *Just Another Day* (2009)

Movie (actor): *Blade Runner 2049* (2017), *Dredd* (2012), *Next Day Air* (2009), *Not Easily Broken* (2009), *Dirty* (2005), *Paid in Full* (2002), *Remember the Titans* (2000), *Train Ride* (2000), *The Siege* (1998), *Above the Rim* (1994)

Television movies (actor): *The New Edition Story* (2017), *The Breaks* (2016), *The Watsons Go to Birmingham* (2013), *Hendrix* (2000), *Rhapsody* (2000), *Spenser: Small Vices* (1999)

Television (actor): *The Breaks* (2017), *Justified* (2014), *Southland* (2010), *The Wire* (2002–08)

Reginald "Reggie" C. Hayes (1969), actor. Prior to representing males so well while outnumbered by extraordinary women on the television series *Girlfriends* from 2000–08, Hayes made quite an impression in the fantasy film *Being John Malkovich* in 1999. He graduated from Illinois State University with a BA in Theater. Before film and television, he perfected his craft on stage as a member of the Illinois Shakespeare Festival. Hayes devotes time to charitable ventures. He and his sister, Frances, founded and awarded HOPE scholarships to students at the University of Illinois.

Awards: Image Award (2007, 2006, 2005)

Movies: *Carter High* (2015), *Charlie's Angels* (2000), *Being John Malkovich* (1999), *Chicago Cab* (1997), *A Family Thing* (1996)

Television movie: *The Devon Taylor Show* (2013)

Television: *Hart of Dixie* (2013–14), *Let's Stay Together* (2013), *Girlfriends* (2000–08), *Getting Personal* (1998)

Dennis Haysbert (1954), actor. Born the eighth of nine children in San Mateo, California, Haysbert graduated from the American Academy of Dramatic Arts in Pasadena, California. As television spokesperson for Allstate Insurance, Haysbert has become a very familiar face.

Known for his deep, rich voice, Haysbert worked at a grocery store to support himself through school and read self-help books to boost his visualization of success. Starting out with guest starring and reoccurring roles on episodic television, he made quite an impact in 2001–06 as President David Palmer on the television series *24*. Haysbert proved he can carry a project when he took the lead as Sergeant Major Jonas Blane in the television action drama *The Unit* in 2006–09. His initial theatrical film recognition came with *Major League* in 1989. He received critical acclaim in the controversial 2002 film *Far from Heaven* and for his portrayal of Nelson Mandela in *The Color of Freedom* in 2007.

Awards: Black Reel Award (2013, 2003), Temecula Valley International Film Festival Award (2006), Satellite Award (2003), Washington DC Area Film Critics Association Award 2002), Academy of Science Fiction, Fantasy & Horror Films, USA Award (2000)

Movies (actor): *Experimenter* (2015), *Think Like a Man Too* (2014), *Life of a King* (2013), *Wreck It Ralph* (2012), *LUV* (2012), *The Details* (2011), *Beach* (2007), *Goodbye Bafana* (2007), *Jarhead* (2005), *Sinbad: Legend of the Seven Seas* (2003), *Far from Heaven* (2002), *Love & Basketball* (2000), *What's Cooking?* (2000), *Random Hearts* (1999), *The Minus Man* (1999), *Major League: Back to the Minors* (1998), *Absolute Power* (1997), *Insomnia* (1996), *Waiting to Exhale* (1995), *Heat* (1995), *Major League II* (1994), *Suture* (1993), *Love Field* (1992), *Mr. Baseball* (1992), *Navy Seals* (1990), *Major League* (1989)

Television movies (actor): *Secrets of Pearl Harbor* (2004), *The Writing on the Wall* (1996), *Widow's Kiss* (1996), *K-9000* (1991), *A Summer to Remember* (1985), *The Return of Marcus Welby, M.D.* (1984), *Grambling's White Tiger* (1981)

Television (producer and actor): *The Unit* (2008–09)

Television (actor): *Reverie* (2018), *Incorporated* (2016-17), *Undercover* (2016), *Backstrom* (2015), *24* (2001–06), *Justice League* (2001–03), *Static Shock* (2001–03), *Soul Food* (2001), *Now and Again* (1999–2000), *Superman* (1998–1999), *American Playhouse: Hallelujah* (1993), *Return to Lonesome Dove* (1993), *Queen* (1993), *Just the Ten of Us* (1988–89), *The Young and the Restless* (1986), *Off the Rack* (1984–85), *Code Red* (1981–82), *Buck Rogers in the 25th Century* (1980–81), *Quincey M.E.* (1980–81)

Taraji P. Henson (1970), actress. Henson's great aptitude for filling each role as if it was created for her alone has earned high praise. An electrical engineering major, she realized while working her way through school as a singer and dancer on a cruise ship that performing was the way she should go. She graduated with a degree in theater from Howard University. Another college job was as a secretary in the Pentagon. Henson was born in Washington, DC. In 2001, taking on the role of Yvette in *Baby Boy*, she gained recognition. By 2005, she was a household name in the highly successful *Hustle & Flow*. Around that same time, television's *Boston Legal* also fueled her acting career. As Cookie Lyon on television series *Empire*, Henson shows no sign of slowing down.

Awards: Image Award (2018, 2017, 2016, 2015, 2014, 2012, 2009), BET Award (2017, 2016, 2015), Golden Globe (2016), MTV Movie + TV Award (2017), Screen Actors Guild Award (2017), Black Reel Award (2012, 2006), BET Award (2011, 2009, 2006), Austin Film Critics Association Award (2008), Gotham Award (2007), Black Movie Award (2005), Locarno International Film Festival Award (2001)

Movie (producer, actress): *Proud Mary* (2018)

Movies (actress): *Acrimony* (2018), *Hidden Figures* (2016), *Think Like a Man Too* (2014), *No Good Deed* (2014), *Think Like a Man* (2012), *Larry Crowne* (2011), *The Good Doctor* (2011), *The Karate Kid* (2010), *Date Night* (2010), *Hurricane Season* (2009), *Not Easily Broken* (2009), *The Curious Case of Benjamin Button* (2008), *The Family That Preys* (2008), *Talk to Me* (2007), *Smokin' Aces* (2006), *Something New* (2006), *Four Brothers* (2005), *Hair Show* (2004), *The Adventures of Rocky & Bullwinkle* (2000). *Streetwise* (1998)

Television (producer and host): *Taraji's White Hot Holidays* TV Special (2016-17), *Taraji and Terrence's White Hot Holidays TV Special* (2015)

Television movies (actress): *Taken from Me: The Tiffany Rubin Story* (2011), *Murder, She Wrote: The Last Free Man* (2001), *Satan's School for Girls* (2000)

Television (actress): *Empire* (2015–18), *Person of Interest* (2011–13), *Eli Stone* (2008), *Boston Legal* (2007–08), *The Division* (2003–04), *Felicity* (1998–1999), *Smart Guy* (1997–98), *ER* (1998)

Robert Hooks (1937), actor. Hooks is in the vanguard of African American film actors to work consistently in non-stereotypical roles in crossover studio-driven films. He was born in Washington, DC, the youngest of Edward and Bertha Hooks five children. After graduating Temple University, he headed straight for the New York stage and won a New York Drama Critics Award for his Broadway debut performance in the original roduction of *A Raisin in the Sun*. Hooks cofounded the Negro Ensemble Company (NEC) with Douglas Turner Ward and created the DC Black Repertory Group. He also established New York's Group Theatre Workshop to mentor disadvantaged youth. Alumni of NEC include Lawrence Fishburne, Lynn Whitfield, and Denzel Washington, to name a very few. On *N.Y.P.D.* in 1967, he was the first African American to carry a lead role in a major television series. His star rose further in 1972 as Mr. T in the Blaxploitation era's *Trouble Man*. Hooks has kept afloat with a huge succession of television projects. He has been inducted into the Black Filmmakers Hall of Fame, the recipient of the Pioneer Award and NAACP Image Award for Lifetime Achievement. He is the father of director and producer Kevin Hooks.

Awards: Primetime Emmy Award (1981)

Movies: *Fled* (1996), *Posse* (1993), *Passenger 57* (1992), *Star Trek III: The Search for Spock* (1984), *Fast-Walking* (1982), *Airport '77* (1977), *Aaron Loves Angela* (1975), *Trouble Man* (1972), *Last of the Mobile Hotshots* (1970), *Hurry Sundown* (1967), *Sweet Love, Bitter* (1967)

Television movies: *Seventeen Again* (2000), *Free of Eden* (1998), *Glory & Honor* (1998), *Abandoned and Deceived* (1995), *Heat Wave* (1990), *Appearances* (1990), *D.C. Cops* (1986), *The Execution* (1985), *Words by Heart* (1983), *Sister, Sister* (1982), *The Sophisticated Gents* (1981), *Hollow Image* (1979), *A Woman Called Moses* (1978), *The Courage and the Passion* (1978), *To Kill a Cop* (1978), *Just an Old Sweet Love Song* (1976), *Ceremonies in Dark Old Men* (1975), *Trapped* (1973), *Two for the Money* (1972), *Crosscurrent* (1971), *Vanished* (1971), *Carter's Army* (1970)

Television: *The Actor's Choice* (2016), *The Hoop Life* (1999–2000), *The Commish* (1995), *M.A.N.T.I.S.* (1994–95), *Dynasty* (1984),

Backstairs at the Whitehouse (TV miniseries) (1979), *N.Y.P.D.* (1967–69), *Profile in Courage: Frederick Douglas* (1965)

Ernie Hudson (1945), actor, producer. A masterful intellect and physique to match, Hudson invested a substantial amount of time in pursuit of higher education. The familiar face of the *Ghostbuster* and *Miss Congeniality* film sequels, as well as television's *Desperate Housewives* and *Oz*, was born in Benton Harbor, Michigan. After a hitch in the Marines, the first in his family to graduate high school, Hudson graduated from Wayne State University where he studied speech and English, then earned an MFA on full scholarship from Yale School of Drama. He completed PhD coursework at the University of Minnesota at Minneapolis while taking a break from acting. While at Wayne State, he utilized his skills as a playwright with Concept East and cofounded the Actors Ensemble Theatre.

Awards: Action on Film International Film Festival, USA Award (2011), F. Lauderdale International Film Festival Award (2006), Satellite Award (1999), Sci-Fi Universe Magazine, USA Award (1995)

Movie (producer and actor): *Everything's Jake* (2000)

Movies (actor): *God's Not Dead 2* (2016), *Doonby* (2013), *Turning Point* (2012), *Game of Death* (2010), *Pastor Brown* (2009), *Nobel Son* (2007), *Halfway Decent* (2005), *Miss Congeniality 2: Armed and Fabulous* (2005), *Miss Congeniality* (2000), *A Stranger in the Kingdom* (1999), *Butter* (1998), *The Basketball Diaries* (1995), *The Crow* (1994), *Sugar Hill* (1993), *The Hand That Rocks the Cradle* (1992), *Ghostbusters II* (1989), *Weeds* (1987), *Ghostbusters* (1984), *Penitentiary II* (1982), *The Main Event* (1979), *The Human Tornado* (1976), *Leadbelly* (1976)

Television movies (actor): *Call Me Crazy: A Five Film* (2013), *Beautiful People* (2012), *Final Approach* (2007), *Lackawanna Blues* (2005), *Hostage Rescue Team* (2001), *Michael Jordan: An American Hero* (1999), *Women of San Quentin* (1983), *Last of the Good Guys* (1978)

Television (actor): *Grace and Frankie* (2015-18), *Graves* (2016), *Transformers Prime* (2010–13), *The Secret of the American Teenager* (2008–13), *Law & Order* (2009–10), *Desperate Housewives* (2006–07), *10–8: Officers on Duty* (2003–04), *Oz* (1997–2003), *Wild Palms* (1993),

Broken Badges (1990–91), *The Last Precinct* (1986), *The Super Powers Team: Galactic Guardians* (1985), *St. Elsewhere* (1984), *Highcliffe Manor* (1979)

Samuel L. Jackson (1948), actor, producer. Be it action hero Shaft in 2000 or as Nick Fury in *The Avengers* in 2012, movie audiences can't get enough of Jackson. A graduate of Morehouse College, he received a dramatic arts degree. Jackson was born in Washington, DC, and raised Chattanooga, Tennessee. He cofounded Just Us Theatre and is an alumnus of the Negro Ensemble Company. While performing in a stage production of *A Soldier's Story*, he was noticed by director Spike Lee. Though he had been cast in a few movie and television roles, his collaboration with Lee in *School Daze, Do the Right Thing, Mo' Better Blues*, and *Jungle Fever* was the catalyst that propelled his nonstop career. Jackson is married to actress LaTanya Richardson. They have a daughter, Zoe.

Awards (select): CinemaCon, USA (2018), BET Award (2016), Black Reel Award (2014, 2013), Image Award (2013, 2011, 2006, 1997), MTV Movie Award (2013), American Cinematheque Gala Tribute (2008), Capri Legend Award (2008), Bambi Award (2006), BET Comedy Award (2005), Palm Springs International Film Festival Award (2005), Star on the Walk of Fame (2000), Acapulco Black Film Festival Award (1999, 1998), Berlin International Film Festival Award (1998), Independent Spirit Award (1998, 1995), Blockbuster Entertainment Award (1997), BAFTA (British Academy of Film and Television) Award (1995), Cannes Film Festival Award (1991), New York Film Critics Circle Award (1991)

Movies (producer and actor): *Cleaner* (2007), *Eve's Bayou* (2001)

Movies (actor): *Shaft* (2019), *The Hitman's Bodyguard* (2017), *The Legend of Tarzan* (2016), *Chi-Raq* (2015), *The Avengers: Age of Ultron* (2015), *Kingsman: The Secret Service* (2014), *Captain America: The Winter Soldier* (2014), *RoboCop* (2014), *Oldboy* (2013), *Django Unchained* (2012), *The Avengers* (2012), *Captain America: The First Avenger* (2011), *Iron Man 2* (2010), *Mother and Child* (2009), *Soul Men* (2008), *Lakeview Terrace* (2008), *Black Snake Moan* (2006), *Snakes on a Plane* (2006), *Coach Carter* (2005), *Basic* (2003), *Changing Lanes*

(2002), *Shaft* (2000), *Jackie Brown* (1997), *A Time to Kill* (1996), *Losing Isaiah* (1995), *True Romance* (1993), *Menace II Society* (1993), *Juice* (1992), *Strictly Business* (1991), *Jungle Fever* (1991), *Mo' Better Blues* (1990), *School Daze* (1988), *Ragtime* (1981), *Together for Days* (1972)

Television movie (actor): *The Sunset Limited* (2011), *Against the Wall* (1994), *Dead or Alive: The Race for Gus Farace* (1991), *The Trial of the Moke* (1978).

Television (producer and actor): *Afro Samurai: Resurrection* (TV movie) (2009), *Afro Samurai* (TV miniseries) (2007)

Television (actor): *The Boondocks* (2005–10), *Freedom: A History of Us* (2003), *Ghostwriter* (1992)

Steve James (1952–1993), actor, stuntman, writer. Following a start in commercials, James began his film career as a stuntman. Born in New York City, he graduated from CW Post College an arts and film major. He choreographed fight scenes and was a black belt in Fu Jow Pai (Tiger Claw) Kung Fu. James considered actor Jackie Chan a major influence. In 1980, the role of Michael Jefferson in *The Exterminator* boosted his career, followed by *The Brother from Another Planet* in 1984 and *American Ninja* in 1985. James's thriving career was cut short when he succumbed to cancer at age forty-one.

Movie (writer and actor): *Street Hunter* (1990)

Movies (actor): *Weekend at Bernie's II* (1993), *McBain* (1991), *Mister Johnson* (1990), *Riverbend* (1989), *American Ninja 3: Blood Hunt* (1989), *I'm Gonna Git You Sucka* (1988), *Hero and the Terror* (1988), *Johnny Be Good* (1988), *American Ninja 2: The Confrontation* (1987), *Hollywood Shuffle* (1987), *Avenging Force* (1986), *Behind Enemy Lines* (1986), *The Delta Force* (1986), *To Live and Die in L.A.* (1985), *American Ninja* (1985), *Mask* (1985), *The Brother from Another Planet* (1984), *Vigilante* (1983), *The Soldier* (1982), *Times Square* (1980), *The Exterminator* (1980), *The Warriors* (1979), *The King of Kung Fu* (1978), *The Land That Time Forgot* (1975), *The Education of Sonny Carson* (1974)

Movie stuntman (credited): *The Brother from Another Planet* (stunt coordinator) (1984), *Hanky Panky* (1982), *Fighting Back* (1982), *Wolfen* (1981), *Oliver's Story* (1978), *The Education of Sonny Carson* (1974)

Movie stuntman (unaccredited): *Ragtime* (1981), *Fort Apache the Bronx* (1981), *He Knows You're Alone* (1980), *Dressed to Kill* (1980), *The Wanderers* (1979), *The Wiz* (1978)

Television movies (actor): *M.A.N.T.I.S.* (1994), *Hammer, Slammer, & Slade* (1990), *C.A.T. Squad: Python Wolf* (1988), *C.A.T. Squad* (1986), *The Atlanta Child Murders* (TV miniseries) (1985), *Fatal Vision* (1984), *Muggable Mary, Street Cop* (1982)

Terrence "J" Jenkins (1982), actor, television host, writer. Camera friendly, Jenkins was involved in media before he graduated from Northern Nash Rocky High School. Prior to graduating in mass communications from North Carolina A&T State University, he was a disc jockey at the campus radio station. He was born in Queens, New York, and raised in North Carolina. Jenkins first achieved major media recognition as television cohost with Rocsi Diaz for Black Entertainment Television's *106 & Park Top 10 Live*. The cohosting job did not come easy. He had multiple auditions in New York and Atlanta. His popularity on *106 & Park* led to movie offers where 2010 appearances in *Stomp the Yard 2: Homecoming* and *Burlesque* opened a path for an acting career. Always in demand, he was named cohost for E! News in 2013. Jenkins is the author of the book, The Wealth of My Mother's Wisdom, and CEO of his entertainment consulting firm, Jenkins Entertainment Group.

Writer (book): *The Wealth of My Mother's Wisdom* (2013)

Movies (actor): *The Perfect Match* (2016), **Think Like a Man Too** (2014), *Baggage Claim* (2013), *Sparkle* (2012), *Think Like a Man* (2012), *Burlesque* (2010), *Stomp the Yard 2: Homecoming* (2010)

Television documentary (production assistant): *Michael Jackson: 30th Anniversary Celebration* (2001)

Television (host, actor): *E! News* (2013–15), *106 & Park Top 10 Live* (2006–13), *The Game* (2011), *Kourtney & Kim Take Miami* (2009–10)

Anne-Marie Johnson (1960), actress, impressionist, and former First vice president of the Screen Actors Guild. Johnson holds the distinguished position of having been first national vice president of the Screen Actors Guild from 2005 to 2010 and serving on the board of directors. Recognized in film and television for her prominent comedic skills, Johnson was born in Los Angeles, California. She graduated from the University of California–Los Angeles with a degree in acting and theater. Though her body of work includes a substantial amount of television roles, the late 1980s and early 1990s were stellar showcasing of her talent on the silver screen. She starred in *I'm Gonna Git You Sucka* in 1988, followed by *The Five Heartbeats and Strictly Business* in 1991. Before and after cinematic film roles, she costarred in a plethora of television series from *Hill Street Blues* and **What's Happening Now!** in 1984–85 to **That's So Raven** in 2006.

Award: Ralph Morgan Award, (2016)

Movies: *About Fifty* (2011), *Suicide Dolls* (2010), *Pursuit of Happiness* (2001), *Down in the Delta* (1998), *Strictly Business* (1991), *True Identity* (1991), *The Five Heartbeats* (1991), *Robot Jox* (1989), *I'm Gonna Get You Sucka* (1988), *Hollywood Shuffle* (1987)

Television movies: *Uncorked* (2009), *Asteroid* (1997), *Dream Date* (1989), *High School U.S.A.* (1984)

Television: *For the People* (2018), *Imposters* (2018), *Days of Our Lives* (2012-2016), *House of Payne* (2007–09), *That's So Raven* (2006), *Girlfriends* (2003–04), *The System* (2003), *JAG* (1997–2002), *Melrose Place* (1995–96), *In Living Color* (1993–94), *In the Heat of the Night* (1988–1993), *What's Happening Now!* (1985–88), *Hill Street Blues* (1984–85), *Double Trouble* (1984–85)

Dwayne "the Rock" Johnson (1972), actor, producer, and professional wrestler. Johnson became a sought-after actor as a result of being television's reigning World Wrestling Federation champion. Sporadic television appearances that called for acting led to *The Scorpion King* in 2002. *The Rundown* in 2003 and *Walking Tall* in 2004 confirmed Johnson's interest in acting was not a passing fling. He has been cast in one leading role after the other often in the action genre. He graduated on full football scholarship from the University of Miami with a bachelor of general studies degree in criminology and physiology. Johnson was born in Hayward, California, to a boxing hierarchy on both his father and mother's side. His father, Rocky Johnson, was a professional wrestler while his mother, Ata Johnson, is the daughter of

Lia Maiva, a boxing promoter.

Awards: Kids' Choice Award, USA (2018, 2013), People's Choice Award (2017), Teen Choice Award (2017), CinemaCon, USA (2012), Teen Choice Award (2001)

Movie (producer, actor): *Rampage* (2018), *Jumani: Welcome to the Jungle* (2017), *Snitch* (2013), *Journey 2: The Mysterious Island* (2012), **Racing Dreams** (documentary, 2009)

Movies (actor): *Baywatch* (2017), *The Fate of the Furious* (2017), *Fast & Furious 7* (2015), *Hercules: The Thracian Wars* (2014), *Fast & Furious 6* (2013), *G.I. Joe: Retaliation* (2013), *Fast Five* (2011), *Faster* (2010), *The Other Guys* (2010), *Tooth Fairy* (2010), *Race to Witch Mountain* (2009), *Get Smart* (2008), *The Game Plan* (2008), *Gridiron Gang* (2006), *Doom* (2005), *Be Cool* (2005), *Walking Tall* (2004), *The Rundown* (2003), *The Scorpion King* (2002), *The Mummy Returns* (2001)

James Earl Jones (1931), actor. His robust, melodic voice is recognized when he is unseen. Stage, screen, television, commercials, voiceovers, there is no medium Jones hasn't conquered. Prior to his acting, he overcame a childhood tendency from age six to twelve to stutter. Born in Arkabutla, Mississippi, Jones started out a premed major, switched to drama, and earned a BA from the University of Michigan, where he also made his stage debut. He continued his academic training in the dramatic arts at the American Theatre Wing in New York and received a diploma after time spent in the United States Army. He rose to first lieutenant. While Jones has been well compensated in the film industry, his talent has been enormously utilized on the New York stage. After more than ten years of proving himself Off-Broadway from carrying a spear to the lead in Shakespeare's *Othello* and touring Europe in *The Emperor Jones*, he assured a successful career for himself when he landed the part of Jack Johnson in the Broadway production of *The Great White Hope*. He won a Tony Award in 1969 for the role. He won two Obie Awards for work Off-Broadway in 1962 and 1965. In 1987, he also received the Tony Award for Best Actor in playwright August Wilson's *Fences*. After his 1964 big-screen debut in *Dr. Strangelove or: How I Learned to Stop Worrying and Love the Bomb* and recreating his Academy Award–nominated role in the screen version of *The Great White Hope*, Jones's illustrious career has been unstoppable. In the role of Roop opposite Diahann Carroll in the 1974 movie *Claudine*, he was absolutely endearing. His lofty performance history includes numerous television appearances, commercial voiceovers, and the voice of Darth Vader in the *Star Wars* movie serials.

Awards: CinEuphoria Award (2018), Behind the Voice Actors Award (2017, 2015), Academy Award (2012), Chicago Film Critics Association Award (2011), Screen Actors Guild Award (2009), Character and Morality in Entertainment Award (2006), DVD Exclusive Award (2006, 2003), Method Fest Award (2001), Daytime Emmy Award (2000), Kansas City Film Critics Circle Award (1996), Joseph Plateau Award (1995), National Board of Review, USA Award (1995), USA Film Festival Award (1995), Image Award (1993, 1975), CableACE Award (1991), Primetime Emmy Award (1991), Golden Globes Award (1971)

Movies: *The Lion King* (2019), *The Angriest Man in Brooklyn* (2014), *Gimme Shelter* (2013), *Welcome Home, Roscoe Jenkins* (2008), *Finder's Fee* (2001), *The Annihilation of Fish* (1999), *On the Q.T.* (1999), *Gang Related* (1997), *A Family Thing* (1996), *Jefferson in Paris* (1995), *Clear and Present Danger* (1994), The *Meteor Man* (1993), *Patriot Games* (1992), *Convicts* (1991), *The Hunt for Red October* (1990), *Field of Dreams* (1989), *Coming to America* (1988), *Gardens of Stone* (1987), *Soul Man* (1986), *Conan the Barbarian* (1982), *A Piece of the Action* (1977), *The Greatest* (1977), *The Bingo Long Traveling All-Stars & Motor Kings* (1976), *The River Niger* (1976), *Claudine* (1974), *The Man* (1972), *The Great White Hope* (1970), *Dr. Strangelove or: How I Learned to Stop Worrying and Love the Bomb* (1964) Movies (voice): *Quantum Quest: A Cassini Space Odyssey* (2010), *Jack and the Beanstalk* (2010), *Click* (2006), *Scary Movie 4* (2006), *Robots* (2005), *Judge Dredd* (1995), *The Lion King* (1994), *Star Wars: Episode VI–Return of the Jedi* (1983), *Star Wars: Episode V–The Empire Strikes Back* (1980), *Star Wars: IV–A New Hope* (1977)

Television movies: *The Lion Guard: Return of the Roar* (2015), *The Magic 7* (2009), *The Reading Room* (2005), *Feast of All Saints* (2001), *Santa and Pete* (1999), *Summer's End* (1999), *The Second Civil War* (1997), *The Vernon Johns*

Story (1994), *Percy & Thunder* (1993), *Lincoln* (narrator voice) (1992), *The Vegas Strip War* (1984), *The Me Nobody Knows* (introduction) (1980), *Guyana Tragedy: The Story of Jim Jones* (1980), *Paul Robeson* (1979), The Star Wars Holiday Special (voice) (1978), *The Greatest Thing That Almost Happened* (1977)

Television: *Star Wars Rebels* (2014-16), *Everwood* (2003–04), *Merlin* (TV miniseries) (1998), *Homicide: Life on the Street* (1997), *Under One Roof* (1995), *Pros and Cons* (1991–92), *Gabriel's Fire* (1990–91), *Mathnet* (1987–1991), *Me and Mom* (1985), *The Atlanta Child Murders* (TV miniseries) (1985), *Freedom to Speak* (TV miniseries) (1981), *Paris* (1979–80), *Roots: The Next Generations* (TV miniseries) (1979), *Roots* (TV miniseries) (1977), *Dr. Kildare* (1966)

Rashida Jones (1976), actress, musician, writer. Jones has often been described as the embodiment of intelligence, beauty, and humor. A student of religion and philosophy, Jones graduated from Harvard University. Born in Los Angeles, California, she is the daughter of music and media mogul Quincy Jones and actress Peggy Lipton. Active in college stage productions, upon graduation, her first screen break was a television miniseries *The Last Don* in 1997. The television series *Parks and Recreation* was a showcase for Jones' comedic flair. Tapping into other talents, Jones and Will McCormick cowrote the screenplay for the 2012 film release *Celeste & Jesse Forever*, which Jones also produced. She is also a musician and singer, performing and contributing to a number of television series and film soundtracks. Recognized for her political activism, Jones is involved in a diverse number of philanthropic causes that include homelessness, medical research, childhood cancer, and AIDS.

Awards: Palm Springs International Film Festival Award (2011), Hollywood Film Festival Award (2010), Phoenix Film Critics Society Award (2010)

Movie (writer, producer, soundtrack, actress): *Celeste & Jesse Forever* (2012)

Movie (soundtrack): *The Ten* (2007)

Movies (actress): *Cuban Fury* (2014), *Decoding Annie Parker* (2013), *The Muppets* (2011), *Our Idiot Brother* (2011), The *Social Network* (2010), *Cop Out* (2010), *I Love You, Man* (2009), *The Ten* (2007), *Little*

Black Book (2004), *Roadside Assistance* (2001), *East of A* (2000)
   Television (producer): *Claws* (2017)
   Television (producer, director): *Angie Tribeca* (2017)
   Television documentary (director): *Quincy* (2018)
   Television (soundtrack): *Parks and Recreation* (2010–13), *The Office* (2007–11), *Late Night with Jimmy Fallon* (2009–10)
   Television (actress): *Angie Tribeca* (2016-18), *Parks and Recreation* (2009–14), *The Awesomes* (2013), *The Office* (2006–11), *Unhitched* (2008), *Wanted* (2005), *NY-LON* (2004), *Boston Public* (2000–02)

Paula Kelly (1943), actress, dancer. From birth, Kelly was surrounded by show business. Her mother by the same name, Paula Kelly, was a jazz singer. After majoring in music in high school, Kelly earned a master's degree from the Juilliard School of Music as a dance major. Her career blossomed from the stage in New York and London to film and television. She was a recognized dancer before adding "actor" to her resume. Born in Jacksonville, Florida, Kelly was among the first African American actresses to take on roles that were not definitively meant for African Americans. In 1969, she recreated her role as Helene on the Broadway stage in the film *Sweet Charity*. She's also in the forefront of taking on controversial roles such as the other half of a same sex couple trying to find acceptance in the 1989 television movie *The Women of Brewster Place*. The superbly played role of Theresa earned her a Primetime Emmy nomination. She is the recipient of the Los Angeles Drama Critics Circle Award and the NAACP Image Award.

   Movies: *Once Upon a Time…When We Were Colored* (1995), *Drop Squad* (1994), *Jo Dancer, Your Life Is Calling* (1986), Drum (1976), *Uptown Saturday Night* (1974), *Lost in the Stars* (1974), *Tough Guys* (1974), *The Spook Who Sat by the Door* (1973), *Soylent Green* (1973), *Trouble Man* (1972), *Top of the Heap* (1972), *Cool Breeze* (1972), *The Andromeda Strain* (1971), *Sweet Charity* (1969)
   Television movies: *Run for the Dream: The Gail Devers Story* (1996), *The Women of Brewster Place* (1989), *Peter Pan* (1976) Television: *South Central* (1994), *Santa Barbara* (1984–85), *Night Court* (1984), *Police Woman* (1975–77)

Boris Kodjoe (1973), actor, producer. Kodjoe's original goal of being a professional tennis player was sidetracked by a back injury. Following through on his tennis scholarship, he graduated with a BA in Marketing from Virginia Commonwealth University. The former model-turned-actor is best known as Damon Carter in the groundbreaking family television drama *Soul Food* from 2000–2004. He made quite an impression on the big screen as the sensitive Frankie Henderson in *Madea's Family Reunion* in 2006. Kodjoe and wife, actress Nicole Ari Parker, ushered in the 2004–2005 television season with their own comedy show, *Second Time Around*. In 2008, he took to the Broadway stage in a Debbie Allen–directed production of *Cat on a Hot Tin Roof*. Born in Vienna, Austria, Kodjoe is fluent in French, English, and German. Kodjoe and Parker founded Sophie's Voice Foundation in 2008 in honor of their daughter, Sophie, who was diagnosed with spina bifida at birth. They are also parents to son, Nicholas. Kodjoe is the recipient of the Supermodel Award during the 1998 fall fashion shows and was named one of the 50 Most Beautiful People in the World by *People* magazine in 2002. Kodjoe is an advocate for many social issues and is committed to the elimination of racism and the celebration of diversity.

Movie (producer and actor): *Doing Hard Time* (2004)

Movies (actor): *Addicted* (2014), *Baggage Claim* (2013), *Resident Evil: Retribution* (2012), *Resident Evil: Afterlife* (2010), *The Confidant* (2010), *Surrogates* (2009), *All About Us* (2007), *Madea's Family Reunion* (2006), *The Gospel* (2005), *Brown Sugar* (2002), Love & Basketball (2000)

Television Movie (producer, actor): *Downsized* (2017)

Television movies (actor): *A Killer Among Us* (2012), *Scruples* (2012), *If You Lived Here, You'd Be Home Now* (2006)

Television (producer, actor): *Cape Town* (2016)

Television (actor): *Code Black* (2016-18), *Members Only* (2015), *Real Husbands of Hollywood* (2013–15), *Undercovers* (2010–11), *Second Time Around* (2004–05), *Soul Food* (2000–04), *Boston Public* (2003)

Eriq La Salle (1962), actor, director, producer, and novelist. La Salle maintains career progression in varied directions. He was born in Hartford, Connecticut. La Salle realized he was interested in acting as a young teen.

He attended the Juilliard School and completed his BFA degree at New York University's Tisch School of the Arts. Upon graduation, he was cast in Joseph Papp's Shakespeare in the Park production of *Henry V* and continued acting Off-Broadway until opportunities in film and television quickly followed. La Salle's film career hit the ground running with substantial roles in his first two films, *Rappin'* and *Cut and Run* in 1985. After his breakout role as Darryl Jenks in *Coming to America* in 1988 and television role of Dr. Peter Benson in the mega television hit *ER*, La Salle entered the rare position of Hollywood talent with numerous options. The choices were aptly put to work as a director and producer of television and film projects. He authored two mystery thriller novels published in 2012, *Laws of Innocence* and *Laws of Depravity*.

Awards: Black Reel Award (2003), Image Award (2002, 2000, 1999), Screen Actors Guild Award (1999, 1998, 1997, 1996)

Movies (producer and actor): *The Salton Sea* (2002)

Movies (director and actor): *Crazy as Hell* (also producer) (2002), *Psalms from the Underground* (short) (1996)

Movies (actor): *Johnny Was* (2006), *Inside Out* (2005), *Biker Boyz* (2003), *One Hour Photo* (2002), *Five Corners* (1987), *Where Are the Children?* (1986), *Cut and Run* (1985), *Rappin'* (1985)

Television movie (producer and actor): *Mind Prey* (1999)

Television movies (director and actor): *Rebound: The Legend of Earl 'The Goat' Manigault* (1996)

Television movie (director): *Notes from Dad* (2013)

Television movies (actor): *Relative Stranger* (2009), *Conviction* (2005), *Empty Cradle* (1993), *Hammer, Slammer, & Slade* (1990), *Out of the Darkness* (1985)

Television series (director): *Chicago P.D.* (2016-18), Numerous guest director spots from 2000 to 2018, which includes writing and directing an episode of the *Twilight Zone* in 2003.

Television (actor): *Under the Dome* (2015), *Blackout* (2012), *A Gifted Man* (2011–12), *How to Make It in America* (2011), *The System* (2004), *ER* (1994–2002, 2009)

Sanaa Lathan (1971), actress. Conceived into the world of entertainment, Lathan is the daughter of celebrated television director,

Stan Lathan. She graduated with a BA in English from the University of California, Berkeley and earned a master's from the Yale School of Drama. After graduation, Lathan immediately took to the New York stage and then Los Angeles. Though she did not grow up always knowing she wanted to act, she has made great strides in the profession. While in New York, Lathan perfected her craft performing in a number of Shakespearian plays. After a couple of years in Los Angeles doing television and the 1998 movie *Blade*, her first lead film role came in 2000 as Monica Wright in *Love & Basketball*.

Awards: Black Reel Awards for Television (2017), All Def Movie Award (2016), Image Award (2016, 2001), Acapulco Black Film Festival (2014), American Black Film Festival Award (2004), Black Reel Award (2004, 2001), BET Award (2001)

Movie (producer, actress): *The Perfect Guy* (2015)

Movies (actress): *Native Son* (2019), *The Best Man Wedding* (2016), *The Best Man Holiday* (2013), *Contagion* (2011), *Wonderful World* (2009), *Powder Blue* (2009), *The Family That Preys* (2008), *Something New* (2006), *AVP: Alien vs. Predator* (2004), *Out of Time* (2003), *Brown Sugar* (2002), *Love & Basketball* (2000), *The Best Man* (1999), *The Wood* (1999), *Catfish in the Black Bean Sauce* (1999), *Life* (1999), *Blade* (1998), *Drive* (1997)

Television movies (actress): *Tilda* (2011), *A Raisin in the Sun* (2008), *Disappearing Acts* (2000), *Miracle in the Woods* (1997)

Television (actress): *Family Guy* (2010-2018), *Shots Fired* (2017), *The Cleveland Show* (2009–13), *Boss* (2012), *Nip/Tuck* (2006), *LateLine* (1998–99)

Harry Lennix(1964), actor. Lennix's entrée into the world of cinema was decidedly different. He was a music and English teacher in the Chicago school district for several years while simultaneously acting on stage. He graduated with a BS from Northwestern University. The recipient of three Joseph Jefferson Awards for stage productions *Ma Rainey's Black Bottom* and *Caught in the Act*, Lennix's first film role was in *The Package* in 1989. The 1991 role of Dresser in *The Five Heartbeats* led to a long profitable film career. He has fared equally well in television. Lennix was born in Chicago, Illinois.

Awards: Best Actors Film Festival (2017), American Movie Award (2016), Northeast Film Festival, US (2014), Action on Film International Film Festival, USA Award (2011), Black Reel Award (2003), NAMIC Vision Award (2003), Satellite Award (2000)

Movies (producer, actor): *Romeo and Juliet in Harlem* (2017)

Movies (actor): *Timeless* (2016), *Chi-Raq* (2015), *Back to School Mom* (2015), *Man of Steel* (2013), *State of Play* (2009), *Stomp the Yard* (2007), *Ray* (2004), *Suspect Zero* (2004), *Barbershop 2: Back in Business* (2004), *The Matrix Revolutions* (2003), *The Matrix Reloaded* (2003), *Don't Explain* (2002), *Collateral Damage* (2002), *Love & Basketball* (2000), *Get on the Bus* (1996), *Clockers* (1995), *Mo' Money* (1992), *The Five Heartbeats* (1991)

Television (actor): *Billions* (2016-18), *The Blacklist* (2013-18), *Emily Owens M.D.* (2012–13), *Dollhouse* (2009–10), *Little Britain USA* (2008), *24* (2007), *Commander in Chief* (2005–06), *Keep the Faith, Baby* (TV movie) (2002), *Diagnosis Murder* (1997–98), *ER* (1997)

Delroy Lindo (1952), actor. Lindo personifies the rugged intellectual. He was born in Eltham, London, England. After immigrating to Canada, his family finally settled in the San Francisco Bay Area. As a teenager, Lindo attended the acting program at the American Conservatory Theater in San Francisco. Bothered by a personal void of not completing college, he returned after attaining success in the film industry. At age fifty-one, he completed his BA degree at San Francisco State University, open to the idea of eventually pursuing a master's. After graduation, he effortlessly shifted back into moviemaking as Carl in the 2005 film *Sahara*. With a sound theatrical-stage foundation, Lindo established a foothold in film, appearing in several Spike Lee productions beginning with the role of West Indian Archie in *Malcolm X*. He was the executive producer of the 2007 holiday comedy *This Christmas* in 2007.

Awards: Image Award (2010), Satellite Award (1999), National Society of Film Critics Award (1996, 1993)

Movie (producer and actor): *Do You Believe?* (2015), *This Christmas* (2007)

Movies (actor): *Point Break* (2015), *The Big Bang* (2011), *Up* (2009), *Domino* (2005), *Sahara* (2005), *The One* (2001), *The Last Castle* (2001),

Gone in Sixty Seconds (2000), *Romeo Must Die* (2000), *The Cider House Rules* (1999), *A Life Less Ordinary* (1997), *Ransom* (1996), *Get Shorty* (1995), *Clockers* (1995), *Crooklyn* (1994), *Malcolm X* (1992)

Television movies (actor): *Marvel's Most Wanted* (2016), *The Exonerated* (2005), *Lakawanna Blues* (2005), *Strange Justice* (1999), *Glory & Honor* (1998), *First Time Felon* (1997), *Soul of the Game* (1996)

Television (actor): *The Good Fight* (20117-18), *Blood & Oil* (2015), *Believe* (2014), *The Chicago Code* (2011), *Kidnapped* (2006–07), *Beauty and the Beast* (1987)

Cleavon Little (1939–1992), actor. The 1974 release of *Blazing Saddles* was the pinnacle of Little's film career. Still, his love for the theater was profound. Of his many stage appearances between 1968 and 1988, it was in 1971 that he won a Tony and Drama Desk Award for his role in *Purlie*. He received his BA from San Diego State University and earned a full master's scholarship to Juilliard School. He continued his training at the American Academy of Dramatic Arts. Little was born in Chickasha, Oklahoma.

Awards: Primetime Emmy Award (1989), Star on the Walk of Fame (1994)

Movies: *Once Bitten* (1985), *Toy Soldiers* (1984), *The Salamander* (1981), *Scavenger Hunt* (1979), *Greased Lightning* (1977), *Blazing Saddles* (1974), *Vanishing Point* (1971), *Cotton Comes to Harlem* (1970), *John and Mary* (1969), *What's So Bad About Feeling Good?* (1968)

Television movies: *In the Nick of Time* (1991), *Separate But Equal* (1991), *Perfect Harmony* (1991), *A House Divided: Denmark Vessey's Rebellion* (1982), *Don't Look Back: The Story of Leroy 'Satchel' Page* (1981), *The Sky Is Gray* (1980), *Money to Burn* (1973)

Television: *True Colors* (1991–92), *Bagdad Café* (1990–91), *The New Temperature Risings Show* (1972–74)

Carl Lumbly (1951), actor. Instilled with a strong work ethic matched with creative discretion, Lumbly brings thoughtful presence to the screen. He was born in Minneapolis, Minnesota. A graduate of Macalester College with a BA in English, Lumbly's entry into the world of acting was happenstance. While working as a journalist, he was approached to audition for a theater company he had showed up to write an article about. He made the cut. He did not take the experience too seriously and moved from Minneapolis to San Francisco to write and saw an ad for auditions for plays *Sizwe Banzi Is Dead* and *The Island* written by South African writer Athol Fugard. He got the roles. After touring with the plays, cinema beckoned. A succession of minor film and television appearances and a reoccurring role on the television series *Cagney & Lacey* in 1981–88 led to notable film roles in *Everybody's All American* in 1988 and *To Sleep with Anger* in 1990. The *Cagney & Lacey* set was also where Lumbly met his wife, actress Vonetta McGee. In 2012, he was featured as Captain Joel Rucker on the television series *Southland*. Television success continues with featured roles on *Supergirl* and *NCIS: Los Angeles.*

Awards: Behind the Voice Actors Award (2013), Los Angeles Drama Critics Circle Award (1980)

Movies: *America Is Still the Place* (2015), *The Alphabet Killer* (2008), *Namibia: The Struggle for Liberation* (2007), *Just a Dream* (2002), *Men of Honor* (2000), *How Stella Got Her Groove Back* (1998), *South Central* (1992), *To Sleep with Anger* (1990), *Judgment in Berlin* (1988), *The Bedroom Window* (1987)

Television (documentary): *Nat Turner: A Troublesome Property* (2003), *Marcus Garvey: Look for Me in the Whirlwind* (2001), *The Massachusetts 54th Colored Infantry* (1991)

Television movies: *Sounder* (2003), *Little Richard* (2000), *The Color of Friendship* (2000), *The Wedding* (1998), *Buffalo Soldiers* (1997), *The Ditchdigger's Daughters* (1997), *On Promised Land* (1994), *Brother Future* (1991), *Moe's World* (1990), *Conspiracy: The Trial of the Chicago 8* (1987), *Undercover with the KKK* (1979)

Television: *Supergirl* (2017-18), *NCIS: Los Angeles* (2017-18), *The Returned* (2015), *Zoo* (2015), Southland (2012), *Black Panther* (2010), *Alias* (2001–06), *Justice League* (2001–06), M.A.N.T.I.S. (1994–97), *EZ Streets* (1996–97), *Going to Extremes* (1992–93), *L.A. Law* (1989–90), *Cagney & Lacey* (1981–88)

Anthony Mackie (1978), actor. Mackie is as fortunate as he is talented. Once he graduated from Juilliard School, he hit the New York stage in 2002 and within a year won an Obie Award for his Off-Broadway performance in the play *Talk* written by Carl Hancock Rux. In 2002, he also made his cinematic debut in *8 Mile*. From that point he has been cast in key roles in top-tier independent and blockbuster films. In 2009, he played Tupac Shakur in the movie *Notorious*. He also played Shakur while in college in an Off-Broadway play titled *Up Against the Wind* in 2001. Mackie joined a star-studded cast for action packed *Captain America: The Winter Soldier* in 2014 and continues his Falcon superhero role in Avengers*: Infinity War*. He was born in New Orleans, Louisiana.

Awards: Black Reel Award (2011, 2010), Chicago International Film Festival Award (2011), Gotham Award (2009), Washington DC Area Film Critics Association Award (2009)

Movies: *Avengers: Infinity War* (2018), *Detroit* (2017), Captain America: *Civil War* (2016), *Avengers: Age of Ultron* (2015), *Shelter* (2014), *Black or White* (2014), *Captain America: The Winter Soldier* (2014), *Repentance* (2014), *The Fifth Estate* (2013), *Runner* (2013), *Pain & Gain* (2013), *The Inevitable Defeat of Mister& Pete* (2013), *Gangster Squad* (2013), *The Adjustment Bureau* (2011), *Notorious* (2009), *The Hurt Locker* (2008), *Freedomland* (2006), *Half Nelson* (2006), *Million Dollar Baby* (2004), *She Hate Me* (2004), *The Manchurian Candidate* (2004), *Brother to Brother* (2004), *Hollywood Homicide* (2003), *8 Mile* (2002)

Television movie: *Sucker Free City* (2004)

S. Epatha Merkerson (1952), actress. Known for sixteen televised seasons in the role of Lieutenant Anita Van Buren on the long-running, serial-spawning *Law & Order* franchise, Merkerson made history being the longest tenured female and African American character in the history of primetime television. A native of Saginaw, Michigan, Merkerson graduated with a BFA from Wayne State University and was later presented with an honorary doctorate of humane letters. For her New York stage performances she won an Obie Award for *I'm Not Stupid* and a Helen Hayes Award for *The Old Settler*. Merkerson's introduction to television was as Reba the mail lady of *Pee-Wee's Playhouse*. Her cinematic debut was as Dr. Jamison in Spike Lee's innovative film *She's Gotta Have It* in 1986. Merkerson has long been an advocate of lung cancer awareness, smoking cessation, and education.

Awards: Best Actors Film Festival Award (2016), Image Award (2011,

2010, 2006), Black Reel Award (2006), Golden Globe Award (2006), Gracie Allen Award (2006), Prism Award (2006), Screen Actors Guild Award (2006), Character and Morality in Entertainment Award (2005), Primetime Emmy Award (2005)

Documentary (producer, director): *The Contradictions of Fair Hope* (2012)

Movies (actress): *Year by the Sea* (2016), *Peeples* (2013), *Lincoln* (2012), *Mother and Child* (2009), *Black Snake Moan* (2006), *Jersey Girl* (2004), *Radio* (2003), *Random Hearts* (1999), *Jacobs Ladder* (1990), *Loose Cannons* (1990), *She's Gotta Have It* (1986)

Television movies (actress): *The Gabby Douglas Story* (2014), *Girl, Positive* (2007), *Lackawanna Blues* (2005), *A Girl Thing* (2001), *Breaking Through* (1996), *A Mother's Prayer* (1995), *A Place for Annie* (1994), *It's Nothing Personal* (1993), *Moe's World* (1990) Television (actress): *Chicago Med* (2015-18), *Chicago Fire* (2015-17), *Deception* (2013), *Law & Order* (1991–2010), American Masters (TV documentaries) (1999, 2008), *The Closer* (2010), *Here and Now* (1992–93), *Mann & Machine* (1992), *Pee-Wee's Playhouse* (1986–89)

Melba Moore (1945), actress, singer. A native New Yorker, Moore was created to entertain, be it stage, film, or television. With father, big band leader Teddy Hill, mother, singer Bonnie Davis, and stepfather, jazz pianist Clement Mooreland, Moore's path to music was inherent. Moore graduated with a BA in Musical Education from Montclair Teachers College and taught in the Newark school system. While teaching and performing on the side, she auditioned for the Broadway musical *Hair*. Various roles in the musical opened up to her until she landed the lead. From *Hair* she crossed over to the lead in another Broadway musical *Purlie*, for which she won numerous awards including a Tony. Moore has contributed as a singer to many movie soundtracks and, in 1972 television, cohosted the *Melba Moore-Clifton Davis Show*. In 1974, she stepped into the lead role of Irina in the dramatic cinematic love story *Lost in the Stars*. Her participation in the recording of the official African American national anthem, "Lift Every Voice and Sing," in 1986 was groundbreaking. A continuous presence on the Broadway stage and in her one-woman show *I'm Still Standing*, Moore starred in the film *The*

Fighting Temptations in 2003.
Movie (producer and director): *Melba Moore: Live in Concert* (2007)
Movies (actress): *The Fighting Temptations* (2003), *Def by Temptation* (1990), *All Dogs Go to Heaven* (voice-over) (1989), *Hair* (1979), *Lost in the Stars* (1974)
Television movies (actress): *Purlie* (1981), *The American Woman: Portraits of Courage* (1976)
Television (actress): *Falcon Crest* (1987), *Melba* (1986), *American Playhouse*, "Charlotte Forten's Mission: Experiment in Freedom" (1985), *The Love Boat* (1979–1984)

Shemar Moore (1970), actor. A very pronounced trait is Moore's steadfastness. He gets with a show and remains for a lengthy amount of time. Television has been very good for the eventual film star beginning with his television-series debut in *Birds of Prey* from 2002–03. His appearances on *The Young and the Restless* from 1995–2005 earned him several Image Awards. In the mix is four years hosting *Soul Train* followed by the role of profiler Derek Morgan on *Criminal Minds* from 2005–15. The former model-turned-actor was born in Oakland, California, and graduated with a BA in Communications from Santa Clara University. The transition to film was relatively smooth with one of his most notable appearances in *Diary of a Mad Black Woman* in 2005 and *The Brothers* in 2001.
Awards: Image Award (2015, 2006, 2005, 2002, 2001, 2000, 1999, 1998), Daytime Emmy Award (2000)
Movie (producer, actor): *The Bounce Back* (2016)
Movies: *Diary of a Mad Black Woman* (2005), *The Seat Filler* (2004), *The Brothers* (2001), *Box Marley* (2000), *Butter* (1998), *Hav Plenty* (1997)
Television movies (actor): *Reversible Errors* (2004), *How to Marry a Billionaire: A Christmas Tale* (2000), *Mama Flora's Family* (1998)
Television (producer, actor): *S.W.A.T.* (2017-18)
Television (actor): *Criminal Minds* (2005–17), *Birds of Prey* (2002–03), *Soul Train* (host) (1995–2003), *The Young and the Restless* (1995–2005)

Joe Morton (1947), actor. Morton has long been an admirable presence on the big screen. From his 1984 portrayal as a mute alien in *A Brother from Another Planet* to his reoccurring role of Rowan Pope in the television hit *Scandal*, Morton delivers. He is a standout in roles that call for the cerebral character. Born in New York City, Morton attended Hoftra University majoring in drama. He took to the Broadway stage after a quick stint Off-Broadway. He made his Broadway debut in the production of *Hair*. Morton was appointed to the Denzel Washington Endowed Chair for Theatre at Fordham University in 2012 to teach drama.

Awards: Image Award (2018, 2015, 2014), Primetime Emmy Award (2014), NAACP Award (1993, 1990), Sitges-Catalonian International Film Festival Award (1984)

Movies: *Home* (2013), *The Mulberry Tree* (2010), *American Gangster* (2007), *The Night Listener* (2006), *Back in the Day* (2005), *Paycheck* (2003), *Ali* (2001), *Blues Brothers 2000* (1998), *Executive Decision* (1996), *Speed* (1994), *The Inkwell* (1994), *Terminator 2: Judgment Day* (1991), *Tap* (1989), *The Good Mother* (1988), *The Brother from Another Planet* (1984)

Television movies: *Gone but Not Forgotten* (2005), *Jasper Texas* (2003), *Ali: An American Hero* (2000), *Mutiny* (1999), *Miss Ever's Boys* (1997), *Legacy of Lies* (1992), *Challenger* (1990), *Howard Beach: Making a Case for Murder* (1989), *Alone in the Neon Jungle* (1988), *Hostile Witness* (1988)

Television: *Proof* (2015), *Scandal* (2013–18), *Eureka* (2006–12), *The Good Wife* (2009–11), *The American Experience* (documentary narrator,1999–2010), *E-Ring* (2005–06), *Law & Order* (1992–2005), *Smallville* (2001–02), *Prince Street* (1997–2000), *Mercy Point* (1998–99), *Under One Roof* (1995), *Tribeca* (1993), *A Different World* (1992), *Equal Justice* (1990–91), *The Equalizer* (1987–89), *Grady* (1975–76)

Denise Nicholas (1944), actress, writer. Renaissance woman Nicholas' career personifies the burgeoning African American cultural arts movement of the late 1960s into the '70s that paved the way for expansion in the twenty-first century. Nicholas honed her craft with some of the most esteemed theater companies of the era that include the Negro Ensemble Company, Free Southern Company, and New Federal Theatre. Born in Detroit, Michigan, she began her college study at Tulane University in fine arts. She left to pursue acting with the Free Southern Theater during the civil rights movement. Nicholas resumed her studies and earned a BA in Drama at the University of Southern California twenty years later. She taught there for a while before returning to television in the role of Harriet Delong in, *In the Heat of the Night* from 1989 to 1995. She also wrote several of the show's episodes. Nicholas's entrée to the silver screen came as Michelle in the classic horror *Blacula* in 1972. In 2005, she published the award-winning novel *Freshwater Road*.

Award: Image Award (1976)

Movies (actress): *Proud* (2004), *Ritual* (2000), *Ghost Dad* (1990), *Marvin & Tige* (1983), *Capricorn One* (1977), *A Piece of the Action* (1977), *Let's Do It Again* (1975), *Mr. Ricco* (1975), *Blacula* (1972)

Television movies (actress): *On Thin Ice: The Tai Babilonia Story* (1990), *Mother's Day* (1989), *And the Children Shall Lead* (1985), *The Sophisticated Gents* (1981)

Television (writer): *In the Heat of the Night* (1992–94)

Television (actress): *Living Single* (1997), *In the Heat of the Night* (1989–1995), *The Love Boat* (1980–82), *Baby, I'm Back* (1977–78), *Room 222* (1969–1974), *N.Y.P.D.* (1967–69)

Bill Nunn (1953-2016), actor. Nunn made his screen presence felt with his bountiful and diverse performances. Be it the role of a school principal in *Won't Back Down*, a newsman in the *Spider-Man* trilogy, or Radio Raheem in *School Daze*, Nunn resists being typecast. A native of Pittsburgh, Pennsylvania, he received his BA in English from Morehouse College. His first intention being a writer, Nunn became a teacher after graduating college. He made his major acting debut as Grady in fellow Morehouse College alumnus, Spike Lee's, *School Daze* in 1988.

Movies: *Won't Back Down* (2012), *Spider-Man 3* (2007), *Idlewild* (2006), *Spider-Man 2* (2004), *Runaway Jury* (2003), *Spider-Man* (2002), *Lockdown* (2000), *He Got Game* (1998), *Kiss the Girls* (1997), *The Last Seduction* (1994), *Sister Act* (1992), *New Jack City* (1991), *Mo' Better Blues* (1990), *Do the Right Thing* (1989), *School Daze* (1988)

Television movies: *A Raisin in the Sun* (2008), *Passing Glory* (1999), *Always Outnumbered* (1998), *Mr. and Mrs. Loving* (1996), *The Affair* (1995), *White Lie* (1991), *The Littlest Victims* (1989)

Television: *Sirens* (2014-15)

Adepero Oduye, pronounced "add-eh-pair-o oh-due-yay," (1978), actress, writer. For Oduye, success hinged on a strong will combined with charm and grace. She was determined to fulfill her dream. It was ten years of minor roles and casting in small independent projects before achieving recognition in a barrier breaking role in the 2011 release of *Pariah*. Oduye became more of a familiar face in the role of Annelle in the cable television remake of *Steel Magnolias* in 2012. The Brooklyn, New York born Nigerian American graduated from Cornell University a premed major. After graduation, Oduye pursued acting, taking classes and performing on stage. *The Feels* television series has allowed her to showcase her writing skills.

Awards: NYC Web Fest (2017), African American Film Critics Association Award (2012), Black Reel Award (2012), Denver Film Festival Award (2011)

Movies (actress): *Geostorm* (2017), *12 Years a Slave* (2013), *Pariah* (2011), *Half Nelson* (2006), *On the Outs* (2004)

Television movies (actress): *Steel Magnolias* (2012), *Wifey* (2007)

Television (writer, actress): *The Feels* (2017)

Nate Parker (1979), actor, producer. Parker's film career was determined by sheer fate. He had already graduated with honors from the University of Arizona with a degree in management science and information systems (a.k.a. business and computer programming) when a talent manager discovered him. From Arizona, Parker accompanied a friend to Texas for a modeling audition when he was unexpectedly approached. Parker immediately headed for Los Angeles and found intermittent work in commercials while using his computer skills to design websites and business cards. Born in Norfolk, Virginia, Parker's college pursuit began on a wrestling scholarship. He is recognized in cinema circles for his deep intensity and show of respect when auditioning for a role. When he faced Denzel Washington to audition for the role of Harry

Lowe in the 2005 film *The Great Debaters*, Parker handed Washington a written biography he created for the character upon leaving. The role of Neil in the *Secret Life of Bees* in 2008 was a definite step-up in establishing his career. His debut as a movie producer was with the 2016 release of *Birth of a Nation*.

Awards: CinemaCon, USA (2016), Sundance Film Festival (2016), Black Reel Awards (2015), 168 Film Festival, US (2013), African American Film Critics Association (2012), Hamptons International Film Festival Award (2012)

Movie (producer, actor) *The Birth of a Nation* (2016)

Movies (actor): *Beyond the Lights* (2014), *Non-Stop* (2014), *Red Hook Summer* (2012), *Arbitrage* (2012), *Red Tails* (2012), *Blood Done Sign My Name* (2010), *Rome & Jewel* (2008), *The Secret Life of Bees* (2008), *Felon* (2008), *The Great Debaters* (2007), *Pride* (2007), *Dirty* (2005)

Nicole Ari Parker (1970), actress. Parker's parents may have wanted a traditional career path for Parker; she had other ideas. Though she did portray an attorney in the hit television series *Soul Food*, having studied and performed with the Washington Ballet Company, she ultimately earned a degree in acting from New York University's Tisch School of the Arts. Fueled by stage roles in Off-Broadway productions including *Chicago* and *Romeo and Juliet*, her career took a leap with independent films. She boldly stepped into the role of Becky Barnett in *Boogie Nights* in 1997. By 2000 Parker's career headed mainstream with *Remember the Titans*.

Awards: Urbanworld Film Festival Award (1999), Florida Film Critics Award (1998)

Movies (actress): *Almost Christmas* (2016), *Repentance* (2014), *35 and Ticking* (2011), *Pastor Brown* (2009) *Imagine That* (2009), *Black Dynamite* (2009), *Welcome Home, Roscoe Jenkins* (2008), *King's Ransom* (2005), *Brown Sugar* (2002), *Remember the Titans* (2000), *Dancing in September* (2000), *Blue Streak* (1999), *Harlem Aria* (1999), *Loving Jezebel* (1999), *Mute Love* (1999), *Spark* (1998), *Boogie Nights* (1997), *The Incredibly True Adventure of Two Girls in Love* (1995)

Television movie (producer, actress): *Downsized* (2017)

Television movies (actress): *Big Mike* (2011), *The Loretta Claiborne*

Story (2000), *Mind Prey* (1999), *Exiled* (1998), *Subway Stories: Tales from the Underground* (1997), *Rebound: The Legend of Earl 'The Goat' Manigault* (1996), *Divas* (1995)

Television (actress): *Empire* (2017-18), *Time After Time* (2017), Rosewood (2015-16), *Murder in the First* (2014), *Revolution* (2013), *The Deep End* (2010), *Second Time Around* (2004–05), Soul *Food* (2000–04), *The System* (2003), *Cosby* (1999–2000)

Paula Jai Parker (1969), actress, director, producer. For the most part a comedic actress, Parker couldn't leave for New York fast enough to perform as a stand-up comic after graduation from Howard University. Once she became a regular on *The Apollo Comedy Hour* television series in 1992–93, it didn't take long to answer the call of Hollywood. Parker's film debut was the role of Joi in the 1995 film *Friday*. That same year she won the CableACE Award for the role of Tang in the television movie *Cosmic Slop*. Parker's memorable roles have been in the films *Hustle & Flow* and *Phone Booth*. She has stepped behind the camera to take on roles of producer and director on movie projects, *The White Sistas* (2017) and *She's Got a Plan* (2016).

Awards: Idyllwild International Festival of Cinema (2017), Laughlin International Film Festival (2016), Women Film Critics Circle Awards (2005), CableACE Award (1995)

Movie (producer, director, actress): *The White Sistas* (2017)

Movie (producer, actress): *She's Got a Plan* (2016)

Movies (actress): *Pastor Shirley* (2013), *Life of a King* (2013), *King of the Underground* (2011), *Cover* (2007), *The Genius Club* (2006), *Idlewild* (2006), *Hustle & Flow* (2005), *She Hate Me* (2004), *Phone Booth* (2002), *High Crimes* (2002), *Why Do Fools Fall in Love* (1998), *Sprung* (1997), *Get on the Bus* (1996), *Tales from the Hood* (1995), *Friday* (1995)

Television movies (actress): *The Proud Family Movie* (2005), *Always Outnumbered* (1998), *Riot* (1997), *Cosmic Slop* (1994) Television (actress): *Black Jesus* (2018), *Family Time* (2012–18), *Ray Donovan* (2016), *Recovery Road* (2016), *Side Order of Life (*2007), *The Proud Family* (2001–2005), *Snoops* (1999–2000), *The Weird Al Show* (1997), *The Wayans Bros.* (1995–96), *Townsend Television* (1993), *The Apollo Comedy Hour* (1992–93)

Paula Patton (1975), actress, producer. After working behind the camera as a documentary filmmaker, Patton realized her latent ambition to be out front. Soon after graduating from the University of Southern California (magna cum laude) film school, Patton embarked on an assignment with the Public Broadcasting System filming documentaries. The experience led to producing *Medical Diaries* from 2000–02 for the Discovery Health Channel. Acting classes proved to be time well invested as Patton's acting career moved swiftly, debuting in the role of Detective Angela Kellogg in television movie *Murder Book* in 2005. A big-screen break followed that same year with a starring role in the movie *Hitch*. Patton was born in Los Angeles, California. By the time Patton completed the lead female role Angel Davenport in the cult musical *Idlewild*, she had achieved name recognition.

Award: Boston Society Film Critic Award (2009)

Movies (producer, actress): *Traffik* (2018), *The Perfect Match* (2016)

Movies (actress): *The Do-Over* (2016), *Warcraft: The Beginning* (2016), *About Last Night* (2014), *Baggage Claim* (2013), *2 Guns* (2013), *Disconnect* (2012), *Mission Impossible: Ghost Protocol* (2011), *Jumping the Broom* (2011), *Just Wright* (2010), *Precious* (2009), *Mirrors* (2008), *Swing Vote* (2008), *Déjà Vu* (2006), *Idlewild* (2006), *London* (2006), *Hitch* (2005)

Television movie (actress): *Runner* (2015), *Murder Book* (2005)

Television (producer): *Medical Diaries* (2000–02)

Television (actress): *Somewhere Between* (2017)

Holly Robinson Peete (1964), actress, author. Parents, Matthew Robinson Jr., a television producer, and mother, Delores, a show business manager, raised Peete. She was born in Philadelphia, Pennsylvania. Her parents put emphasis on higher education when navigating an industry that can be, at times, uncertain. Primarily a television actress, she tested the waters with a part in the 1979 television movie *Dummy*. She then proceeded to earn a BA in French and psychology from Sarah Lawrence College. In the 1986 movie *Howard the Duck*, as with the television series *21 Jump Street* in 1987–91, Peete was able to exhibit her singing talent. She gained recognition in the role of Vanessa Russell on the television series *Hangin' with Mr. Cooper* (1992–97). She is the author of several books including the award winning *"My Brother Charlie"* and *"Get Your Own Damn Beer, I'm Watching the Game."* Peete and her husband, ex-professional football player Rodney Peete, are advocates in bringing awareness to Parkinson's disease and autism. The HollyRod Foundation was founded in 1997 to support individuals and families living with Parkinson's disease and autism.

Awards: NAACP Image Award (2011), Quill Award for Sports (2006)

Movies (actress): *21 Jump Street* (2012), *Speed-Dating* (2010), *Howard the Duck* (1986)

Television movies (actress): *Morning Show Mystery: Mortal Mishaps* (2018), *Michael Jackson: Searching for Neverland* (2017), *Matters of Life & Dating* (2007), *Football Wives* (2007), *Earthquake* (2004), *After All* (1999), *Killers in the House* (1998), *The Jacksons: An American Dream* (1992), *Dummy* (1979)

Television (producer): *Meet the Peetes* (2018), *For Peete's Sake* (2016-17)

Television (actress): *Chicago Fire* (2016-17), *Mike & Molly* (2011–14), *Love, Inc.* (2005–06), *Like Family* (2003–04), *For Your Love* (1998–2002), *One on One* (2001–02), *Hangin' with Mr. Cooper* (1992–97), *21 Jump Street* (1987–91)

Sydney Tamiia Poitier (1973), actress. Being the daughter of iconic actor Sydney Poitier and wife, actress Joanna Shimkus, obviously has many advantages, yet Poitier chose to follow through with graduating from New York University Tisch School of the Arts. After graduation she also studied at Stella Adler School of Acting. With leanings toward independent films, Poitier made her screen debut in *Park Day* in 1998. A couple of family collaborations include a 1998 television movie *Free of Eden* with her father and *The Devil Cats* in 2004, in which she produced and acted while sister Anika Poitier wrote and directed. Poitier generated well-deserved notice in the 2007 "Death Proof" segment of the Quentin Tarantino movie *Grindhouse*. She was born in Los Angeles, California.

Award: Locarno International Film Festival (2005)

Movies (actress): *Clinical* (2017), *Blues* (2008), *Death Proof* (2007), *The List* (2007), *Grindhouse* (2007), *Hood of Horror* (2006), *Nine Lives*

(2005), *MacArthur Park* (2001), *True Crime* (1999), *Park Day* (1998)
   Movie (actress and producer): *The Devil Cats* (2004)
   Television movies (actress): *Noah's Ark* (1999), *Free of Eden* (1998)
   Television (actress): *Carter* (2018), *Chicago P.D.* (2014), *Kendra* (2012), *Knight Rider* (2008–09), *Veronica Mars* (2004), *Joan of Arcadia* (2003–04), *Abby* (2003), *First Years* (2001)

Keshia Knight Pulliam (1979), actress. *The Cosby Show* brought Pulliam mega success from 1984–1992. She had been a working actor since the age of nine months. Her initial exposure was in print advertisements and commercials. Pulliam's first appearance on screen was in *The Last Dragon* in 1985. Pulliam took time from acting after *The Cosby Show* to focus on education. She attended Spelman College and earned a BA in Sociology with a concentration in film. Born in Newark, New Jersey, she has fared quite well in Tyler Perry productions, starring in the television series *House of Payne* and on the big screen in *Madea Goes to Jail*. For her work on *House of Payne* from 2007–12, she won three Image Awards for Best Supporting Actress in a Comedy Series.
   Awards: Image Award (2012, 2010, 2009, 1988), TV Land Award (2011), Kids' Choice Award (1991), Young Artist Award (1989), People's Choice Award (1988)
   Movies: *Madea Goes to Jail* (2009), *Death Toll* (2008), *Cuttin' Da Mustard* (2008), *The Gospel* (2005), *Beauty Shop* (2005), *The Last Dragon* (1985)
   Television movies: *Will to Love* (2015), *The Love Letter* (2013), *Christmas at the Water's Edge* (2004), *What About Your Friends: Weekend Getaway* (2002), *Polly: Comin' Home!* (1990), *A Connecticut Yankee in King Arthur's Court* (1989), *Polly* (1989), *The Little Match Girl* (1987), *Back to Next Saturday* (1985)
   Television: *3 Year Plan* (2018), *House of Payne* (2007–12), *A Different World* (1987–1988), *The Cosby Show* (1984–1992)

Sheryl Lee Ralph (1956), actress, singer, producer. A former Miss Black Teenage New York, Ralph originated the lead role of Deena Jones in the Broadway musical production of *Dreamgirls* in 1981. Ralph had television exposure and a role in the movie *A Piece of the Action* before the original stage production of *Dreamgirls* launched her career. Before earning a BA in English and Literature from Rutgers University at age nineteen, she was a premed major. Ralph was born in Waterford, Connecticut. Her talent for singing was captured on the album *In the Evening* in 1984. The activist side of Ralph was brought to light in a one-woman show entitled *Sometimes I Cry*, a focus on the lives of women infected with HIV. In 2012, Ralph published her autobiography, *Redefining Diva: Life Lessons from the Original Dreamgirl*.

Awards: LA Femme International Film Festival (2014), Independent Spirit Award (1991), Tony Award (1982)

Movie (producer and actress): *Blessed and Cursed* (2010)

Movies (actress): *Step Sisters* (2018), *Christmas in Compton* (2012), *Frankie D* (2007), *Baby of the Family* (2002), *Lost in the Pershing Point Hotel* (2000), *Deterrence* (1999), *White Man's Burden* (1995), *Sister Act 2: Back in the Habit* (1993), *The Distinguished Gentleman* (1992), *Mistress* (1992), *To Sleep with Anger* (1990), *The Mighty Quinn* (1989), *A Piece of the Action* (1977)

Television movies (actress): *Niecy Nash's Wedding Bash* (2011), *Witch Hunt* (1994), *No Child of Mine* (1993), *Sister Margaret and the Saturday Night Ladies* (1987), *The Neighborhood* (1982)

Television (actress): *The Quad* (2018), *One Mississippi (2017)*, *Instant Mom* (2013–15), *JD Lawrence's Community Service* (2013), *Barbershop* (2005), *Moesha* (1996–2001), *The District* (2000–01), *Street Gear* (1994–95), *George* (1993–94), *Designing Women* (1992–94), *New Attitude* (1990), *It's a Living* (1986–89)

Documentary (producer) *The Last Laugh* (2015)

Phylicia Rashad (1948), actress. In the role of professional upwardly mobile Clair Huxtable on *The Cosby Show* from 1984–92, Rashad shattered stereotype and upgraded the image of African American women via the powerful medium of television. Before the role of attorney, Clair Huxtable on *The Cosby Show*, she was Courtney Wright on the long-running daytime series *One Life to Live*. She is a stage veteran on and off Broadway. Rashad graduated from Howard University magna cum laude with a BA in Fine Arts. She was born in Houston, Texas, and the daughter of Dr. Andrew Allen and Mrs. Vivian Ayers-Allen. Rashad is sister to actress, director, and choreographer Debbie Allen and musician Andrew Arthur Allen Jr. She made her screen debut in a 1972 comedy based on women's rights called *The Broad Coalition*. She appeared in *Once Upon a Time...When We Were Colored* in 1995. In 2004, she was the first African American actress to win a Tony Award for Best Performance by a Leading Actress in a Play for her role as Lena Younger in the Broadway stage revival of *A Raisin in the Sun*. She reprised the role in 2008 when the stage version aired on television. In 2011, Rashad won the Black Reel Award for Best Supporting Actress in the movie *For Colored Girls* released in 2010.

Awards: Black Reel Award (2011), TV Land Award (2011), Image Award (2009, 1997, 1988), New York Women in Film and Television Award (2001), People's Choice Award (1989, 1985)

Movies: *Creed II* (2018), *Creed* (2015), *Good Deeds* (2012), *For Colored Girls* (2010), *Frankie & Alice* (2010), *Just Wright* (2010), *The Visit* (2000), *Loving Jezebel* (1999), *Once Upon a Time...When We Were Colored* (1995), *The Broad Coalition* (1972)

Television movies: *Tour de Pharmacy* (2017), *For Justice* (2015), *Steel Magnolias* (2012), *Change of Plans* (2011), *A Raisin in the Sun* (2008), *The Old Settler* (also producer) (2001), *Free of Eden* (1998), *Polly: Comin' Home!* (1990), *Polly* (1989), *Uncle Tom's Cabin* (1987)

Television: *Jean-Claude Van Johnson* (2016-17), *Empire* (2016-17), *Do No Harm* (2013), *The Cleveland Show* (2012–13), *Cosby* (1996–2000), *The Cosby Show* (1984–92), *A Different World* (1988–90), *Santa Barbara* (1985), *One Life to Live* (1984–84)

Daphne Reid a.k.a. **Daphne Maxwell Reid** (1948), actress, producer. The first African American model to grace the cover of *Glamour* magazine, Reid made her first screen appearance in the movie *Protocol* in 1984. She was introduced to the mainstream as Vivian Banks in the television comedy *The Fresh Prince of Bel-Air* from 1993–96. Reid has collaborated in quite a few film and television productions with husband, Tim Reid. Reid graduated from Northwestern University with a degree in interior design and architecture. She was also the first African American homecoming queen while in attendance. With her husband, Reid co-owns New Millennium Studios in Petersburg, Virginia.

Award: Women in Film & Video Women of Vision Award (2006)
Movie (producer): *For Real* (2003)
Movie (co-director and actress): *Once Upon a Time...When We Were Colored* (1995)
Movies (actress): *Out of Gas* (2018), *By the Grace of Bob* (2016), *Asunder* (1999)
Television movies (actress): *Polly and Marie* (2007), *Alley Cats Strike* (2000), *You Must Remember This* (1992), *The Long Journey Home* (1987), *Coach of the Year* (1980)
Television (actress): *Eve* (2002–06), *The Fresh Prince of Bel-Air* (1993–96), *Frank's Place* (1987–88), *Simon & Simon* (1983–87)

Tim Reid (1944), actor, producer, director, writer. From the very beginning of his career in film and television, Reid took control and actively participated behind as well as in front of the camera. While on the television series that propelled his career, *WKRP in Cincinnati*, he wrote several episodes and influenced positive image change for his character Venus Flytrap from a gross stereotype. Reid emphasized the importance of a cohesive community taking control of destiny when he co-directed and produced the 1995 film *Once Upon a Time...When We Were Colored*. He was born in Norfolk, Virginia, in an environment that was not very conducive to insuring success. He has acknowledged that as a street kid he knew how to maneuver and get by. When he found his way to college, he credits caring faculty at the Historically Black College, Norfolk State University for turning him around. Reid graduated with a BS in Business and Marketing. After graduation he worked corporate for a while then tried stand-up comedy, which led to commercials then television. He is married to actress and business partner Daphne Maxwell Reid.

Awards: Christopher Award (1999), PGA Oscar Micheaux Award (1999), St. Louis International Film Festival Award (1995), Image Award (1990), Viewers for Quality Television Award (1988)
Movie (producer) *Out of Gas* (2018)
Movies (producer and director): *Asunder* (1999), *Once Upon a Time When...We Were Colored* (1995)
Movie (director, writer, actor): *For Real* (2003)
Movies (actor): *93 Days* (2016), *Tri* (2016), *By the Grace of Bob*

(2016), *The Cost of Heaven* (2010), *Trade* (2007), *Preaching to the Choir* (2005), *Out-of-Sync* (1995), *The Fourth War* (1990), *Dead Bang* (1989), *Mother, Jugs & Speed* (1976)

Television movies (producer): *Blue Moon* (1999), *About Sarah* (1998)

Television movies (actor): *The Rooftop Christmas Tree* (2016), *Chasing Waterfalls* (2016)

Television (producer and director): *The Contender* (2000), *Linc's* (1998–99)

Television (producer, writer, actor): *Frank's Place* (1987–88)

Television (writer): *Simon & Simon* (1985,1987), *WKRP in Cincinnati* (1980–82)

Television (actor): *Greenleaf* (2017), *Treme* (2010–12), *That '70s Show* (2004–06), *Sister, Sister* (1994–99), *Simon & Simon* (1983–87), *Teachers Only* (1983), *WKRP in Cincinnati* (1978–82)

Ving Rhames (1959), actor, producer. Beneath his tough exterior resides an actor who resists stereotype. Rhames attended the State University of New York at Purchase. He graduated with a BFA from Juilliard School. Upon graduation, he performed Shakespeare in the Park and performed roles in regional theater written by Ibsen and Moliere. He lit the Broadway stage in *The Boys of Winter* in 1984. By 1986 he was cast in two films *Go Tell It on the Mountain* and *Native Son*. The role of Cinque soon followed in the controversial film *Patty Hearst* in 1988. Rhames was born in New York, New York. In 2005, Rhames produced and took the lead role in a resurrected version of the *Kojak* television series. He has a reoccurring role as computer expert operative Luther Stickell in the *Mission: Impossible* film franchise.

Awards: DVD Exclusive Award (2006), Lucarno International Film Festival Award (2001), ShoWest Convention, USA Award (2000), Golden Globe Award (1998)

Movies (producer and actor): *King of the Avenue* (2010), *Phantom Punch* (2008), *Animal 2* (2008), *Ascension Day* (2007), *Back in the Day* (2005)

Movies (actor): *Mission: Impossible-Fallout* (2018), *Father Figures* (2017), *Guardians of the Galaxy Vol.2* (2017), *Mission: Impossible-Rogue Nation* (2015), *Percentage* (2014), *Won't Back Down* (2012), *'Master*

Harold'...and the Boys (2010), *Idlewild* (2006), *Mission Impossible III* (2006), *Dark Blue* (2002), *Undisputed* (2002), *Baby Boy* (2001), *Mission Impossible II* (2000), *Out of Sight* (1998), *Rosewood* (1997), *Mission Impossible* (1996), *Pulp Fiction* (1994), *The Saint of Fort Washington* (1993), *Jacob's Ladder* (1990), *The Long Walk Home* (1990), *Casualties of War* (1989), *Patty Hearst* (1988), *Native Son* (1986), *Go Tell It on the Mountain* (1984)

Television movies (actor): *Football Wives* (2007), *RFK* (2002), *Sins of the Father* (2002), *Holiday Heart* (2000), *Don King: Only in America* (1997), *When You Remember Me* (1990)

Television (producer and actor): *Kojak* (2005)

Television (actor): *Monday Mornings* (2013), *Gravity* (2010), *The District* (2003–04), *The System* (2003), *Freedom: A History of Us* (documentary, 2003), *ER* (1994–96), *Men* (1989)

LaTanya Richardson (1949), actress. A native of Atlanta, Georgia, Richardson appears to be a woman of substance because she is. After graduating from Spelman College with a BA in Drama, she was encouraged by premier theatrical stage producer Joseph Papp to leave Georgia and perfect her craft with his New York Shakespeare Festival. Richardson also fortified her talent with major African American theater companies such as the New Federal Theatre and Negro Ensemble Company. While in
New York, she earned a master's degree in drama at New York University. Making a move to Los Angeles with her husband, actor Samuel Jackson, Richardson became active in film and television. Between 1991 and 1992, film roles came in quick succession starting with *Hangin' with the Homeboys* followed by *The Super*, *Fried Green Tomatoes*, *Juice*, and *Malcolm X*. She has served on the Spelman College Board of Trustees and assisted in raising millions for scholarships. Spelman awarded Richardson an honorary doctorate in 2012. She is a producer of the ESPY (Excellence in Sports Performance Yearly) Awards on ESPN.

Movies: *Mother and Child* (2009), *Blackout* (2007), *All About Us* (2007), *Freedomland* (2006), *The Fighting Temptations* (2003), *U.S. Marshals* (1998), *Lone Star* (1996), *Losing Isaiah* (1995), *When a Man Loves a Woman* (1994), *Sleepless in Seattle* (1993), *Lorenzo's Oil* (1992),

Malcolm X (1992), *Juice* (1992), *Fried Green Tomatoes* (1991), *The Super* (1991), *Hangin' with the Homeboys* (1991)

Television documentary (narrator): *American Masters: Lorraine Hansberry* (2018)

Television movies: *The Watsons Go to Birmingham* (2013), *Within These Walls* (2001), *Introducing Dorothy Dandridge* (1999), *The Deliverance of Elaine* (1996), *Midnight Run for Your Life* (1994), *Shameful Secrets* (1993), *The Nightman* (1992)

Television: *Grey's Anatomy* (2017), *Show Me a Hero* (2015), *Blue Bloods* (2014-15), *100 Centre Street* (2001–02)

Sy Richardson (1941), actor, writer. Richardson lived quite a bit of life before venturing out to further his education or pursue acting. His acting debut was a quirky adult-themed rendition of a fairytale in the 1977 film *Cinderella*. He has often been cast in offbeat independent productions such as *Sid and Nancy* in 1986 and the role of the coroner in the television series *Pushing Daisies*. Before graduation from the University of Colorado–Boulder with a BS in Journalism, specializing in advertising, Richardson sang doo-wop with Lil June and the Januarys. He also served a two year stint in the navy and drove a bus seven years for the Chicago Transit Authority. With the journalism degree, he worked for several Colorado news publications before performing on stage in the Heritage Square Opera House in Golden, Colorado, and touring vaudeville shows before heading to Los Angeles for film work. His writing skills shone in 1993 in the screenplay *Posse* in which he also acted. Richardson has written several books including *PEP for Christian Entertainers*. PEP is an acronym for prayer, education, and persistence. He was a former member of the board of directors for the Screen Actors Guild. Richardson was born in Cincinnati, Ohio.

Movie (screenwriter and actor): *Posse* (1993)

Movies (actor): *Message from a Mistress* (2017), *House Arrest* (2012), *Larry Crown* (2011), *Our Family Wedding* (2010), *All About Us* (2007), *Surviving Christmas* (2004), *Human Nature* (2001), *The Glass Shield* (1994), *Men at Work* (1990), *To Sleep with Anger* (1990), *Colors* (1988), *Sid and Nancy* (1986), *My Brother's Wedding* (1983) Television movies (actor): *L.A. Sheriff's Homicide* (2003), *After Diff'rent Strokes: When*

the Laughter Stopped (2000)
Television (actor): *Pushing Daisies* (2007–09)

Wendy Raquel Robinson (1967), actress. While Robinson has appeared in several films, television has been a great medium to showcase her talent. Before her long illustrious run on the *Steve Harvey Show* from 1996 to 2002, there was *Minor Adjustment* in 1995 to 1996. Starring roles in *Something New* in 2006, *Two Can Play That Game*, and *Miss Congeniality* confirmed Robinson's cinematic appeal. Born in Los Angeles, California, she graduated cum laude with a BFA from Howard University. No stranger to the stage, Robinson received a NAACP Image Award for best choreographer and actress for the play *Vanities*. Robinson is cofounder of Amazing Grace Conservatory, a theatrical training institute for the youth dedicated to "building self-esteem through self-expression."

Award: Image Award (2014)

Movies (producer, actress) *Boy Bye* (2016), *A Weekend with the Family* (2016) Movies (actress): *Grandma's House* (2016), *He's Mine Not Yours* (2011), *35 and Ticking* (2011), *Something New* (2006), *Rebound* (2005), *With or Without You* (2003), *Two Can Play That Game* (2001), *Miss Congeniality* (2000), *A Thin Line Between Love and Hate* (1996), *The Walking Dead* (1995)

Television (actress): *The Game* (2006–2015), *All of Us* (2004–05), *The Steve Harvey Show* (1996–2002), *Getting Personal* (1998), *Minor Adjustments* (1995–96)

Tracee Ellis Ross (1972), actress, producer, director. A brilliant talent, Ross has put in work for every measure of her success. She is primarily known for her role as Joan Clayton in the megahit television series *Girlfriends*, which aired from 2000–2008. Ross was initially a journalist and occasional model after graduation from Brown University, in theater. While taking acting classes at William Esper Studio, she achieved her first film roles in independent movies *Far Harbor* in 1996 and *Sue* in 1997. Major studio films include *Daddy's Little Girls* in 2007 and *Labor Pains* in 2009. Born in Los Angeles, California, Ross is the daughter of businessman Robert Silberstein and superstar performer Diana Ross. Brown University awarded Ross an honorary doctorate of fine art in 2015.

She is known to volunteer her time teaching self-esteem workshops for at-risk teenage girls in Los Angeles, Michigan, and New York. In 2004, she was the recipient of the Volunteer of the Year Award by the Urban League and received the Impact Award from Aviva Family and Children Services in Los Angeles in 2009.

Awards: Image Award (2018, 2016, 2015, 2012, 2009, 2007), Golden Globes, USA (2017), BET Comedy Award (2005) Movies (actress): *Labor Pains* (2009), *Daddy's Little Girls* (2007), *I-See-You.Com* (2006), *In the Weeds* (2000), *Hanging Up* (2000), *A Fare to Remember* (1998), *Sue* (1997), *Far Harbor* (1996) Television movies (actress): *Bad Girls* (2012), *Five* (2011), *Life Support* (2007), *Race Against Fear* (1998)

Television (producer and actress): *Reed Between the Lines* (2011)

Television (producer): *Black-ish* (2018)

Television (actress): *Black-ish* (2014–18), *CSI: Crime Scene Investigation* (2011), *Girlfriends* (2000–08)

Maya Rudolph (1972), actress, comedienne, singer. Initially it seemed as if all roads would lead to a career in music for Rudolph. The 2000–2016 *Saturday Night Live* alum was a backup singer and keyboardist in a couple of bands before embarking on a career in acting. Rudolph's parents are music heavyweights—composer, songwriter, producer, Richard Rudolph and vocalist Minnie Riperton. Her brother, Marc Rudolph, is also in the music business. Rudolph performed with the band Weezer and spin-off band the Rentals before taking acting roles on the television series *Chicago Hope* in 1996–97 and in the movie *Gattaca* in 1997. Born in Gainesville, Florida, Rudolph graduated from University of California–Santa Cruz with a BA in photography. Cast in roles in the independent film *Friends with Kids* to the studio-driven *Bridesmaids* in 2011, Rudolph's film career is solid.

Award: Behind the Voice Actors Award (2016), Film Independent Spirit Award (2015), MTV Award (2012)

Movie (music supervisor and actress): *Duets* (2000)

Movies (actress): *Life of the Party* (2018), *Popstar: Never Stop Never Stopping* (2016), *The Angry Birds Movie* (2016), *Sisters* (2015), *Inherent Vice* (2014), *The Nut Job* (voice) (2014), *Turbo* (2013), *Grown Ups 2* (2013), *Friends with Kids* (2011), *Bridesmaids* (2011), *Grown*

Ups (2010), *Away We Go* (2009), *50 First Dates* (2004), *Duplex* (2003), *Gattaca* (1997)

Television movie (actress): *A Christmas Story Live!* (2017), *Tour de Pharmacy* (2017)

Television (producer, writer, actress): *Maya & Marty* (2016)

Television (actress): *Big Hero 6 The Series* (2017-18), *Big Mouth* (2017), *The Awesomes* (2014-15), *The Spoils Before Dying* (2015), *The Maya Rudolph Show* (2014), Saturday *Night Live* (2000–16), *Up All Night* (2011–12), *Kath & Kim* (2008–09), *City of Angels* (2000), *Chicago Hope* (1996–97)

Keesha Sharp (1973), actress. Sharp has been outspoken about the importance of the arts in school being acknowledged as an important discipline. She maintains art is a societal escape to relive tension. In high school, Sharp studied music and won a scholarship to study theater at the Boston Conservatory where she earned a BFA with honors. Before she gained prominence on television shows *Are We There Yet?* in 2010–12 and *Girlfriends* in 2002–08, Sharp established a firm foundation appearing in stage productions that led to film. A plum role was Pam in the movie *Why Did I Get Married?* In 2012, she directed "The Concussion Episode" of *Are We There Yet?* A starring role in the television version of *Lethal Weapon* proved to be a definite uptick to Sharp's career.

Award: NYLA International Film Festival, US (2014)

Movies: *Marshall* (2017), *You Have a Nice Flight* (2017), *Why Did I Get Married?* (2007), *Never Die Alone* (2004), *Leprechaun: Back 2 tha Hood* (2003)

Television: *Lethal Weapon* (2016-18), *American Crime Story* (2016), *Bad Teacher* (2014), *Are We There Yet?* (2010–12), *Girlfriends* (2002–08), *Everybody Hates Chris* (2005–06)

Henry Simmons (1970), actor. Simmons quickly realized that a career in financial management was not for him and took acting classes after graduating from Franklin Pearce College with a BA in Business. With his six-foot-four height and athletic skills, he was admitted to Franklin Pearce on a basketball scholarship. Simmons auditioned while holding down his job as a financial management trainee until he got a role in the movie

Above the Rim in 1994. Born in Stamford, Connecticut, it was drilled into him and his two sisters to work hard and be the best they could be. The reoccurring role of Detective Baldwin Jones on network television's *NYPD Blue* elevated him into the ranks of the recognizable actor. More film roles followed starting with *Something New* and *Madea's Family Reunion*, both released in 2006. Simmons won the best actor award at the American Black Film Festival for the role of Dr. Walter Chambers in the movie *South of Pico* in 2007.

Award: American Black Film Festival (2007)

Movies: *No Good Deed* (2014), *From the Rough* (2012), *World's Greatest Dad* (2009), *South of Pico* (2007), *The Insurgents* (2006), *Madea's Family Reunion* (2006), *Something New* (2006), *Are We There Yet?* (2005), *Taxi* (2004), *A Gentleman's Game* (2002), *On the Q.T.* (1999), *Above the Rim* (1994)

Television movies: *Stalkers* (2013), *Georgia O'Keeffe* (2009), *Lackawanna Blues* (2005), *Spartacus* (2004)

Television: *Agents of S.H.I.E.L.D.* (2014–18), *Ravenswood* (2013–14), *Man Up* (2011–12), *Shark* (2006–08), *NYPD Blue* (2000–05)

Anna Deavere Smith (1950), actress, writer, professor. Smith, an award-winning playwright, is recognized for being an innovator and advocate of performance art as a tool to raise social consciousness. Smith's talent is a magnet for reoccurring roles on popular television series such as, *For The People* and *Black-ish*. She is highly praised for her role as producer, writer and actress in the 2018 television movie *Notes from the Field.* In 2013, she received the Dorothy and Lillian Gish Prize, one of the most prestigious awards in American art. Smith's quest to promote peace led to several one-woman shows created for the stage including *Fires in the Mirror*, which fetched an Obie Award, Drama Desk Award, and Drama-Logue Award in 1992. *Twilight: Los Angeles* (1992) also won multiple awards. These plays and other work resulted in Smith receiving the "genius" MacArthur Award in 1996. She was born in Baltimore, Maryland, and graduated with a BA from Beaver College in Pennsylvania and an MFA from the American Conservatory Theater in San Francisco, CA. Television audiences know her as Gloria Akalitus on *Nurse Jackie*. Her films include *Rachel Getting Married* in 2008, *The*

Kingdom in 2007, and *The Human Stain* in 2003. Smith has published books *House Arrest: A Search for American Character In and Around the White House, Past and Present*; *Talk to Me: Listening Between the Lines*; and *Fires in the Mirror: Crown Heights, Brooklyn and Other Identities*. She is the recipient of an array of honorary doctorate degrees and has taught at numerous educational institutions.

Awards: Black Reel Award (2004), Washington DC Area Film Critics Association Award (2003)

Movie (writer, producer, actress): *Twilight: Los Angeles* (2000)

Movies (actress): *Rachel Getting Married* (2008), *The Kingdom* (2007), *Rent* (2005), *The Human Stain* (2003), *The American President* (1995), *Philadelphia* (1993), *Dave* (1993), *Unfinished Business* (1987), *Soup for One* (1982)

Television movie (producer, writer, actress) *Notes from the Field* (2018)

Television movies (actress): *Life Support* (2007), *Expert Witness* (2003)

Television (writer and actress): *American Playhouse* (1993)

Television (actress): *For The People* (2018), *Black-ish* (2015-18), *Nurse Jackie* (2009–15), *The West Wing* (2000–06), *Presidio Med* (2002), *The Practice* (2000)

Kellita Smith (1969), actress. Smith worked traditional sales and office jobs after graduating from Santa Rosa Junior College with a degree in political science then decided to enroll in an acting workshop. She took to the stage and won the NAACP Theatre Award for her part in the production of *Feelings*. Smith was born in Chicago, Illinois, and partially raised in Oakland, California. Of her long list of television appearances, she is best known as wife Wanda McCullough on *The Bernie Mac Show* (2001–06). Roles in film include *Roll Bounce* and *King's Ransom* both in 2005 and *Hair Show* in 2004. Smith appears as First Lady Katherine Johnson in the television series *The First Family*.

Movies: *Three Can Play That Game* (2007), *Roll Bounce* (2005), *King's Ransom* (2005), *Hair Show* (2004), *Kingdom Come* (2001), *Retiring Tatiana* (2000), *The Crossing Guard* (1995)

Television movies: *She's Not Our Sister* (2011), *Masquerade* (2000)

Television: *In the Cut* (2016-18), *Z Nation* (2014), *The First Family* (2012–13), *The Bernie Mac Show* (2001–06), *The Jamie Foxx Show* (1997–99), *Malcolm & Eddie* (1997), *Sister, Sister* (1995), *Martin* (1992–95)

Roger Guenveur Smith, actor, writer. Smith attracts thought provoking roles, none more riveting than the one-man stage play and film he wrote and starred in, *A Huey P. Newton Story*. His performance won an Obie Award and Peabody Award. Born in Berkeley, California, Smith graduated from Occidental College with a degree in American studies. While in the graduate program at Yale University, he majored in American studies with a concentration in African American studies. Smith then went to Yale Drama School. He also studied at the Keskidee Arts Centre in London, England, on fellowship. Early in his film career, Smith collaborated with filmmaker Spike Lee in *School Daze* in 1988, *Do the Right Thing* in 1989, and *Malcolm X* in 1992. Spike Lee directed the television documentary *A Huey P. Newton Story* in 2001. Smith switched to antihero as Nate in the 2007 film *American Gangster*.

Award: Black Reel Award (2002)

Movie documentary (writer and actor): *A Huey P. Newton Story* (2001)

Movie (writer, actor): *Rodney King* (2017)

Movies (actor): *Marshall* (2017), *The Birth of a Nation* (2016), *Chi-Raq* (2015), *But Not for Me* (2015), *Empire State* (2013), *CornerStore* (2011), *Mooz-Lum* (2011), *Better Mus' Come* (2010), *Fighting* (2009), *Cover* (2007), *American Gangster* (2007), *All About the Benjamins* (2002), *Summer of Sam* (1999), *He Got Game* (1998), *Eve's Bayou* (1997), *Get on the Bus* (1996), *Tales from the Hood* (1995), *Panther* (1995), *Poetic Justice* (1993), *Malcolm X* (1992), *Deep Cover* (1992), *King of New York* (1990), *Do the Right Thing* (1989), *School Daze* (1988)

Television movies (actor): *Behind the Movement* (2018), *The Warden* (2001), *Hamlet* (2000), *Incognito* (1999), *The Color of Courage* (1999)

Television (actor): *K Street* (2003), *All My Children* (1997–98), *A Different World* (1990)

Wesley Snipes (1962), actor, producer. In high school, Snipes focused on being an actor. Born in Orlando, Florida, and raised for a good portion of his youth in South Bronx, New York, study and mastering various forms of martial arts were key to nurturing his disciplined nature. Having performed in a number of stage productions in high school and college, Snipes graduated with a BA from State University of New York at Purchase. Soon after a talent competition, he caught the attention of an agent. After a few small television roles, he landed his first screen role in *Wildcats* in 1986. Cast in the role of Nino Brown in *New Jack City*, it was clear Snipes was an emerging major talent. By the time he starred in *Blade: Trinity* in 2004, his commanding salary was stratospheric. Snipes has stepped up frequently as a producer, including all three films in the *Blade* series.

Awards: Screen Nation Award (2016), Black Reel Award (2011), Blockbuster Entertainment Award (1999), Star on the Walk of Fame (1998), Image Award (1997, 1993), Venice Film Award (1997), CableACE Award (1989), WorldFest-Houston Award (1992)

Movies (producer and actor): *Blade: Trinity* (2004), *Undisputed* (2002), *Blade II* (2002), *The Art of War* (2000), *Blade* (1998), *Down in the Delta* (1998), *John Henrik Clarke: A Great and Mighty Walk* (1996)

Movies (actor): *Chi-Raq* (2015), *The Expendables 3* (2014), *Brooklyn's Finest* (2009), *Chaos* (2005), *Zig Zag* (2002), *One Night Stand* (1997), *Murder at 1600* (1997), *Money Train* (1995), *Sugar Hill* (1993), *White Men Can't Jump* (1992), *Jungle Fever* (1991), *Mo' Better Blues* (1990), *King of New York* (1990)

Television (producer and actor): *Disappearing Acts* (2000), *Futuresport* (1998), *Masters of the Martial Arts Presented by Wesley Snipes* (1998)

Television (actor): *The Player* (2015)

Octavia Spencer (1972), actress, producer. The sixth African American female to win an Academy Award, in 2012 for Best Supporting Actress in *The Help*, Spencer did not start out with a career in front of the camera in mind. After graduation from Auburn University with a BA in Liberal Arts, she earned a living in casting and as a crewmember on film sets. What would become a major turn of events took place in 1996 when Spencer was part of the crew for the movie *A Time to Kill*, and the director thought she would be right for a minor role. From that point on, she has been a continuous working actress in film and television. Her recognition grew with reoccurring roles in several popular television situation comedies such as *Ugly Betty* and *Halfway Home* in 2007. Since becoming a winner of numerous awards in 2013, Spencer took on the role of producer as well as actor in *Fruitvale Station*. She published her first book in a series, a children's mystery titled *Randi Rhodes, Ninja Detective* in 2013. Spencer was born in Montgomery, Alabama.

Awards (select): Image Award (2018, 2012), Palm Springs International Film Festival (2018, 2012), Hasty Pudding Theatricals, USA (2017), Screen Actors Guild award (2017, 2012), African American Film Critics Association (2014, 2011), Black Reel Award (2014), Academy Award (2012), BAFTA Award (2012), Black Reel Award (2012), Broadcast Film Critics Association Award (2012), Golden Globe Award (2012), Hollywood Film Festival Award (2011), National Board Review, USA Award (2011), Satellite Award (2011), Southeastern Film Critics Association Award (2011), Washington DC Area Film Critics Association Award (2011)

Movie (executive producer and actress): *Fruitvale Station* (2013)

Movies (actress): *The Shape of Water* (2017), *Gifted* (2017), *The Shack* (2017), *Hidden Figures* (2016), *Insurgent* (2015), *Get on Up* (2014), *Black or White* (2014), *Paradise* (2013), *Smashed* (2012), *The Help* (2011), *Dinner for Schmucks* (2010), *Jesus People: The Movie* (2009), *Seven Pounds* (2008), *Beauty Shop* (2005), *Big Mama's House* (2000)

Television (actress): *Red Band Society* (2014–15), *Mom* (2013–15), *Call Me Crazy: A Five Film* (TV movie) (2013), *Raising the Bar* (2009), *Halfway Home* (2007), *Ugly Betty* (2007), *LAX* (2004–05), *The Chronicle* (2001–02), *City of Angels* (2000)

Regina Taylor (1960), actress, playwright. Taylor achieved award winning recognition as the non-stereotype domestic worker Lilly Harper on the television drama *I'll Fly Away* from 1991–93. Taylor was the first African American woman to play Juliet on Broadway in *Romeo and Juliet*. She is also an accomplished playwright. Of her collection of plays, she won the American Critics Association Steinberg New Play Award for *Oo-Bla-Dee*, a story of Black female jazz musicians in the 1940s. After a substantial number of roles on television, in 1995 Taylor returned to film with roles in *Losing Isaiah* and *Clockers*. A graduate of Southern Methodist University, Taylor was born in Dallas, Texas.

Awards: Image Award (2008, 1995), Golden Globe Award (1993), Viewers for Quality Television Award (1993, 1992)

Movies: *Saturday Church* (2017), *The Negotiator* (1998), *Spirit Lost* (1997), *Courage Under Fire* (1996), *A Family Thing* (1996), *The Keeper* (1995), *Clockers* (1995), *Losing Isaiah* (1995), *Jersey Girl* (1992), *Lean on Me* (1989)

Television movies: *Who Is Clark Rockefeller?* (2010), *In from the Night* (2006), *Cora Unashamed* (2000), *Strange Justice* (1999), *Hostile Waters* (1997), *Children of the Dust* (1995), *I'll Fly Away: Then and Now* (1993), *Howard Beach: Making a Case for Murder* (1989), *Crisis at Central High* (1981)

Television: *Fly* (2018), *The Unit* (2006–09), *The Education of Max Bickford* (2001–02), *I'll Fly Away* (1991–93)

Lynne Thigpen, (1948–2003), actress, voice-over, singer. Thigpen was adamant about not being typecast. Her final appearances on film was *Anger Management* in 2003 and the remake of *Shaft* in 2000. Thigpen was also a television favorite. She achieved notoriety with the children's television program *Where in the World Is Carmen San Diego?* from 1991–95 as the chief and as computer phenomenon Ella Mae Farmer on the television drama *The District* from 2000 to 2003. Success in the stage musical *Godspell* in 1971 led to a career in film and television. Later she did reenact the role of Lynne in the movie *Godspell: A Musical Based on the Gospel According to St. Matthew* in 1973. She also sang on the movie soundtrack. Thigpen earned her BA in English and speech and a teaching certificate from the University of Illinois at Urbana, Champaign. She taught high school English and started work on a master's degree when she decided to head for the New York stage. Within three months of arriving in New York, she was cast in the stage production of *Godspell*. She was born and raised in Joliet, Illinois. Thigpen's rich, deep voice has been utilized on voice-over projects and recorded books. For her stage work, she won a Tony Award in 1997 for *An American Daughter*, which she also reenacted for television in 2000. She took home Obie Awards for the Off-Broadway plays *Jar the Floor* and August Wilson's *Fences*. Lynne Thigpen Elementary School in Joliet, Ill was named in her honor.

Movies: *Bicentennial Man* (1999), *The Insider* (1999), *Blankman* (1994), *Naked in New York* (1993), *Bob Roberts* (1992), *Article 99* (1992), *Lean on Me* (1989), *Running on Empty* (1988), *Streets of Fire* (1984), *Tootsie* (1982), *The Warriors* (1979)

Television movies: *The Boys Next Door* (1996), *Separate but Equal* (1991), *Fear Stalk* (1989), *Rockabye* (1986)

Television: *The District* (2000–03), *All My Children* (1983–2000), *Bear in the Big Blue House* (voice,1997–2003), *Where in Time Is Carmen Sandiego?* (1996), *L.A. Law* (1991–92), *FM* (1989–90), *Thirtysomething* (1989)

Sean Patrick Thomas (1970), actor. Although he was groomed for law school, after auditioning and appearing in a few college productions at University of Virginia, Thomas received a degree in English and went on to earn an MFA from New York University's Tisch School of the Arts. After the MFA program, he did some stage work and waited tables until an opportunity came for a gang-member role on the television daytime drama *All My Children*. He deplored the typecasting to which he was to be relegated and moved to Los Angeles where he got commercial work while substitute-teaching. An inroad to film came with roles in *Courage Under Fire* in 1996 and *Conspiracy Theory* in 1997. Major career turning points came with the films *Cruel Intentions* in 1999 and *Save the Last Dance* in 2001. He was simultaneously cast in the television series *The District* from 2000–2004. Thomas was born in Wilmington, Delaware.

Awards: Black Reel Award (2013), Washington DC Area Film Critics Association Award (2002), MTV Award (2001), Young Hollywood Award (2001)

Movies: *Barbershop: The Next Cut* (2016), *Deep in the Darkness* (2014), *Finding Neighbors* (2013), *Murder on the 13th Floor* (2012), *Honeydripper* (2007), *The Fountain* (2006), *Barbershop 2: Back in Business* (2003), *Barbershop* (2002), *Save the Last Dance* (2001), *Cruel Intentions* (1999), *Conspiracy Theory* (1997), *Courage Under Fire* (1996)

Television movies: *Vixen: The Movie* (2017), *Merry Ex-Mas* (2016), *The Selection* (2013), *A Raisin in the Sun* (2008)

Television: *Vixen* (2015-16), Ringer (2012), *The District* (2000–04)

Guy Torry (1969), actor, comedian. After graduating from Southeast Missouri State University with a BS in Marketing, Torry decided to travel to Los Angeles, California, and check in on his brother, Joe Torry, who was establishing himself as an actor. Torry was immediately entrenched in the comedy scene. As a result of appearances on television series *Family Matters* and *Martin*, his writing talent was recognized. He contributed to numerous comedy series. Utilizing his marketing skills, he created a weekly showcase called Phat Tuesdays at the Los Angeles Comedy Store for up-and-coming talent. *Don't Be a Menace to South Central While Drinking Your Juice in the Hood* in 1996 marked Torry's screen debut with *American History X*, bringing him prominence as an actor. When Torry isn't working in film or making television appearances, he is on the road for his comedic stand-up performances. Torry was born in St. Louis, Missouri.

Movies: *Axe to Grind* (2015), *Darnell Dawkins: Mouth Guitar Legend* (2010), *Funny Money* (2006), *Slow Burn* (2005), *Runaway Jury* (2003), *With or Without You* (2003), *Don't Say a Word* (2001), *Pearl Harbor* (2001), *American History X* (1998), *Ride* (1998), *Sunset Park* (1996), *Don't Be a Menace to South Central While Drinking Your Juice in the Hood* (1996)

Television movies: *Just Love* (2016), *Dead & Deader* (2006), *The '70s* (2000), *Introducing Dorothy Dandridge* (1999)

Television: *As Told by Ginger* (2000–04), *The Strip* (1999–2000), *The Good News* (1997–98)

Joe Torry (1965), actor, comedian. After college, Torry made his way to Los Angeles and into some of the most significant movies of the time. By the time he appeared in *Strictly Business* in 1991, *Poetic Justice* in 1993, and *House Party 3* in 1994, his film and television career took off. Hosting *Def Comedy Jam* in 1995 was a huge career boost. He continued to prove a mighty comic television host with *Uptown Comic* in 2012. Born and raised in St. Louis, Missouri, Torry earned a BA in Mass Communications from Lincoln University. Lincoln has also awarded him the President's Lifetime Achievement Award and an honorary PhD. He gives back to the community, primarily in his hometown, with the establishment of Giving Back the Love Foundation. The foundation informs and assists thousands of children and families on the importance of health-care awareness and education. He persists in outreach activities in and outside his hometown community.

Movie (actor and producer): *Pawn Shop* (2012)

Movies (actor): *Perfectly Single* (2018), *Unreported* (2016), *Soul Ties* (2015), *Act of Faith* (2014), *The Power of Love* (2013), *Who's Watching the Kids* (2012), *Why Am I Doing This?* (2009), *The Mannsfield 12* (2007), *Hair Show* (2004), *Lockdown* (2000), *Sprung* (1997), *Fled* (1996), *Tales from the Hood* (1995), *House Party 3* (1994), *Poetic Justice* (1993), *Strictly Business* (1991)

Television movies (actor): *Getting Played* (2006), *Commitments* (2001), *The Flamingo Rising* (2001)

Television (actor): *Zane's the Jump Off* (2013), *Uptown Comic* (host) (2012), *Def Comedy Jam* (host) (1995)

Lorraine Toussaint (1960), actress, producer. Toussaint works nonstop. She brings quality to the quantity of her work. An American citizen, Toussaint was born in Trinidad, West Indies. As a young girl living in New York, she got involved in acting classes. Toussaint ultimately graduated with a BFA from Juilliard School. Not long after graduation, she appeared in a string of television movies and series until she was cast in her first film, *Breaking In*, in 1989. While simultaneously appearing on television, she graced the silver screen in *Hudson Hawk* in 1991 and *Point of No Return* in 1993. In 2008, Toussaint was executive producer of *Accidental Friendship* for which actress Chandra Wilson won a Prism Award for her performance. Intermittent film work while dominating television continued right up to a major role in the award-winning independent film *Middle of Nowhere* in 2012. Toussaint's work ethic is summed up in her belief that the craft of acting can be hard work and would-be actors should find something else to do if not fully dedicated.

Awards: Screen Actors Guild Award (2015), Critics Choice Television Award (2015), Black Film Critics Circle Award (2014), La Femme

International Film Festival (2008)

Movies (actress): *Girls Trip* (2017), *Selma* (2014), *Middle of Nowhere* (2012), *The Soloist* (2009), *Black Dog* (1998), *Dangerous Minds* (1995), *Bleeding Hearts* (1994), *Point of No Return* (1993), *Hudson Hawk* (1991), *Breaking In* (1989)

Television movie (executive producer): *Accidental Friendship* (2008)

Television movies (actress): *The Doctor* (2011), *The Line* (2010), *Their Eyes Are Watching God* (2005), *America's Dream* (1996)

Television (actress): *Into the Badlands* (2018), *Orange is the New Black* (2014-2018), *Forever* (2014–15), The *Young and the Restless* (2012–14), *The Fosters* (2013–17), *Body of Proof* (2013), *Friday Night Lights* (2009–11), *Saving Grace* (2007–10), *Ugly Betty* (2007), *Threat Matrix* (2003–04), *Law & Order* (1990–2003), *Crossing Jordan* (2002–03), *Any Day Now* (1998), *Leaving L.A.* (1997), *Amazing Grace* (1995), *Where I Live* (1993)

Gabrielle Union (1972), actress, producer. Union was on the path to becoming a lawyer when she was recruited to be a model while working as a student office worker at a modeling agency. She took on modeling assignments to pay student loans after earning a BS in Sociology with honors from the University of California, Los Angeles. Little did she know that modeling would change the trajectory of her original career goal. Modeling led to guest-starring television appearances followed by being cast in a succession of youth-cultured films such as *She's All That* in 1999 then *Love & Basketball* and *Bring It On* in 2000. Movie blockbuster *Bad Boy II* in 2003 cast Union in the role of Syd. In the television series *Being Mary Jane* (2013–18), Union plays lead character Mary Jane Paul. Born in Omaha, Nebraska, Union is an advocate for finding a cure for cancer and victims of assault.

Awards: CinemaCon, USA (2018), Image Award (2014), Palm Beach International Film Festival (2006), BET Comedy Award (2004), American Black Film Festival Award (2003), Black Reel Award (2001), Young Hollywood Award (2001)

Movies (actress): *Breaking In* (2018), *The Public* (2018), *Almost Christmas* (2016), *Top Five* (2014), *Think Like a Man Too* (2014), *Think Like a Man* (2012), *In Our Nature* (2012), *Good Deeds* (2012), *Cadillac*

Records (2008), *Meet Dave* (2008), *Daddy's Little Girls* (2007), *Neo Ned* (2005), *Breakin' All the Rules* (2004), *Bad Boys II* (2003), *Cradle 2 the Grave* (2003), *Deliver Us from Eva* (2003), *Two Can Play That Game* (2001), *The Brothers* (2001), *Bring It On* (2000), *Love & Basketball* (2000), *10 Things I Hate About You* (1999), *She's All That* (1999)

Television movies (actress): *With This Ring* (2015), *Little in Common* (2011), *Body Politic* (2009), *Football Wives* (2007), *Something the Lord Made* (2004), *Close to Home* (2001), *H-E Double Hockey Sticks* (1999), *1973* (1998)

Television (producer, actress): *Being Mary Jane* (2013–18)

Television (actress): *The Lion Guard* (2016-18), *Flashforward* (2009–10), *Life* (2009), *Night Stalker* (2005–06), *City of Angels* (2000), *7th Heaven* (1996–99)

Courtney B. Vance, actor, producer. Vance maintains a balancing act between the mediums of stage, film, and television. Staying true to his stage roots, Vance won a Tony Award for Best Featured Actor in the play *Lucky Lady* in 2013. Initially, he was a history major at Harvard University. After joining a theatrical group, Vance became enamored with acting. Once he earned his BA, he continued and graduated from Yale School of Drama with an MFA. Conquering the New York stage, Vance won an Obie Award for his role in the off-Broadway production *My Children, My Africa!* in 1990. From the beginning of his film career, Vance has consistently been cast in substantial roles from *Hamburger Hill* in 1987 and *The Adventures of Huck Finn* in 1993 to the role of Bobby Seale in *Panther* in 1995. In 1999, he joined the ranks of producer with *Love and Action in Chicago*. Easy recognition and wide audience appeal were achieved in the network television role of Assistant District Attorney, Ron Carver on *Law & Order: Criminal Intent*. He earned numerous accolades for his award-winning role as Johnnie Cochran in *American Crime Story (*2016-18). Vance hails from Birmingham, Michigan.

Awards: Image Award (2017), Black Reel Award (2017, 2013), Primetime Emmy Award (2016), Critics Choice Television (2016), Online Film & Television Association (2016), DVD Exclusive Award (2001)

Movie (producer and actor): *Love and Action in Chicago* (1999)

Movies (actor): *Isle of Dogs* (2018), *The Mummy* (2017), *Terminator*

Genisys (2015), *Joyful Noise* (2012), *Final Destination 5* (2011), *Extraordinary Measures* (2010), *Hurricane Season* (2009), *Space Cowboys* (2000), *Ambushed* (1998), *Blind Faith* (1998), *The Preacher's Wife* (1996), *Dangerous Minds* (1995), *Panther* (1995), *The Adventures of Huck Finn* (1993), *The Hunt for Red October* (1990), *Hamburger Hill* (1987)

Television movies (actor): *The Immortal Life of Henrietta Lacks* (2017), *Let It Shine* (2012), *Whitewash: The Clarence Brandley Story* (2002), *12 Angry Men* (1997), *The Piano Lesson* (1995), *Percy & Thunder* (1993), *In the Line of Duty: Street War* (1992)

Television (actor): *State of Affairs* (2014–15), *Revenge* (2012), *FlashForward* (2009–10), *ER* (2008–09), *Law & Order: Criminal Intent* (2001–06)

Mario Van Peebles (1957), actor, director, producer. Peebles continues to make the most of his filmmaker father's, Melvin Van Peebles, influence. There appears to be a friendship and mutual respect between the two who share the same interests from art to economics. Before Van Peebles made an indelible impression as an actor and director in *New Jack City* in 1991 and *Posse* in 1993, he was an analyst for the New York City Mayor's Office of Management and Budget. He graduated from Columbia University with a BS in Economics. Once he decided to explore his creative side, he started as a model and photographer. His mother, Maria Magdalena Van Peebles, is a photographer. Van Peebles has struck a balance as actor, director, and producer. Producing the movie *Panther* in 1995 was a bold move. A confluence of his ability as actor, producer, and director merged in the award-winning film *Baadasssss!* released in 2003. The medium of television as an actor and director has been a staple.

Awards: Black Reel Award (2005), Philadelphia Film Festival Award (2004), Phoenix Film Festival Award (2003), Locarno International Film Festival Award (1995), Image Award (1989) Movies (director, actor, producer): *We the Party* (2012), *Baadasssss!* (2003), *Panther* (1995)

Movie (producer, writer, actor): *Los Locos* (1997)

Movies (director, actor): *All Things Fall Apart* (2011), *Posse* (1993), *New Jack City* (1991)

Movie (writer, director, actor): *Armed* (2018)

Movies (actor): *Ali* (2001), *Identity Crisis* (1989), *Hotshot* (1987), *Heartbreak Ridge* (1986), *Rappin'* (1985), *Sweet Sweetback's Baadasssss Song* (1971)

Television movie (actor, producer, director): *Gang in Blue* (1996)

Television movies (actor): *Crown Heights* (2004), *44 Minutes: The North Hollywood Shoot-Out* (2003), *The Street Lawyer* (2003), *10,000 Black Men Named George* (2002), *Sally Hemings: An American Scandal* (2000), *Stompin' at the Savoy* (1992), *A Triumph of the Heart: The Ricky Bell Story* (1991), *The Sophisticated Gents* (1981)

Television (producer, writer, director, actor): *Superstition* (2017-18)

Television (director): *Being Mary Jane* (2015-17), *Empire* (2015-16)

Television (actor): *Bloodline* (2017), *Damages* (2007–09), *All My Children* (2008), *Rude Awakening* (2000–01), *Sonny Spoon* (1988), *L.A. Law* (1986)

Michael Warren (1946), actor. Warren transitioned from being on a phenomenal basketball team in 1967 to 1968 to success in movies and television. Warren played for the University of California–Los Angeles Bruins and graduated from UCLA with a BA in theatre arts. He appeared and was a basketball technical adviser for the 1971 film *Drive, He Said*. By the time Warren followed up *Butterflies Are Free* in 1972 and *Cleopatra Jones* in 1973, his foundation as an actor was pretty much set. He became widely known for his role as Officer Bobby Hill on the long running television drama *Hill Street Blues* from 1981 to 1987.
The new millennium ushered in reoccurring roles in the television series *Lincoln Heights* and *Single Ladies*. Warren was born in South Bend, Indiana.

Awards: Indiana Basketball Hall of Fame (1992), UCLA Athletic Hall of Fame (1990)

Movies: *Anderson's Cross* (2010), *Mother and Child* (2009), *Trippin'* (1999), *Storyville* (1992), *Heaven Is a Playground* (1991), *Fast Break* (1979), *Norman...Is That You?* (1976), *Cleopatra Jones* (1973), *Butterflies Are Free* (1972), *Drive, He Said* (1971), *Halls of Anger* (1970)

Television movies: *After All* (1999), *The Wedding* (1998), *Buffalo Soldiers* (1997), *Stompin' at the Savoy* (1992), *The Kid Who Loved*

Christmas (1990), *A Little Bit Strange* (1999), *The Child Saver* (1988)

Television: *Single Ladies* (2011), *Lincoln Heights* (2007–09), *Soul Food* (2002–04), *City of Angels* (2000), *In the House* (1995–96), *Hill Street Blues* (1981–87), *Paris* (1979–80), *Sierra* (1974)

Denzel Washington (1954), actor, producer, director. Washington is one of the most outstanding cinematic talents of the era. His biography is a testament to a great American story. A wholesome, carefully guided childhood eventually paved the way to college that led to stage, television, and film. After dabbling into various majors at Fordham University, Washington finally settled on graduating with a BA in Journalism. Before graduation, he led a stage production at a youth summer camp, and after receiving accolades for his performance, he was convinced acting was the right career choice. When he returned to Fordham's campus, he won lofty parts in plays by Shakespeare and Eugene O'Neill. Off-Broadway he won an Obie Award for his performance in *A Soldier's Play* in 1982. He recreated the role in 1984 for the big screen in *A Soldier's Story*. Washington had joined the ranks of recognizable actor by the time he completed the television series *St. Elsewhere*, which ran from 1982–1988. Within a twelve-year span that include three other Academy Award nominations, Washington won the Academy Award twice as best supporting actor in 1990 for the film *Glory* and best actor in 2002 for *Training Day*. He was again nominated in 2013 for best actor in the movie *Flight*. Washington has successfully collaborated in a number of projects with filmmaker Spike Lee, an audience favorite being *Malcolm X* in 1992. He proved himself as a director and producer with *Antwone Fisher* in 2002. In 2007, he occupied the director's chair again with *The Great Debaters*. Washington is the recipient of several honorary doctorates that include his alma mater, Fordham University, Morehouse College, and University of Pennsylvania. His charitable gifts to numerous organizations resulted in him and his wife, Pauletta, receiving the BET Humanitarian Award in 2005. They also jointly share the Women in Film Crystal Award for Humanitarianism in 2000. Washington was born in Mount Vernon, New York.

Awards (select): Screen Actors Guild Award (2017), Image Award (2017, 2013, 2011, 2008, 2003, 2002, 2001, 2000, 1998, 1997, 1996,

1995, 1994, 1992, 1988), Black Reel Award (2013, 2003, 2002, 2001, 2000), Tony Award (Broadway stage) (2010), BET Award (2008, 2005, 2004, 2001), AFI Award (2002), Academy Award (2002, 1990), Berlin International Film Festival Award (2000, 1993), Golden Globe Award (2000, 1990), Women in Film Crystal Award (2000) Sundance Film Festival (1993) Movie (producer, director, actor): *Fences* (2016), *Antwone Fisher* (2002)

Movie (director and actor): *The Great Debaters* (2007)

Movies (producer and actor): *The Equalizer 2* (2018), *Roman J. Israel, Esq.* (2017), *The Equalizer* (2014), *Safe House* (2012), *The Book of Eli* (2010)

Documentaries (producer): *Half Past Autumn: The Life and Works of Gordon Parks* (television, 2000), *Hank Aaron: Chasing the Dream* (film, 1995)

Movies (actor): *The Magnificent Seven* (2016), *2 Guns* (2013), *Flight* (2012), *Unstoppable* (2010), *The Taking of Pelham 1 2 3* (2009), *American Gangster* (2007), *Déjà Vu* (2006), *Inside Man* (2006), *Man on Fire*, (2004), *John Q* (2002), *Training Day* (2001), *Remember the Titans* (2000), *The Hurricane* (1999), *He Got Game* (1998), *The Preachers Wife* (1996), *Devil in a Blue Dress* (1995), *Philadelphia* (1993), *Malcolm X* (1992), *Mississippi Masala* (1991), *Mo' Better Blues* (1990), *Glory* (1989), *Cry Freedom* (1987), *A Soldier's Story* (1984) Television (actor): *St. Elsewhere* (1982–88), *Wilma* (TV Movie, 1977)

Kerry Washington (1977), actress, producer. However a film or television project fares, Washington emerges as a standout. She was awarded a Teen Choice Award early in her career for a breakout performance in the movie *Save the Last Dance* in 2001. Recognized for her extraordinary range, the role of Della Bea Robinson in the Academy Award–winning *Ray* in 2004 gave Washington's career a meteoric boost. She was born in New York City and graduated from George Washington University with a double major in anthropology and sociology. Early in her acting career, she was a substitute teacher in Harlem between acting jobs. Starring in the politically themed television sensation *Scandal*, Washington is a political activist in real life and spoke at the 2012 Democratic National Convention. She is the recipient of the NAACP

President's Award in 2013.

Awards: Black Reel Award (2017, 2011), GLADD Media Award (2015), Image Award (2014, 2013, 2005), BET Award (2013), TV Guide Award (2013), Urbanworld Film Festival Award (2002), Teen Choice Award (2001)

Movies (actress): *Cars 3* (2017), *Peeples* (2013), *Django Unchained* (2012), *A Thousand Words* (2012), *For Colored Girls* (2010), *Night Catches Us* (2010), *Mother and Child* (2009), *Lakeview Terrace* (2009), *Miracle at St. Anna* (2008), *Fantastic 4: Rise of the Silver Surfer* (2007), *The Last King of Scotland* (2006), *Fantastic Four* (2005), *Mr. and Mrs. Smith* (2005), *Ray* (2004), *She Hate Me* (2004), *Save the Last Dance* (2001), *Our Song* (2000)

Television movie (actress): *Confirmation* (2016)

Television (producer): *Scandal* (2017-18)

Television (actress): *Scandal* (2012–18), *Black Panther* (voice, 2010), *Boston Legal* (2005–06), *100 Centre Street* (2001)

Kim Wayans (1961), actress, comedienne, writer, producer, director. A member of an entertainment dynasty, Wayans possesses a wide range of talent. At times she has collaborated with brothers Keenan, Damon, Shawn, and Marlon. Belonging to an immensely talented family who share some of the same interests has its perks. Wayans made a successful turn as a dramatic actress in the 2011 independent film success *Pariah*. A graduate of Wesleyan University, she towed her parents' line with regard to higher education before heading for Hollywood. As a comedienne, she performed stand-up in various clubs before the role in her first film *Hollywood Shuffle* in 1987. Work in television has been very lucrative for Wayans with the longest exposure on *In Living Color* from 1990 to 2001. Between 2002 and 2005, she put her producing, writing, and directing skills to work for the television comedy *My Wife and Kids*. Wayans and her husband, Kevin Knotts, are coauthors of the children's Amy Hodgepodge *All Mixed Up!* book series, which explores the multiracial experience.

Award: TV Land Award (2012)

Movies (actress): *Pariah* (2011), *Dance Flick* (2009), *Juwanna Mann* (2002), *Don't Be a Menace to South Central While Drinking Your Juice* in the Hood (1996), A Low Down Dirty Shame (1994), I'm Gonna Get You Sucka (1988), Hollywood Shuffie (1987)

Television movies (executive producer and voice): Thugaboo: Sneaker Madness (2006)

Television movies (actress): Thugaboo: A Miracle on D-Roc's Street (2006)

Television (producer, writer, director): My Wife and Kids (2002–05)

Television (actress): The Breaks (2017), Reckless (2014), In Living Color (1990–2001), In the House (1995–99), Waynehead (1996–97), A Different World (1987–88)

Forest Whitaker (1961), actor, producer, director. The ability to turn adversity into an asset made Whitaker one of the most influential people in twenty-first century cinema. A devastating back injury while attending Cal Poly Pomona on a football scholarship forced Whitaker to change his career course. His talent as an opera tenor got him accepted into the music conservatory at University of Southern California where he subsequently graduated with a degree from the USC School of Dramatic Arts. After graduation, Whitaker went to New York to pay the requisite stage dues. While working in a play, he was given an opportunity to appear on film. In 1982, the same year he graduated college, he got the role of Charles Jefferson in the movie *Fast Times at Ridgemont High*. From then on, he has worked continuously in studio-driven and independent films, winning awards along the way. As a producer and director, he expanded his love of storytelling. Before he got involved with the business of producing *Fruitvale Station* in 2013, he took the plunge in 1991 with *A Rage in Harlem*. Whitaker's directing skills proved admirable in the movie classic *Waiting to Exhale* in 1995 and *Hope Floats* in 1998. A major turning point came with him winning the Academy Award for Best Performance by an Actor in the lead role for *The Last King of Scotland* in 2007. Whitaker heads an all-star cast in 2013's movie, *Lee Daniels'The Butler*. Whitaker is recognized for his activism, which is reflected in his politics and charitable contributions. He is an ambassador for peace and reconciliation with the United Nations Educational, Scientific, and Cultural Organization (UNESCO). He cofounded the International Institute for Peace at Rutgers University.

Awards (select): AFI Award (2014), Image Award (2014, 2007), Independent Spirit Award (2014), PGA Award (2014), News and Documentary Emmy Award (2012), Peabody Award (2010), Academy Award (2007), BET Award (2007), Black Reel Award (2007), Golden Globes Award (2007), Screen Actors Guild Award (2007), Star on the Walk of Fame (2007), Primetime Emmy Award (2003), Blockbuster Entertainment Award (1997), Cannes Film Festival Award (1988)

Movie (actor, producer, director): *First Daughter* (2004)

Movie (producer, actor): *Sorry to Bother You* (2018), *Dope* (2015), *Repentance* (2014), *Powder Blue* (2009), *A Rage in Harlem* (1991) Movie (producer): *Fruitvale Station* (2013) Movie (documentary): *I Am You* (2014)

Movies (director): *Hope Floats* (1998), *Waiting to Exhale* (1995)

Movies (actor): *Black Panther* (2018), *Southpaw* (2015), *Two Men in Town* (2014), *Out of the Furnace* (2013), *Black Nativity* (2013), *Lee Daniels' The Butler* (2013), *Zulu* (2013), *Pawn* (2013), *The Last Stand* (2013), *Repo Men* (2010), *Our Family Wedding* (2010), *Hurricane Season* (2009), *The Great Debaters* (2007), *The Last King of Scotland* (2006), *Phone Booth* (2002), *Ghost Dog: The Way of the Samurai* (1999), *Phenomenon* (1996), *Smoke* (1995), *Blown Away* (1994), *The Crying Game* (1992), *A Rage in Harlem* (1991), *Johnny Handsome* (1989), *Bird* (1988), *Good Morning Vietnam* (1987), *Platoon* (1986), *The Color of Money* (1986), *Fast Times at Ridgemont High* (1982) Television movie (producer, director): *Black Jaq* (1988) Television movie (producer) *Roxanne Roxanne* (2017)

Television movie (director): *Strapped* (1993)

Television movies (actor): *Deacons for Defense* (2003), *Feast of All Saints* (2011), *Witness Protection* (1999), *Rebound: The Legend of Earl 'The Goat' Manigault* (1996), *Lush Life* (1993)

Television (host, producer): *The Twilight Zone* (2002–03)

Television series documentary (producer): *Brick City* (2009–11)

Television (actor): *Empire* (2017-18), *Criminal Minds: Suspect Behavior* (2011), *The Shield* (2006–07), *ER* (2006–07), *North and South, Book II* (1986), *North and South* (1985)

Lynn Whitfield (1953), actress, producer. Whitfield always knew what she wanted to do. A descendant of a long line of college graduates, there was never any question she would earn the BFA from Howard University. While in college, Whitfield took to the stage with the DC Black Repertory Company. She was born in Baton Rouge, Louisiana. Her mother and father were very involved in a community theater that her father organized. After college, Whitfield moved to New York and appeared in a number of Off-Broadway productions before heading to Los Angeles. After a national tour of Ntozake Shange's *For Colored Girls Who Have Considered Suicide/When the Rainbow Is Enuf*, television and film projects soon followed. Able to strike a balance between film and major television, Whitfield's career picked up momentum in 1985 with *The Slugger's Wife* and *Silverado*. By 1986, she would lead in the television movie *Johnnie Mae Gibson: FBI*. Whitfield is the recipient of a number of awards including a Primetime Emmy for *The Josephine Baker Story*, which first aired in 1991. Whitfield took a comedic turn in *Head of State* in 2003. She joined the ranks of producer in 2012 with the film *Redemption of a Dog* and *Deaf Ghost* in 2014. Whitfield is an advocate in raising awareness of the importance of foster care with focus on the more mature youth.

Awards: Gracie Allen Award (2017), Black Reel Award (2005), Image Award (2005, 2000, 1998, 1994, 1993), Primetime Emmy Award (1991)

Movie (producer and actress): *Deaf Ghost* (2014), *Redemption of a Dog* (2012)

Movies (actress): *King's Faith* (2013), *All Things Fall Apart* (2011), *The Rebound* (2009), *Kings of the Evening* (2008), *Madea's Family Reunion* (2006), *Head of State* (2003), *Stepmom* (1998), *Eve's Bayou* (1997), *A Thin Line Between Love and Hate* (1996), *Silverado* (1985)

Television movies (actress): *Somebody's Child* (2012), *The Cheetah Girls 2* (2006), *The Cheetah Girls* (2003, 2004), *Love Songs* (1999), *Dangerous Evidence: The Lori Jackson Story* (1999), *The Wedding* (1998), *The Cosby Mysteries* (1994), *Stompin' at the Savoy* (1992), *The Josephine Baker Story* (1991), *The Women of Brewster Place* (1989), *The George McKenna Story* (1986), *Johnnie Mae Gibson: FBI* (1986)

Television (actress): *Greenleaf* (2016-18), *Mistresses* (2015-16), *Hit the Floor* (2014-16), *How to Get Away with Murder* (2014–15), *Without* *a Trace* (2002–06), *Equal Justice* (1991), *Heartbeat* (1988)

Cynda Williams (1966), actress, singer. Until Williams was cast in the role of Clarke Bentancourt in the 1990 film *Mo' Better Blues*, she never considered film acting as a career. Born in Chicago, Illinois, Williams graduated with a BA in Theater Art from Ball State University. After graduation, she went to New York City with Broadway musical theater aspirations in mind. Focused on her gospel-music roots, it was a jolt when after doing her own singing in *Mo' Better Blues*, she had a hit with single "Harlem Blues" and was a highly sought-after jazz performer. The pull of acting proved to be irresistible and led to a major role in the movie *One False Move* in 1992. *Introducing Dorothy Dandridge* in 1999 and *The Wedding* in 1998 contributed to Williams's cache of television movie roles. In 2012, she returned to the stage at the Goodman Theater appearing in the play *Immediate Family*.

Award: Various Artists independent Film Festival (2017)

Movie (documentary): *Reel Black Love* (2012)

Movies: *Every 21 Seconds* (2018), *A Chance in the World* (2017), *The Hills* (2017), *Turning Point* (2012), *Tru Loved* (2008), *Frankie D* (2007), *With or Without You* (2003), *MacArthur Park* (2001), *Caught Up* (1998), *Black Rose of Harlem* (1996), *One False Move* (1992), *Mo' Better Blues* (1990)

Television movies: *Violation* (2003), *Hidden Blessings* (2000), *Introducing Dorothy Dandridge* (1999), *The Wedding* (1998), *Gang in Blue* (1996), *Armistead Maupin's Tales of the City* (TV miniseries) (1993)

Vanessa L. Williams (1963), actress, singer, producer. Williams has triumphed in music, stage, film, and television. The first African American to be crowned Miss America in 1984 opened the door for Williams to showcase her gifts. Born in Millwood, New York, music instructor parents Milton and Helen Williams heavily influenced her interest in developing her natural talent for singing and songwriting. To William's credit, after leaving Syracuse University to fulfill Miss America duties, she returned twenty-five years later to finish and earn a BA in Musical Theater. The mother of four wanted to set an example. 1988 marked the release of two number-one singles, "The Right Stuff" and "Dreamin'." William's power as a singer of film scores were given full range on the soundtrack of the Academy Award–winning "Colors of the Wind" from the 1995 film release of *Pocahontas*. As an actress, Williams's career in television and film began in 1984. She made quite an impression in the 1991 film *Harley Davidson and the Marlboro Man* and in the 1992 television movie *Stompin' at the Savoy*. Notable stage appearances were in the Broadway musicals *Kiss of the Spider Woman* in 1994 and *Into the Woods* in 2002. The role of Detective Vasquez in the 2000 film *Shaft* showcased Williams's range as a dramatic actress. As Renee Perry in 2010–2012 television series *Desperate Housewives*, the focus was on her comedic talent.

Awards: Image Awards (2013, 2011, 2008, 2007, 1998), Satellite Award (2011, 2007, 2003), New York Women in Film (2010), Teen Choice Award (2007), Star on the Walk of Fame (2007)

Movie (producer, actress): *And Then Came Love* (2007)

Movies (actress): *Temptation: Confessions of a Marriage Counselor* (2013), *Hannah Montana: The Movie* (2009), *My Brother* (2006), *Johnson Family Vacation* (2004), *Shaft* (2000), *Light It Up* (1999), *The Adventures of Elmo in Grouchland* (1999), *Dance with Me* (1998), *Hoodlum* (1997), *Soul Food* (1997), *Eraser* (1996), *Harley Davidson and the Marlboro Man* (1991), *The Pick-up Artist* (1987)

Television movies (actress): *Fantasy Life* (2015), *The Trip to Bountiful* (2014), *Keep the Faith, Baby* (2002), *A Diva's Christmas Carol* (2000), *Don Quixote* (2000), *Futuresport* (1998), *Bye Birdie* (1995), *Nothing Lasts Forever* (1995), *The Jacksons: An American Dream* (1992), *The Kid Who Loved Christmas* (1990)

Television (producer, actress): *Vanessa Williams Christmas: Live by Request* (TV special) (2004), *The Courage to Love* (TV movie) (2000), *Vanessa Williams & Friends: Christmas in New York* (TV movie) (1996)

Television (actress): *Me, Myself and I* (2018), *Daytime Divas* (2017), *The Librarians* (2016-17), *The Good Wife* (2015), *666 Park Avenue* (2012–13), *Desperate Housewives* (2010–12), *Ugly Betty* (2006–10), *Mama Mirabelle's Home Movies* (2007–08), *South Beach* (2006), *Boomtown* (2003), *L.A. Doctors* (1999)

Alfre Woodard (1952), actress, producer. Woodard is highly praised for the scope of her talent. Woodard knew by her junior year in high school that acting was the career she would pursue. She graduated with a BFA from Boston University. She was born in Tulsa, Oklahoma. After college, Woodard performed on stage in Washington, DC, New York, and Los Angeles. Her first major film role was as Rita in *Remember My Name* in 1978. During her distinctive career, she has been cast in numerous television movies and series, which include the role of Winnie Mandela in the television movie *Mandela* in 1987. Between 1991 and 1999, Woodard produced three critically acclaimed films *Funny Valentines, Down in the Delta*, and *Pretty Hattie's Baby*. She won a Black Reel Award for best supporting actress in the 2013 television movie *Steel Magnolias*. Woodard took home a Golden Globe in 1998 for best performance in the television movie *Miss Evers' Boys* and was nominated for an Academy Award for the movie *Cross Creek* in 1983. Woodard is the recipient of four Primetime Emmy Awards. She appears as Mistress Harriet Shaw in the 2013 movie *12 Years a Slave*.

Awards (select): Society of Camera Operators (2015), Black Reel Award (2013, 2007), Image Award (2013, 2004, 2001, 1998, 1996, 1992, 1990, 1989, 1984), Screen Actors Guild Award (2006, 1998, 1996), Character and Morality in Entertainment Award (2005), Primetime Emmy Award (2003, 1997, 1987, 1984), Golden Globe Award (1998), CableACE Award (1997, 1989), Women in Film Crystal Award (1995), Independent Spirit Award (1993) Movie documentary (producer): *Soft Vengeance: Albie Sachs and the New South Africa* (2014)

Movies (producer and actress): *Funny Valentines* (1999), *Down in the Delta* (1998), *Pretty Hattie's Baby* (1991)

Movies (actress): *Captain America: Civil War* (2016), *12 Years a Slave* (2013), *American Violet* (2008), *Take the Lead* (2006), *Something New* (2006), *Beauty Shop* (2005), *Radio* (2003), *Baby of the Family* (2002), *K-PAX* (2001), *Love & Basketball* (2000), *Crooklyn* (1994), *Bopha* (1993), *Passion Fish* (1992), *Grand Canyon* (1991), *Extremities* (1986), *Go Tell It on the Mountain* (1984), *Cross Creek* (1983), *Remember My Name* (1978).

Television movies (actress): *Steel Magnolias* (2013), *Holiday Heart* (2000), *The Piano Lesson* (1995), *Race to Freedom: The Underground*

Railroad (1994), *A Mother's Courage: The Mary Thomas Story* (1989), *The Child Saver* (1988), *Mandela* (1987), *Words by Heart* (1985), *The Sophisticated Gents* (1981), *The Trial of the Moke* (1978),

Television (actress): *Luke Cage* (2016-18), *Empire* (2018), *State of Affairs* (2014–15), *Copper* (2013), *True Blood* (2010–12), *Memphis Beat* (2010–11), *Three Rivers* (2009–10), *Black Panther* (voice, 2010), *My Own Worst Enemy* (2008), *Desperate Housewives* (2005–06), *St. Elsewhere* (1985–88), *Sara* (1985), *American Playhouse* (1982–85), *Tucker's Witch* (1982–83)

Jeffrey Wright (1965), actor, producer. Having achieved mammoth success on the Broadway stage and several awards including a 1994 Tony Award for his featured role in *Angels in America: Perestroika*, Wright's progression to film was a smooth transition. His first role in 1990 was as a prosecuting attorney in the film *Presumed Innocent*. By 1996, he was the lead in the award winning film biography of avant-garde artist *Basquiat*. Born in Washington, DC, Wright's initial intention was to become a lawyer. He graduated with a BA in Political Science from Amherst College. Prior to graduation from Amherst, he discovered a love for acting and accepted a scholarship for a master's degree in theater arts from New York University, then left after two months to stake a claim in the professional world of acting. In 2007, he struck gold producing and starring in *Blackout*, a film which chronicle events that took place during a neighborhood blackout in Brooklyn.

Awards: Tribeca Film Festival (2018), NAMIC Vision Award (2014), Black Reel Award (2008, 2006, 2004), Chicago International Film Festival Award (2007), San Diego Film Critics Society Award (2005), Golden Globe Award (2004), Primetime Emmy Award (2004), AFI Award (2002), Toronto Film Critics Association Award (2000)

Movie (producer and actor): *Blackout* (2007)

Movies (actor): *Hold the Dark* (2018), *O.G.* (2018), *Friday's Child* (2018), *The Public* (2018), *The Hunger Games: Mockingjay–Part 2* (2015), *The Hunger Games: Mockingjay–Part 1* (2014), *The Hunger Games: Catching Fire* (2013), *The Inevitable Defeat of Mister Pete* (2013), *Broken City* (2013), *The Ides of March* (2011), *Source Code* (2011), *Cadillac Records* (2008), *Quantum of Solace* (2008), *W.* (2008),

Casino Royale (2006), *Syriana* (2005), *The Manchurian Candidate* (2004), *Sin's Kitchen* (2004), *Ali* (2001), *Shaft* (2000), *Hamlet* (2000), *Basquiat* (1996), *Presumed Innocent* (1990)

Television documentaries (actor): *Independent Lens: Bobby Seale/Chicago 10* (2008), *The American Experience: New Orleans* (2007)

Television movies (actor): *Confirmation* (2016), *Lakawanna Blues* (2005), *Boycott* (2001)

Television (actor): *Westworld* (2016-18), *Boardwalk Empire* (2013), *Angels in America* (TV miniseries) (2003), *Homicide: Life on the Street* (1997), *The Young Indiana Jones Chronicles* (1993)

FROM ATHLETE TO CINEMA

Athletes who graduated and transitioned to film.

Kareem Abdul-Jabbar (1947), athlete, actor, writer, producer. Renowned basketball player Abdul-Jabbar was cast in *Airplane!* in 1980 after guest-starring in a succession of television series. On a scholarship from University of California, Los Angeles where he played for the Bruins, he graduated with a BA in History. The only child of Ferdinand, a New York transit officer, and Cora Alcindor, Abdul-Jabbar was born in New York City. Mentored by Bruce Lee in the martial-art discipline of Jeet Kune Do, Abdul-Jabbar gives commentary in several documentaries about Lee, which include *The Curse of the Dragon* in 1993. He has written two autobiographies, one with Peter Knobler titled *Giant Steps: An Autobiography of Kareem Abdul-Jabbar* in 1983. The other book is written with Mignon McCarthy called *Kareem* published in 1990. In 2012, Abdul-Jabbar published a children's book on the history of black inventors called *What Color Is My World?* and in 2013, delivered young-adult fiction *Sasquatch in the Paint* about a thirteen-year-old pushed to play basketball. Abdul-Jabbar has won numerous athletic awards and honors.
    Awards (select non-athletic): Presidential Medal of Freedom (2016), Double Helix Medal (2011), Image Award (2013)
    Documentary (writer and producer): *On the Shoulders of Giants* (2011), *On the Shoulders of Giants: The Story of the Greatest Team You Never Heard Of* (2010)
    Movies (actor): *Forget Paris* (1995), *Airplane!* (1980), *The Fish That Saved Pittsburgh* (1979)
    Television movie (producer): *The Vernon Jordan Story* (1994), *All Star Tribute to Kareem Abdul-Jabbar* (1989)
    Television movies (actor): *Rebound: The Legend of Earl 'The Goat' Manigault* (1996), *Jake Spanner Private Eye* (1989)
    Television (as himself): *The Comedy Get Down* (2017), *Mike & Mike* (2010–13), *Splash* (2013)

Jim Brown (1936), actor, producer, athlete, activist. Heir to the Triple Crown as an inductee into the Pro Football Hall of Fame, College Football Hall of Fame, and Lacrosse Hall of Fame, Brown has succeeded in every field opted for. In 1964, he made the transition from pro football to film in *Rio Conchos*. By 1967, he was starring in a blockbuster film *The Dirty Dozen*. In the years 1972–73 during the Blaxploitation era, he took the lead in *Slaughter*, *Black Gunn*, and *Slaughter's Big Rip-Off*. Brown was again, cast in mainstream films including *Mars Attacks!* in 1996. He allied with filmmaker Spike Lee in *She Got Game* in 1998 and *She Hate Me* in 2004. Brown was born in St. Simmons, Georgia. He graduated with a BA from Syracuse University. His social activism centers on informing and building economic skills for independent living in the African American community. In 1988, Brown founded Amer-I-Can, a life-management skills organization that targets youth and the incarcerated. In 1970, Brown won an Image Award for Outstanding Actor in a Motion Picture for the movie *El Condor*.

Movie documentaries (producer,): *Frontliners* (2010), *Richard Pryor...Here and Now* (1983)

Movie (producer and actor): *Pacific Inferno* (1979)

Television movie (producer): *The Magnificent Magical Magnet of Santa Mesa* (1977)

Movies (actor): *Draft* Day (2014), Dream *Street* (2010), *She Hate Me* (2004), *Any Given Sunday* (1999), *He Got Game* (1998), *Mars Attacks!* (1996), *Original Gangstas* (1996), *L.A. Heat* (1989), *I'm Gonna Git You Sucka* (1988), *The Running Man* (1987), *Fingers* (1978), *Vengeance* (1977), *Take a Hard Ride* (1975), *Three the Hard Way* (1974), *I Escaped from Devil's Island* (1973), *The Slams* (1973), *Slaughter's Big Rip-Off* (1973), *Black Gunn* (1972), *Slaughter* (1972), *El Condor* (1970), *...tick...tick...tick* (1970), *100 Rifles* (1969), *The Split* (1968), *Ice Station Zebra* (1968), *Dark of the Sun* (1968), *The Dirty Dozen* (1967), *Rio Conchos* (1964)

Television movies (actor): *Sideliners* (2006), *Sucker Free City* (2004), *Hammer, Slammer & Slade* (1990), *Lady Blue* (1985) Television (actor): *Soul Food* (2004), *CHiPs* (1979, 1983)

Terry Crews (1968), actor. Prior to acting, Crews was a professional football player with the Philadelphia Eagles, Washington Redskins, San Diego Chargers, and Los Angeles Rams. On a full athletic scholarship, he graduated an art major from Western Michigan University. He was born in Flint, Michigan. Being a wholesome comic and a family man are cornerstones to Crews' success. Major notice came with *Everybody Hates Chris* (2005–09). His reality show, *The Family Crews* (2010–11) enhanced his audience appeal. *The Expendables 2* (2012) was yet another opportunity to showcase his magnificent physique.

Movies: *Deadpool 2* (2018), *Sorry to Bother You* (2018), *Blended* (2014), *The Expendables 3* (2014), *Cloudy with a Chance of Meatballs 2* (voice, 2013), *The Expendables 2* (2012), *Bridesmaids* (2011), *Lottery Ticket* (2010), *The Expendables* (2010), *Gamer* (2009), *Middle Men* (2009), *Terminator Salvation* (2009), *Get Smart* (2008), *Balls of Fury* (2007), *Who's Your Caddy?* (2007), *How to Rob a Bank* (2007), *Inland Empire* (2006), *Idiocracy* (2006), *The Longest Yard* (2005), *White Chicks* (2004), *Soul Plane* (2004), *Malibu's Most Wanted* (2003), *Deliver Us from Eva* (2003), *Friday After Next* (2002), *Serving Sara* (2002), *The 6th Day* (2000)

Television: *Brooklyn Nine-Nine* (2013–18), *Arrested Development* (2013), *Are We There Yet?* (2010–12), *The Newsroom* (2012), *The Family Crews* (2010–11), *Everybody Hates Chris* (2005–09)

Shaquille O'Neal (1972), athlete, actor, producer, soundtrack, entrepreneur, philanthropist. O'Neal wants and sets out to do it all. He is as intellectual as he is physical. The Olympic gold medal winner, National Basketball Association champion has a BA in General Studies with a minor in political science from Louisiana State University. He left LSU early when he was drafted into professional basketball and returned later to keep a promise to his mother he would graduate. He then earned his Master's in Business administration from the University of Phoenix and his doctorate (EdD) in human resource development from Barry University. All his college degrees don't overshadow his affinity for the world of entertainment, be it acting, producing, or making music. Out of five studio albums, *Shaq Diesel* went platinum in 1993, a year before

his first film role as Neon in *Blue Chips* in 1994. In 1996, O'Neal was executive producer of the movie *Kazaam*. He also produced several *All Star Comedy Jam* segments for television and video in 2009 and 2010. He is the voice of
Smooth Smurf in *The Smurfs 2* and appears as Officer Fluzoo in *Grown Ups 2*, both 2013 film releases. O'Neal was born in Newark, New Jersey.

Awards: CableACE Award (1996), numerous athletic awards including an outdoor statue erected at Louisiana State University at Baton Rouge

Movies (producer and actor): *Steel* (1997), *Kazaam* (1996)

Movies (actor): *Uncle Drew* (2018), *Blended* (2014), *The Lego Movie* (voice, 2014), *Grown Ups 2* (2013), *The Smurfs 2* (voice, 2013), *Scary Movie 4* (2006), *The Wash* (2001), *Freddy Got Fingered* (2001), *Blue Chips* (1994)

Movie soundtrack (performer and/or writer): *Pineapple Express* (2008), *Bring It On: All or Nothing* (2006), *Rebound* (2005), *Pootie Tang* (2001), *Steel* (1997)

Television documentary (producer): *A week in Watts* (2018), *Killer Bees* (2017), *30 for 30* (2016)

Television (producer): *All Star Comedy Jam* (2018, 2014, 2013, 2010, 2009), *The Love Shaq* (TV movie, 2009), *Shaq's Big Challenge* (2007)

Television (director): *Cousin Skeeter*, "Mo' Skeeter Blues" (1998)

Television soundtrack (performer and/or writer): *Beavis and Butt-Head* (1994)

Television (actor): *Southland* (2013)

Carl Weathers (1948), actor, director, producer. Throughout his football career, Weathers knew he wanted to be a film actor. Inspired by Sydney Poitier, Weathers graduated with a BA in Theater from San Diego State University. After sailing through a career as a professional football player for the Oakland Raiders and in Canada for the British Columbia Lions, Weathers was more than happy to make the transition to film. Prior to becoming legendary famous for originating the role of Apollo Creed in the *Rocky* movie franchise, he got his start in the 1975 Blaxploitation films *Bucktown* and *Friday Foster*. Always full of grandiose ideas, his Stormy Weather Productions led to his starring in

Action Jackson in 1988. He developed a track record as a television director with the series *Silk Stalkings* from 1993 to 1997 and *Sheena* in 2001. Weathers is closely associated with the US Olympic Committee and the Big Brothers Association.

Award: Behind the Voice Actors Award (2014)

Movies (actor): *Think Like a Man Too* (2014), *The Comebacks* (2007), *Hurricane Smith* (1992), *Action Jackson* (1988), *Predator* (1987), *Rocky IV* (1985), *Rocky III* (1982), *Rocky II* (1979), *Force 10 from Navarone* (1978), *Semi-Tough* (1977), *Rocky* (1976), *Friday Foster* (1975), *Bucktown* (1975)

Television movie (actor and producer): *The Defiant Ones* (1986)

Television movies (actor): *Dangerous Passion* (1990), *Braker* (1985), *The Bermuda Depths* (1978), *The Hostage Heart* (1977)

Television (producer and director): *Always Night* (2013)

Television (director): *Sheena* (2001), *Silk Stalkings* (1993–97)

Television (actor): *Star vs. the Forces of Evil* (2017-2018), *Chicago Justice* (2017), *Colony* (2016), Arrested *Development* (2004–13), *Brothers* (2009), *In the Heat of the Night* (1993–95), *Street Justice* (1991–93), *Tour of Duty* (1989–90), *Fortune Dane* (1986)

Fred Williamson (1938), actor, producer, director. It didn't take long for professional football player Williamson to take control of his career in film once he entered the arena in 1972. Having played with the San Francisco 49ers, Pittsburgh Steelers, Oakland Raiders, Kansas City Chiefs, and Montreal Alouetts, the Hammer was ready for the change. After a proper introduction to acting in the reoccurring role of Steve Bruce on the hit television show *Julia* in 1969–71, Williamson went on to be cast and create lead roles in film. The films *Black Caesar* and *Hell Up in Harlem* elevated Williamson to major-player status during the Blaxploitation, African American Film Renaissance era. Born in Gary, Indiana, he graduated from Northwestern University, excelling in football, with a BA in Architecture. By the mid-1970s, he formed Po'Boy Production Company and set out to write, direct, produce, and star in his films. *No Way Back* in 1976 is a prime example of his filmmaking endeavors. Fluent in Italian Williamson's production company made a string of films in Italy.

He collaborated with Italian filmmakers in the role of Detective Robert Malone in *Cobra 1*, *2*, and *3* between 1987 and 1990. Staying true to a relentless work ethic, he appeared in *From Dusk Till Dawn* in 1996 and added star power to the television movie *Carmen: A Hip Hopera* in 2001.

Movies (writer, director, actor, producer): *Three Days to a Kill* (1992), *Steele's Law* (1991), *The Messenger* (1986), *Mr. Mean* (1977), *No Way Back* (1976), *Adios Amigo* (1976)

Movies (director, actor, producer): *On the Edge* (2002), *Original Gangtas* (1996), *Foxtrap* (1986), *Mean Johnny Barrows* (1976)

Movie (writer, director, actor): *The Last Fight* (1983)

Movie (writer, actor): *Joshua* (1976)

Movie (director, actor): *The Kill Reflex* (1989)

Movies (actor): *A Chance in the World* (2017), *.357* (2013), *Street Poet* (2010), *Fighting Words* (2007), *From Dusk Till Dawn* (1996), *Deceptions* (1992), *Black Cobra 3: The Manila Connection* (1990), *Black Cobra 2* (1990), *The Inglorious Bastards* (1978), *Take a Hard Ride* (1975), *Bucktown* (1975), *Three the Hard Way* (1974), *Hell Up in Harlem* (1973), *Black Caesar* (1973), *Tell Me That You Love Me, Junie Moon* (1970), *MASH* (1970)

Television movies (actor): *Carmen: A Hip Hopera* (2001), *Half Nelson* (1995)

Television (actor): *Being Mary Jane* (2017), *Real Husbands of Hollywood* (2014-16), *Hello Paradise* (host, 2007–08), *Fast Track* (1997–98), *Half Nelson* (1985), *Julia* (1969–71)

EARLY PIONEERS OF CINEMA

Zora Neale Hurston (1891–1960), writer, documentary filmmaker. Considered a cinematic foremother, Hurston understood the profound impact media, namely film, can have on lives. Recognized primarily as a writer of novels, poetry, and folklore, Hurston was employed in the early forties as a story consultant at Paramount Studios in Hollywood, California. With the passing of her mother at age nine and a strained relationship with her father, Hurston was on her own at fourteen. Born in Notasulga, Alabama, Hurston's field of study was anthropology. She attended Howard University and earned a BA from Barnard College and an MA from Columbia University. As an anthropological documentary filmmaker from 1928 to 1940, her focus was on life in the rural south. Much of her footage went untitled except for two, *Kossula: Last of the Takkoi Slaves in America* (circa late 1920s to early 1930s) and *Commandment Keeper Church, Beaufort South Carolina, May 1940.*

Awards: Rosenwald Foundation Fellowship (1935), Guggenheim Fellowship (1936), honorary doctorate, Morgan State College (1939), Anisfield-Wolf Book Award (1943), Distinguished Alumni Award, Howard University (1943), Education and Human Relations Award, Bethune-Bookman College (1956) Documentary movie (director): *Commandment Keeper Church, Beaufort South Carolina, May 1940* (1940)

Movie (writer): *The Gilded Six Bits* (short, 2001)
Television movie (writer): *Their Eyes Are Watching God* (2005)

Etta Moten (1901–2004), actress, singer, humanitarian. Initially a singer, Moten was married at age seventeen to Lieutenant Curtis Brooks and, within six years, became the mother of three daughters and divorced. Eventually with the support of her parents, Freeman and Ida Moten, she was able to return to school and graduate with a BFA from the University of Kansas at Lawrence. After graduation, she went to New York where her singing ability won her roles in Broadway productions *Fast and Furious* and *Zombie, Zombie* in 1931. When George Gershwin wrote the play *Porgy and Bess*, it had been said that he wrote the role of Bess with Moten in mind. Her being cast brought the play its first commercial success. Born in Weimar, Texas, Moten was the first African American to perform at the White House and decimate stereotypes in Hollywood. Her appearance in *Gold Diggers of 1933* set a precedent for African American actresses on screen to present in roles other than domestic. In the 1933 film *Flying Down to Rio*, she sang "The Carioca," which was nominated for an Academy Award. Moten married the founder of the Associated Negro Press, Claude Barnett, in 1934, and he adopted her daughters, Sue, Gladys, and Etta Vee. Moten and her husband were committed activists with a focus on Africa. They traveled there frequently as United States representatives and privately. Their African art collection is renowned. After her husband's death in 1967, Moten continued to lecture and travel into her nineties. Upon her death at age 102, her daughter Sue told *Jet* magazine her mother "had a full one hundred years and did everything." She quoted Moten as saying, "Life does not owe me one thing." Actor and singer Harry Belafonte said, "She gave Black people an opportunity to look at themselves on a big screen as something beautiful, when all that was there before spoke to our degradation. In her we found another dimension to being Black in our time."

Awards: Black Filmmakers Hall of Fame Award (1979)

Movies (singer and actress): *A Day at the Races* (1937), *Flying Down to Rio* (1933), *Gold Diggers of 1933* (1933)

Movie soundtracks (singing voice): *Professional Sweetheart* (1933), *Ladies They Talk About* (1933)

Maidie Norman (1912–1998), actress, educator. Norman was one of the first actors to teach the craft on university and college campuses based on a rich background in the field of acting. She earned two degrees, a BA in Literature from Bennett College in North Carolina and an MA in Theater Arts from Columbia University in New York. Most noted for her 1962 role as Elvira in *What Ever Happened to Baby Jane?* She managed to land the lead role in the 1951 crossover studio-driven film *The Well*, which was rare for an African American actress at the time. Restricted to primarily domestic roles at the start of her career, she insisted on using correct pronunciation and shunned what she considered "old slavery time talk." Born to parents Louis and Lila Gamble, Norman, when not acting, continuously lectured and taught drama, African American theater history and African American literature and theater. She was an artist in residence at Stanford University and taught at University of California, Los Angeles and the University of Texas at Tyler. UCLA established the Maidie Norman Research Award for best student essay on African American film or theater. She was married to McHenry Norman until his death. They had one son, McHenry Norman III. She was later married to Weldon D. Canada until her death.

Awards: Honorary doctorate from alma mater, Bennett College (1992), California Educational Theatre Association Professional Artist Award (1985), Black Filmmakers Hall of Fame Award (1977)

Movies: *Movie Movie* (1978), *Airport '77* (1977), *A Star Is Born* (1976), *Maurie* (1973), The Exorcist (voice, uncredited,1973), *The Final Comedown* (1972), *What Ever Happened to Baby Jane?* (1962), *Written on the Wind* (1956), *Susan Slept Here* (1954), *Torch Song* (1953), *Bright Road* (1953), *The Well* (1951), *The Peanut Man* (1947)

Television movies: *Side by Side* (1988), *Secrets of a Mother and Daughter* (1983), *Thornwell* (1981), *The Sty of the Blind Pig* (1974), *Say Goodbye, Maggie Cole* (1972), *Another Part of the Forest* (1972)

Television: *Roots: The Next Generations* (1979), *Alfred Hitchcock Presents*, "Mrs. Bixby and the Colonel's Coat" (1960)

Paul Robeson (1898–1976), actor, concert singer, lawyer, athlete, social activist.

Vexed by vicious racism after initially passing the bar and joining a New York law firm, Robeson left the legal profession vowing to never again get involved with a career that left no room for growth. He returned to the profession that financially helped get him through college and law school, acting on stage and singing. Robeson went on to captivate and set precedence with his artistry worldwide. On the silver screen, the crossover from silent film to talkies was effortless for his eloquent speaking voice and rich, baritone singing. Robeson was born in Princeton, New Jersey, to William and Maria Robeson. His father escaped the plantation, graduated from Lincoln University, and became a minister. Robeson was the youngest of three brothers, William, Reeve, Ben, and a sister, Marian. He graduated with an AB from Rutgers University and earned his law degree from Columbia University. Of his many achievements at Rutgers, he became football All American and was class valedictorian. While at Columbia, he played professional football for the Akron Pros in 1921 and Milwaukee Badgers in 1922. One of the most notable figures of the Harlem renaissance, Robeson was successful on stage and film in the United States and England. Pioneer African American filmmaker Oscar Michaux chose Robeson as the lead in *Body and Soul* in 1925, a silent film that was Robeson's debut. He received high praise when his voice was first heard in the film *The Emperor Jones* in 1933. The majority of Robeson's films are musicals or ones where he sings. By 1942, he grew frustrated with the types of roles film offered and returned exclusively to the stage where he had major success in productions that include *Othello*, *Show Boat*, and *Porgy and Bess*. Robeson married Eslanda Cardoza Goode, and they had a son, Paul Jr.

Awards (film-related): Star on the Walk of Fame (1978), Image Award (1972)

Movies: *Tales of Manhattan* (1942), *Native Land* (1942), *The Proud Valley* (1940), *Jericho* (1937), *King Solomon's Mines* (1937), *Big Fella* (1937), *Song of Freedom* (1936), *Show Boat* (1936), *Sanders of the River* (1935), *The Emperor Jones* (1933), *Borderline* (1930), *Camille* (short) (1926), *Body and Soul* (1925)

Leigh Whipper (1876–1975), actor. A cinematic pioneer who paved the way for African Americans with film aspirations, Whipper was the first African American member of Actor's Equity Association in 1913 and was a founding member of the Negro Actors Guild of America in 1937. Whipper graduated with a law degree (LLB) from Howard University and was admitted to the state bar of South Carolina. He left law to pursue a career in acting, first appearing on the Broadway stage with the Georgia Minstrels, progressing quickly to the classic productions of *Porgy* and *Of Mice and Men*. Oscar Micheaux cast Whipper in his first film roles, which at the time were silent films, *Within Our Gates* in 1920 and *The Symbol of the Unconquered* that same year. As a result of limitations in film for

African Americans and Whipper being extremely selective about the type of roles he played, there would be a twenty-nine-year gap in his acting career. He agreed to a role in the 1939 film version of, *Of Mice and Men*. When he was not acting in film, he produced, directed, and returned to the stage. Whipper was born in Charleston, South Carolina, to free parents. His father, William Whipper, was an entrepreneur and abolitionist. His mother, Francis Rollin Whipper, was a writer and political activist. One of five siblings, three survived past infancy. Whipper retired from film and stage at the age of ninety-five.

Movies (producer): *Come Back* (1922)

Movies (director and producer): *A Regeneration of Souls* (1921), *Renaissance Newsreel* (1921)

Movies (actor): *The Young Don't Cry* (1957), *The Shrike* (1955), *Lost Boundaries* (1949), *Untamed Fury* (1947), *Undercurrent* (1946), *The Hidden Eye* (1945), *Strange Confession* (1944), *The Oxbow Incident* (1943), *White Cargo* (1942), *Heart of the Golden West* (1942), *The Vanishing Virginian* (1942), *Bahama Passage* (1941), *Road to Zanzibar* (1941), *Virginia* (1941), *Robin Hood of the Pecos* (1941), *Of Mice and Men* (1939), *The Symbol of the Unconquered* (1920), *Within Our Gates* (1920)

INTERNATIONAL TALENT ESTABLISHED IN THE UNITED STATES AND INDIGENOUS AFRICAN CINEMA (FOLK LIFE)

Adewale Akinnuoye-Agbaje (1967), actor, producer. Akinnuoye-Agbaje was a successful model in Paris and Milan before he decided to reside in Los Angeles and pursue a career in acting in 1994. Prior to modeling, he earned a law degree from King's College in London and a Master's in Law from the University of London. Though his impeccable skills were utilized in the films *Bourne Identity* in 2002 and *Get Rich or Die Tryin'* in 2005, television was the medium by which he rose in popularity. The catalyst was the role of Simon Adebisi on the television series *Oz* from 1997 to 2000 and as Mr. Eko on *Lost* in 2005 to 2006. Akinnuoye-Agbaje is of Nigerian lineage and was born in London, England.

Award: Screen Actors Guild (2006)

Movie (producer, actor): *Elizabeth Blue* (2017)

Movies (actor): *Suicide Squad* (2016), *Bilal: A New Breed of Hero* (2015), *Concussion* (2015), *Trumbo* (2015), *Annie* (2014), *Pompeii* (2014), *Thor: The Dark World* (2013), *The Inevitable Defeat of Mister & Pete* (2013), *Best Laid Plans* (2012), *G.I. Joe: The Rise of the Cobra* (2009), *Get Rich or Die Tryin'* (2005), *The Bourne Identity* (2002)

Television movie (actor): *Enslavement: The True Story of Fanny Kemble* (2000)

Television (actor): *Major Lazer* (2015), *American Odyssey* (2015), *Hunted* (2012), *Lost* (2005–06), *Oz* (1997–2000)

Safi Faye (1943), ethnologist, director, actress, writer. Faye is recognized as the first African woman from south of the Sahara to make a feature film. Born in Fad'Jal, Senegal, as an ethnologist (scientific study that compares human culture), her films capture daily life from a Senegalese perspective. She first obtained her teacher's certificate from Rufisque Normal School. She then graduated with a diploma in ethnology from the University of Paris followed by a PhD. She also attended the Louis Lumiere Film School. Faye gained international notice in 1975 with the film *KadduBeykat* (*Peasant Letter*). *KadduBeykat* documents the lives of Faye's own ethnic group, the Serer—their origins, family structure, and everyday way of life. *La Passante* (*The Passerby*), a short film made in 1972 was set to music, no dialogue and based on Faye's experience as a foreign woman in Paris.

Awards: Lucas–International Festival of Films for Children and Young People Award (1997), Berlin International Film Festival Award (1979, 1976)

Movie (writer and director): *Mossane* (1997)

Movie documentary (director): *Selbe: One Among Many* (short) (1983), *Fad'jal* (1979)

Movies (director): *KadduBeykat* (1976), *La Passante* (1972)

Movies (actress): *La Passante* (1972), *Little by Little* (1970)

Sanaa Hamri (1975), director. Hamri is one of a handful of renowned female directors in Hollywood. She evolved into film directing as a result of being a video music director. Born in Tangier, Morocco, Hamri is the daughter of Moroccan painter and author Mohammed Hamri. She graduated from Sarah Lawrence College on a scholarship. Hamri has directed or edited over fifty music videos for artists that range from Prince, Mariah Carey, and Jay-Z to Nicki Minaj. Hamri's initial foray onto the big screen was in 2006 with *Something New* starring Sanaa Lathan. Within two years, commercial success followed with *The Sisterhood of the Traveling Pants 2* in 2008 and *Just Right* in 2010. She has received numerous accolades for directing the television mega hit *Empire*. Hamri is also executive producer for *Empire*.

Movie director: *Just Right* (2010), *The Sisterhood of the Traveling Pants 2* (2008), *Something New* (2006)

Television movie (editor): *Mariah Carey: Around the World* (1998)

Television movies (director): *Studio City* (2015), *Lovestruck: The Musical* (2013), *Elixir* (2012), *Acceptance* (2009)

Television (producer) *Empire* (2015-2018)

Television (director): *Empire* (2015-2017), *Shameless* (2011–15), *Elementary* (2013–14), *Nashville* (2013), *Bounce* (2013), *90210* (2012), *Life Unexpected* (2010), *Men in Trees* (2007), *Desperate Housewives* (2007), *Prince: The Art of Musicology* (TV special) (2004)

David Harewood (1965), actor. Recognized for innumerable stage, screen, and television casting in the United Kingdom before making an impressive debut in the United States, Harewood attracts highly distinguished roles. He has taken on the role of Martin Luther King in London's Theatre 503 stage production of *The Mountaintop*. In the 2010 television movie *Mrs. Mandela*, he portrayed Nelson Mandela. He became a familiar face in the United States in the role of David Estes on the television series *Homeland*. Harewood received critical acclaim as Captain Poison in *Blood Diamond* in 2006. He has experienced substantial commercial success on the television series *Supergirl*. A graduate of the Royal Academy of Dramatic Art, he was born in Birmingham, England.

Award: Nashville Film Festival (2016)

Movies: *Tulip Fever* (2017), *The Brothers Grimsby* (2016), *Free in Deed* (2015), *MI-5* (2015), *SuperBob* (2014), *Third Person* (2013), *The Man Inside* 012), *Victim* (2011), *The Hot Potato* (2011), *Blood Diamond* (2006), *Separate Lies* (2005), *The Merchant of Venice* (2004), *I Wonder Whose Kissing You Now* (1998), *Mad Dogs and Englishmen* (1995), *The Hawk* (1993)

Television movies: *The Money* (2014), *Treasure Island* (2012), *Mrs. Mandela* (2010), *Gunrush* (2009)

Television: *Supergirl* (2015-18), *Madiba* (2017), *Selfie* (2014) *Homeland* (2011–12), *Robin Hood* (2009), *The Palace* (2008)

Marianne Jean-Baptiste (1967), actress, writer, producer. The London, England–born performer reserves the distinction of being the first African English actress to ever be nominated for an Academy Award. In 1996, imminent success followed her performance in *Secrets and Lies* for which she was also a Golden Globe nominee. Upon graduation from the Royal Academy of Dramatic Art, she appeared on stage at London's Royal National Theatre and Theatre Royal Stratford East. She wrote a one-woman play, *Ave Africa*. Jean-Baptiste is best known in the United

States as FBI Agent Vivian Johnson in the television series *Without a Trace*. She is also a recognized singer and composer.

Award: La Femme International Film Festival (2009)

Movie (producer and actress): *Jam* (2006)

Movies (actress): *Peter Rabbit* (2018), *Edge of Tomorrow* (2014), *Robo Cop* (2014), *Won't Back Down* (2012), *Violet & Daisy* (2011), *Takers* (2010), *Don't Explain* (2002), *Spy Game* (2001), *Women in Film* (2001), *The Cell* (2000), *28 Days* (2000), *The 24 Hour Woman* (1999), *A Murder of Crows* (1998), *Mr. Jealousy* (1997), *Secrets & Lies* (1996)

Television movies (actress): *Secrets in the Walls* (2010), *Loving You* (2003), *Men Only* (2001), *The Murder of Stephen Lawrence* (1999), *The Wedding* (1998)

Television (writer): *Without a Trace* (2009)

Television (actress): *Training Day* (2017), *Blindspot* (2015-2017), *Broadchurch* (2015), *Private Practice* (2012), *Harry's Law* (2011–2012), *Without a Trace* (2002–09)

Gaston Kaboré (1951), director, writer, producer. Kaboré brought global film prominence to the African country of Burkina Faso. The 1983 film *Wend Kuuni* is a preindustrial fabled tale of a mute child's journey in an unfamiliar village, and *Buud Yam*, released in 1997, is a continuation of his perils as a young adult. Both films are Kaboré's most recognized projects and international award winners. The 1988 film *Zan Boko* explores the effect of urban transition on agricultural life and village tradition. Kaboré began his academic career in Africa as a history major at Centre d'Etudes d'Histoired' Ouagadougou and received his master's in the subject at the Sorbonne in Paris. Convinced that images are important as a means of communication and education, Kaboré decided to study cinematography, while in Paris, at the Ecole Supérieured 'Études Cinématographiques (ESEC) film school. Recognized as the godfather of African cinema, Kaboré was born in Bobo-Dioulasso in Upper Volta. He founded a film school called Imagine in Ouagadougou, the capital of Burkina, with a keen focus on the study of anthropology and sociology.

Awards: Ouagadougou Panafrican Film and Television Festival Award (1997), Torino International Festival of Young Cinema Award (1988), Fribourg International Film Festival Award (1986), Cesar Award,

France (1985)
Movie (director and writer): *Buud Yam* (1997), *Rabi* (1992), *Zan Boko* (also producer, 1998)
Movies (director): *Lumière and Company* (documentary, 1995), *Wend Kuuni* (1983)
Movie (writer and producer): *The Cora Player* (short, 2000)
Television (producer): *Les hommes de l'ombre* (2012), *La nuit Africaine* (TV movie, 1990)

Gugu Mbatha-Raw (1983), actress. Triumphant representation in a new era of bustling talent is acclaim achieved by Mbatha-Raw. Born in Oxford, England, the multiple award winner is a graduate of the Royal Academy of Dramatic Art. With roots in theater Mbatha-Raw has carried leads in stage productions such as *Romeo and Juliet*, for which she was nominated for the Manchester Evening News Theatre Award in 2005. She also appeared on stage as Cleopatra in *Antony and Cleopatra* and as Ophelia in *Hamlet* opposite Judd Law in 2009. After a solid television series track record, her role as Dido Elizabeth Belle in the 2013 hit movie *Belle* brought box office draw recognition and four cinema award wins. The 2014 role of Noni in *Beyond the Lights* was a megawatt career boost.
Awards: Black Reel Award (2015), African American Film Critics Association (2014), Alliance of Women Film Journalist (2014), British Independent Film Award (2014), Capri, Hollywood (2014), Chicago International Film Festival (2014)
Movies: *Irreplaceable You* (2018), *Beauty and the Beast* (2017), *Miss Sloane* (2016), *The Free State of Jones* (2016), *Concussion* (2015), *Jupiter Ascending* (2015), *Beyond the Lights* (2014), Belle (2014), *Larry Crowne* (2011), *Act of God* (2009)
Television movies: *Fallout* (2008), *Legless* (2005)
Television: *Touch* (2012), *Undercovers* (2010–12), *Bonekickers* (2008), *Doctor Who* (2007), *MI-5* (2006), *Vital Signs* (2006)

Steve McQueen III (1969), director, writer, still photography artist. Initially, McQueen's primary focus was his highly recognized still art photography. His first feature film, *Hunger*, in 2008 won numerous awards including the First Time Director Award at Cannes, a first for Britain.

Shame, his second feature in 2011, was also heralded, garnering awards. Born in London, England, McQueen received his BA in Fine Arts from Goldsmiths College. Prior to Goldsmiths, he studied at Chelsea College of Art and Design. He has written and directed several short films before and in between features. In 2013, McQueen won the Breakthrough Director Award at the Hollywood Film Festival for *12 Years a Slave*. The film continued to dominate the awards season of 2014 by winning the Academy Award for Best Motion Picture.

Awards (select): CinEuphoria Award (2015), AFI Award (2014), Black Reel Award (2014), Directors Guild of America Award (2014), Empire Award (2014), Image Award (2014), Independent Spirit Award (2014), PGA Award (2014), Hollywood Film Festival Award (2013), Toronto International Film Festival Award (2013, 2008), Black Reel Award (2012), Venice Film Festival Award (2011, 2008), Toronto Film Critics Association Award (2010), Cinemanila International Film Festival Award (2009), Evening Standard British Film Award (2009), London Critics Circle Film Award (2009), New York Film Critics Circle Award (2009), Writers' Guild of Great Britain (2009), Douglas Hickox Award (2008), Cannes Film Festival Award (2008), Chicago International Film Festival Award (2008), Dinard British Film Festival Award (2008), European Film Award (2008), Geneva Cinéma Tout Ecran (2008), Ghent International Film Festival Award (2008), Jerusalem Film Festival Award (2008), Ljubljana International Film Festival Award (2008), Los Angeles Film Critics Association Award (2008), Stockholm Film Festival Award (2008), Sydney Film Festival Award (2008), Tallinn Black Nights Film Festival Award (2008)

Movies (director and writer): *Shame* (2011), *Hunger* (2008)
Movie (director and producer): *12 Years a Slave* (2013)

Fanta Régina Nacro (1962), director, writer, producer. Nacro is an African filmmaker known for bringing humor to serious subject matters. In the film *Living Positively* in 2003, the subject is AIDS. Nacro, a highly praised, multiple award winner, was born in Burkino Faso, Africa. Nacro earned her first degree in audiovisual science and techniques from a regional film school, Institut d' Education Cinématographique de Ouagadougou (INACEC), in Burkino Faso. Many of Nacro's sixteen films range in running time from five to thirty-five minutes to her first full-length feature, *The Night of the Truth*, made in 2004 running one hundred minutes. According to Nacro, time is never a consideration when she has a story to tell. If the story can be told in five minutes or fifteen minutes, so be it.

Awards: Fribourg International Film Festival Award (2005, 1993), San Sebastian International Film Festival Award (2004), Ouagadougou Panafrican Film and Television Festival Award (2003, 2001, 1999), Rotterdam International Film Festival Award (2003), Clermont-Ferrand International Short Film Festival Award (2002), Tampere International Short Film Festival Award (2002), Amiens International Film Festival Award (2001), Bermuda International Film Festival Award (2001), Cannes Film Festival Award (2001), Marrakech International Film Festival Award (2001), San Francisco International Film Festival Award (1997)

Movie (director, producer, and writer): *The Night of the Truth* (2004)

Movie (director and writer): *Don't Make Trouble!* (2001), *Puk Nini* (1996)

Movie (director): *Vivre positivement* (2003), *Mama Africa* (2002), *Scenarios from the Sahel* (2001), *Le truc de Konaté* (2001), *A Close-Up of Bintou* (2001), *Un certainmatin* (1991)

Thandie Newton (1972), actress. A major talent from across the pond, Newton finished college when her acting career was shifting into high gear. Born in London, England, she earned a BA in Anthropology from Cambridge University. Her career climb was steady in the nineties and escalated with *Mission Impossible II* in 2000. No stranger to television, she appeared in reoccurring roles on *ER* from 2003 to 2009 and *Rogue* from 2013 to 2014. In 2018 Newton took home a Primetime Emmy for her role as Maeve Millay in the HBO series, *Westworld*.

Awards: Primetime Emmy Award (2018), Black Reel Award (2017), Gold Derby Award (2017), Online Film & Television Association (2017), BAFTA Award (2006), Broadcast Film Critics Association Award (2006), Empire Award (2006), London Critics Circle Film Award (2006), Screen Actors Guild Award (2006), Hollywood Film Award (2005)

Movies: *Solo: A Star Wars Story* (2018), *Gringo* (2018), *Half of a Yellow Sun* (2013), *Good Deeds* (2012), *For Colored Girls* (2010),

2012 (2009), *W.* (2008), *RocknRolla* (2008), *Norbit* (2007), *The Pursuit of Happyness* (2006), *Crash* (2004), *The Chronicles of Riddick* (2004), *Mission Impossible II* (2000), *Beloved* (1998), *Gridlock'd* (1997), *Jefferson in Paris* (1995), *Interview with a Vampire: The Vampire Chronicles* (1994)

Television movies: *In Your Dreams* (1996)

Television: *Westworld* (2016-18), *Line of Duty* (2017), *The Slap* (2015), *Rogue* (2013–15), *ER* (2003–09)

Lupita Nyong'o (1983), actress, director, producer, editor. A Kenyan of the Luo tribe born in Mexico City, Mexico, to a highly accomplished family did not deter Nyong'o from putting in the work to achieve cinematic success. The "it" actress of 2014 swept through the year's award season for her performance in *12 Years a Slave*. She attended college in the United States, receiving a degree in film and theater studies at Hampshire College. Nyong'o was awarded her master's degree from the Yale School of Drama just about the time she was cast in the role of Patsy for *12 Years a Slave*. She appeared in many stage productions while at Yale and received the Herschel Williams Prize for acting students with exceptional talent. In 2009, she produced, directed, and edited the highly praised documentary *In My Genes* based on what it's like to be albino in African society. Nyong'o has achieved phenomenal success with the reoccurring role of Maz Kanata in the *Star Wars* franchise. The Maz Kanata character appears in every film medium; movie, animated television movie and television series.

Awards: CinEuphoria Award (2015), Academy Award (2014) BET Award (2014), Black Reel Award (2014), Empire Award (2014), Image Award (2014), Independent Spirit Award (2014), London Critics Circle Film Award (2014), Screen Actors Guild Award (2014), Hollywood Film Festival Award (2013)

Movies (actress): *Star Wars: Episode IX* (2019), *Black Panther* (2018), *Star Wars: The Last Jedi* (2017), *Queen of Katwe* (2016), *The Jungle Book* (2016), *Star Wars: The Force Awakens* (2015), *Non-Stop* (2014), *12 Years a Slave* (2014)

Documentary movie (producer, director, and editor): *In My Genes* (2009)

Television movies (actress): *Star Wars Forces of Destiny: Volume 1,2,3,4* (2017-28)
Television miniseries (actress): *Shuga* (2009–2012)
Television (actress): *Star Wars Forces of Destiny* (2017-18)

Idrissa Ouedraogo (1954-2018), director, writer, producer. Ouedraogo has been outspoken on insisting that films made by Africans not be pigeonholed as "African films." He makes it clear that all films made in Africa are not folkloric or interchangeable. "We are struggling as African filmmakers to show that we are no more different to you than you are to us: the only difference is economical." Two of Ouedraogo's best-known films are *Tilaï* (*The Law*) made in 1990 and *Yaaba* (*Grandmother*) made in 1989. *Tilaï* is a family drama that takes a different spin when a father decides to exercise his tribal right and make his son's love interest his second wife. *Yaaba* explores the friendship of a boy and an old woman who is thought a witch and treated as a village outcast. *Yaaba* was the winner of the International Critics Prize at the Cannes Film Festival. Ouedraogo was born in Banfora, Upper Volta. He holds a BA in General Studies from the African Institute of Cinematographic Studies of Ouagadougou and a DEA (diploma of advanced studies), cinema option, from the University of Paris I Sorbonne. He is also a graduate of Institut des hautes études cinématographiques (IDHEC) of Paris. Ouedraogo began his career making short films financed by the Burkina Faso government. He wrote, directed, and produced French language television series and movies that are African themed.

Awards: Venice Film Festival (2002), Bermuda International Film Festival (1998), OCIC Award (1994), Berlin International Film Festival (1993), Ouagadougou Panafrican Film and Television Festival Award (1991), Cannes Film Festival Award (1990,1989), Tokyo International Film Festival Award (1989), Taormina International Film Festival Award (1987)

Movie (producer): *Thom* (2016)
Movies (producer, director, writer): *Tenga* (2018), *Samba Traoré* (1992), *The Law* (1990), *Yaaba* (1989)
Movies (director, writer): *Kato* (2006), *Anger of the Gods* (2003), *Kini and Adams* (1997)
Movie (segment director): *Stories on Human Rights* (2008)

David Oyelowo (1976), actor, producer. A highly regarded stage actor, Oyelowo was the first actor of African descent to play an English king in a major Shakespearean production. His taking on the role of King Henry VI in 2000 with the Royal Shakespeare Company was acclaimed and criticized. Oyelowo won the Ian Charleston Award for his performance. He was born in Oxford, England, to Nigerian parents and graduated from the London Academy of Music and Dramatic Art where he finished with honors. After his television debut in the television series *MI-5* in 2002–05, his first American movie was *The Last King of Scotland* in 2006. Oyelowo reprised the role of Joseph Asagai in the televised version of the classic *A Raisin in the Sun* in 2008. The year 2012 proved to be a busy year with A-list screenings of *Lincoln*, *Middle of Nowhere*, and *Red Tails* to name a few.

Awards: Black Reel Award (2016, 2015), Central Ohio Film Critics Association (2015), Image Award (2015, 2014), Santa Barbara Film Festival (2015), African American Film Critics Association (AAFCA) (2014), Hollywood Film Festival (2013), RiverRun International Film Festival Award (2012), Royal Television Society, UK Award (2010), Satellite Award (2007)

Movies (producer, actor): *A United Kingdom* (2016), *Nina* (2016), *Captive* (2015), *Five Nights in Maine* (2015

Movies (actor): *Gringo* (2018), *A Wrinkle in Time* (2018), *The Cloverfield Paradox* (2018), *Selma* (2014), *A Most Violent Year* (2014), *Interstellar* (2014), *Lee Daniels' The Butler* (2013), *Complicit* (2013), *Jack Reacher* (2012), *Lincoln* (2012), *The Paperboy* (2012), *The Middle of Nowhere* (2012), *Red Tails* (2012), *96 Minutes* (2011), *The Help* (2011), *Rise of the Planet of the Apes* (2011), *Rage* (2009), *Who Do You Love* (2008), *The Last King of Scotland* (2006)

Television movie (actor): *A Raisin in the Sun* (2008)

Television (producer, actor): *Les Miserables* (2018), *Nightingale* (2014)

Television (actor): *The Lion Guard* (2017-18) *Star Wars Rebels* (2014-18), *Five Days* (2007), *MI-5* (2002–04)

Euzhan Palcy (1958), director, writer, producer. Not swayed by the glamour of Hollywood, Palcy entered the scene as a fierce independent filmmaker. First time out with *Sugar Cane Alley* in 1983, the film won numerous international film awards including the Cesar Award, the French equivalent of the Academy Award. Six years later, her full-length offering *A Dry White Season* was released. In 1998, Palcy directed *Ruby Ridges* for television, a true story based on an African American girl who integrates a school in the 1960s. Born in Martinique, France, she earned her Master's in French literature and Theater from the Sorbonne and a DEA (diplômed 'études appliquées, also a master's) in cinematography from the Louis-Lumière School of Cinema.

Awards: Christopher Award (1999), Brussels International Festival of Fantasy Film Award (1993), Cesar Award (1984), Venice Film Festival (1983)

Movies (director, writer, producer): *Aimé Césaire: A Voice for History* (documentary) (1993), *Siméon* (1993)

Movies (director and writer): *A Dry White Season* (screenplay) (1989), *Sugar Cane Alley* (1983)

Movies (writer): *Dionysos* (1986)

Television movies (director and writer): *Les mariées de l'isle Bourbon* (2007), *Parcours de dissidents* (documentary, 2006), *The Messenger* (also producer, 1975)

Television movies (director and producer): *Ruby Ridges* (1998)

Television movies (director): *The Killing Yard* (2001)

CCH Pounder (1952), actress, producer. Pounder was introduced in 1987 as Brenda in the movie *Bagdad Cafe*. Soon after, she was cast in a reoccurring role in the television series *Women in Prison*. Born in Georgetown, British Guiana, she graduated with a BFA from Ithaca College in Ithaca, New York. As detective-promoted to captain Claudette Wyms on the cable television series *The Shield*, which aired from 2002 to 2008, Pounder's popularity grew. From 2009 to 2013, the nonstop working actress rounds out the cast as Mrs. Irene Frederic in the science-fiction thriller *Warehouse 13*. Her career momentum continues in the role of Loretta Wade in the television series *NCIS: New Orleans*. Pounder is a founder of Artists for a New South Africa, which brings awareness and education regarding HIV and AIDS.

Awards: Behind the Voice Actors Award (2015), Black Reel Award

(2005), Satellite Award (2004, 2003)

Movie (producer): *Ayiti Mon Amour* (2016)

Movies (actress): *The Mortal Instruments: City of Bones* (2013), *Home Again* (2012), *Avatar* (2009), *Orphan* (2009), *Rain* (2008), *Baby of the Family* (2002), *End of Days* (1999), *Funny Valentines* (1999), *Race* (1998), *Face/Off* (1997), *Tales from the Crypt: Demon Knight* (1995), *Benny & Joon* (1993), *Postcards from the Edge* (1990), *Bagdad Cafe* (1987), *Go Tell It on the Mountain* (1984), *Union City* (1980), *All That Jazz* (1979)

Television movies (actress): *Redemption: The Stan Tookie Williams Story* (2004), *Boycott* (2001), *Disappearing Acts* (2000), *Cora Unashamed* (2000), *Final Justice* (1998), *House of Frankenstein* (1997), *If These Walls Could Talk* (1996), *Zooman* (1995), *Lifepod* (1993), *For Their Own Good* (1993), *The Ernest Green Story* (1993), *Murder in Mississippi* (1990), *No Place Like Home* (1989), *On the Edge* (1987), *As Summers Die* (1986), *Resting Place* (1986)

Television (actress): *NCIS: New Orleans* (2014–18); *Sons of Anarchy* (2013–14), *Warehouse 13* (2009–14), *Law & Order: Special Victims Unit* (2001–10), *Brothers* (2009), *The Shield* (2002–08), *Rocket Power* (1999–2000), *Millennium* (1996–98), *ER* (1994–97), *L.A. Law* (1986–92), *Women in Prison* (1987–88)

Madge Sinclair (1938–1995), actress. Stepping out on faith at age thirty, Sinclair left her teaching job in Jamaica to pursue an acting career in New York. Born in Kingston, Jamaica, she was educated at the Shortwood College for Women. With a reputation for being very ambitious and quick to catch on, she performed with the New York Shakespearean Theatre and Joseph Papp's Public Theater. Sinclair's first movie was a starring role as school principal Mrs. Scott in *Conrack* in 1974. She was well known for her role as Bell Reynolds, Kunta Kinte's wife, in the 1977 television miniseries *Roots*. She also stood out as Queen Aoleon in *Coming to America* in 1988. Sinclair was also cast in several long-running television series including *Trapper John, M.D.* (1980–86). In 1991, she won a Primetime Emmy Award for Outstanding Actress in a Drama Series for *Gabriel's Fire*.

Award: Primetime Emmy Award (1991)

Movies: *The Lion King* (voice, 1994), *Coming to America* (1988), *Convoy* (1978), *Leadbelly* (1976), *Cornbread, Earl and Me* (1975), *Conrack* (1974)

Television movies: *Victims* (1982), *Guyana Tragedy: The Story of Jim Jones* (1980), *I Know Why the Caged Bird Sings* (1979), *One in a Million: The Ron LeFlore Story* (1977), *Guess Who's Coming to Dinner* (1975)

Television: *Me and the Boys* (1994–94), *Pros and Cons* (1991–92), *Gabriel's Fire* (1990–91), *The Orchid House* (1991), *Ohara* (1987), *Trapper John, M.D.* (1980–86), Roots (TV miniseries) (1977)

PRODUCERS, DIRECTORS SCREENWRITERS AND CINEMATOGRAPHERS

Behind the camera: producer, director, screenwriter, and cinematographer—the staple of cinema.

Producer: a person or group who provides funding and coordinates various aspects of creating an entertainment performance

Director: directs and controls the artistic making of a film and is responsible for the interpretive aspect

Screenwriters: a person who writes scripts that is the dialogue and actions of a movie and other forms of graphic media including television, video games, and comics

Cinematographer: the profession of motion picture photography, an artist who captures images electronically or on film through the use of visual recording

Mara Brock Akil (1970), producer, writer. Kansas City–bred powerhouse, Brock Akil was born in Los Angeles and is a graduate of Northwestern University where she received a BA in Journalism. The longevity of her film and television presence as a producer, series creator, and writer is the firm foundation on which it is built. It's been a steady climb for Brock Akil in a range of film and television projects starting most notably with the television situation comedy *Moesha* in 1998 and *The Jamie Foxx Show* in 1999 to 2000. Just as comfortable writing as she is producing, Brock Akil combined those talents in the 2012 movie *Sparkle* and television hits *Girlfriends*, *Cougar Town*, and *The Game*. With television series *Love Is_* (2018) and Being *Mary Jane (2014-18)*, Brock Akil continues and will continue to break barriers. She is married to director, writer, and producer Salim Akil. Brock Akil is a member of Delta Sigma Theta Sorority and is known to mentor young aspiring writers.

Awards: Image Award (2016, 2012), Black Reel Award (2014), BET

Comedy Award (2005)
Movie (producer and writer): *Sparkle* (2012)
Television (producer and writer): *Love Is_* (2018), *Black Lightning* (2018), *Being Mary Jane* (2013–17), *The Game* (2006–15), *Cougar Town* (2009–10), *Girlfriends* (2000–07), *Moesha* (1996–98), *South Central* (1994)
Television (producer): *Diggy Simmons MOW* (2013), *The Jamie Foxx Show* (1999–2000), *Moesha* (1998–99)
Television (writer): *Being Mary Jane* (2014-18)

Salim Akil (1964), director, writer, producer. After high school graduation and being sidetracked by some harsh realities, Akil enrolled and graduated with a Bachelor's of Fine Arts from Columbia College in Hollywood, California. A native of Oakland, California, and raised in Richmond, California, Akil used his firsthand knowledge of gangs as inspiration for his first film collaboration *Drylongso* in 1998, which dealt with gang violence in Oakland. Excelling in any cinematic field he decided to focus on, Akil first garnered major attention in 2003 writing and directing episodes of television hits *Soul Food* and *Girlfriends*. He made his directing and producing theatrical screen debut in 2011 with *Jumping the Broom* and has followed up applying his talent to television megahits, such as The *Game* (2006-15), *Being Mary Jane and* Whitney Houston's last film, *Sparkle.*

Award: Image Award (two categories, 2012)
Movie (writer): *Drylongso* (1998)
Movies (producer and director): *Sparkle* (2012), *Jumping the Broom* (2011)
Television movie (producer and director): *Diggy Simmons MOW* (2013)
Television (producer, director, writer): *Black Lightning* (2018), *The Game* (2006–15), *Soul Food* (2000–04)
Television (producer and director): *Being Mary Jane* (2013–15)
Television (director): *Girlfriends* (2003–07)

Stephanie Allain (1959), producer, actress. Committed to seeing her vision through, Allain literally bet the house to start her production company, Homegrown Pictures, in 2002. With Homegrown she was able to guide *Hustle & Flow* to the screen by 2005, followed by *Something New* in 2006. In 2003, Allain produced *Biker Boyz* for DreamWorks SKG Productions. She was born in New Orleans, Louisiana, and graduated from the University of California, Santa Cruz with a BA in English and Creative Writing. As President of Jim Henson Pictures, she produced *Muppets from Space* and *The Adventures of Elmo in Grouchland* between 1996 and 2000, as well as other related brand films. Allain is the director of the Los Angeles Film Festival and sits on the board of directors of Film Independent.

Award: African American Film Critics Association (2014)

Movies (producer): *Burning Sands* (2017), Beyond *the Lights* (2014), *Blackbird* (2014), *Dear White People* (2014), *Peeples* (2013), *Hurricane Season* (2009), *Black Snake Moan* (2006), *Something New* (2006), *Hustle & Flow* 005), *Biker Boyz* (2003), *Rat* (2000), *The Adventures of Elmo in Grouchland* (1999), *Muppets from Space* (1999), *Buddy* (1997)

Movie (producer, actress): *French Dirty* (2015)

Television (producer): *Dear White People* (2017)

Reggie "Rock" Bythewood (1965), writer, director, producer. From rapper to actor, Bythewood finally answered his behind-the-camera calling. Born in New York City, he graduated from Marymount Manhattan College with a BFA in Theater. He put his writing and directing skills to work by cofounding a theater company, The Tribe, before relocating to Los Angeles to pursue a screenwriting career. Bythewood was accepted into Walt Disney's Writers Fellowship Program. The fellowship program opened an opportunity to write for the situation television comedy *A Different World* in 1992–93. He was able to translate what he observed at the Million Man March in 1995 into a screenplay for the movie *Get on the Bus* in 1996. Bythewood took a seat in the director's chair writing and directing *Biker Boyz* in 2003 and shared writing credits with Cheo Hodari Coker for Biggie Small's biography, *Notorious*, in 2009.

Awards: Black Reel Award (2015), Image Award (2015), Black Reel Award (two categories, director and screenplay, 2002)

Movie (producer, writer, director): *Dancing in September* (2000)

Movie (producer): *Beyond the Lights* (2014)

Movie (writer, director): *Biker Boyz* (2003)
Movies (writer): *Notorious* (2009), *Get on the Bus* (1996)
Television (producer, writer): *Shots Fired* (2017)
Television (producer, writer, director): *Gun Hill* (2011)
Television documentary (director): *Daddy's Girl* (2007)
Television (producer, writer): *New York Undercover* (1994–97)
Television (writer): *A Different World* (1992–93)

Debra Martin Chase (1956), producer. With Chase as executive producer of three *The Cheetah Girls* installments for the Disney network, the second installment was most viewed in Disney movie history at the time. The soundtrack for *The Cheetah Girls: One World* went double platinum. Chase is the first African American woman to have a long-standing production deal with a major studio, the Walt Disney Company. Prior to television, her film-producing projects in 1996 were *Courage Under Fire* and *The Preacher's Wife*. Born in Great Lakes, Illinois, Chase earned a BA from Mount Holyoke College and a law degree from Harvard University. After working with a few major corporate law firms and political campaigns, Chase chose to focus on a career in the film industry. Chase is committed to promoting positive imagery and mentoring up and coming talent. In 2003, *Essence* magazine recognized Chase as one of fifty African American women shaping the world. *Ebony* magazine honored her in 2007 with the Television and Film Award for Outstanding Women in Marketing and Communications.

Award: African American Film Critics Association (AAFCA) (2014)
Movies: *Grace Stirs Up Success* (2015), *Sparkle* (2012), *McKenna Shoots for the Stars* (2012), *Just Wright* (2010), *The Sisterhood of the Traveling Pants* (2005), *The Princess Diaries* (2001), *The Preacher's Wife* (1996), *Courage Under Fire* (1996), *Hank Aaron: Chasing the Dream* (documentary, 1995)
Television movies: *Aaliyah, The Princess of R&B* (2014), *Saige Paints the Sky* (2013), *Lovestruck: The Musical* (2013), *Lemonade Mouth* (2011), *The Cheetah Girls: One World* (2008), *The Cheetah Girls 2* (2006), *The Cheetah Girls* (2003, 2004)
Television: *Zoe Ever After* (2016), *1-800-Missing* (2003–06)

Ryan Coogler (1986), director, writer, producer. Richmond, California native, Coogler at one time was working a film project while simultaneously counseling at San Francisco Juvenile Hall. University of Southern California School of Cinematic Arts was where he received his Master of Fine Arts and where many doors of opportunity opened for him. In 2013 His notable film introduction, *Fruitvale Station* is based on factual police shooting of a young African American male at a commuter train station in Oakland, California. Forest Whitaker was the executive producer of the Sundance Film Festival Award winner. Coogler powered on as the writer, director of the block buster hit *Black Panther* movie in 2018.

Awards: Academy of Science Fiction, Fantasy & Horror Films, USA (2018), CinemaCon, USA (2018), *Black Reel Award* (2016), Image Award (2016), Independent Spirit Award (2014), PGA Award (2014), Cannes Film Festival (2013), Deauville Film Festival (2013), Humanitas Prize (2013), Nantucket Film Festival (2013), Sundance Film Festival 2013)

Movies (writer, director): *Black Panther* (2018), *Fruitvale Station* (2013)
Movie (producer, writer): *Creed II* (2018)
Movie (writer): *Creed* (2015)
Movie (producer): *The Castle Tale* (short) (2012)
Movie (director): *Fig* (short) (2009)

Rusty Cundieff (1960), director, writer, actor. Between 1993 and 1997, Cundieff was very involved in the satire-comedy genre of filmmaking. His first major break came as cowriter with Reginald Hudlin for *House Party 2* in 1991. Cundieff's writing, directing, and acting in *Fear of a Black Hat*, *Tales from the Hood*, and *Sprung* solidified his future success in film. Born in Pittsburgh, Pennsylvania, Cundieff is a graduate of the University of Southern California. He has kept extremely busy as a television director. In 2016 he was nominated for an Image Award for his directing the television movie, *White Water*.

Movies (director, writer, actor): *Sprung* (1997), *Tales from the Hood* (1995), *Fear of a Black Hat* (1993)
Movie (writer): *House Party 2* (1991)
Movies (director): *Movie 43* (2013)

Movies (actor): *School Daze* (1988), *Hollywood Shuffle* (1987), *Welcome to the Fun Zone* (Television movie, 1984)

Television movie (director): *White Water* (2015), *The Devon Taylor Show* (2013)

Television (producer, director, writer): *Black Jesus* (2018)

Television (director): *Second Generation Wayans* (2013), *The Wanda Sykes Show* (2009–10), *Chocolate News* (2008), *Somebodies* (2008), *Chappelle's Show* (2003–06)

Julie Dash (1952), director, writer, and producer. With her 1992 film *Daughters of the Dust*, New York City native Dash is recognized as the first African American female filmmaker to have a full-length mainstream theatrical release in the United States. She studied at the American Film Institute and earned a Master's in Fine Art from University of California, Los Angeles Film School after receiving her BA in Film at the Leonard Davis Center for the Performing Arts at City College, New York. While at UCLA, Dash became part of a progressive movement of African and African American filmmakers called the LA Rebellion. She first received recognition with her 1982 film *Illusions*, a short that centers on African American actresses trying to make it in Hollywood in the 1940s. The National Film Registry declared *Daughters of the Dust* a national treasure in 2004. In 2017 Dash stepped into the role of director for the television series *Queen Sugar*.

Awards: American Film Institute, USA Award (1993), Black Filmmaker Foundation Jury Prize (1989), Black American Cinema Society Award (1985)

Movies (producer, director, and writer): *Daughters of the Dust* (1991), *Illusions* (short, 1982)

Movies (director): *Brothers of the Borderland* (short, 2004), *Funny Valentines* (1999), *Praise House* (1991), *Diary of an African Nun* (1997), *Four Women* (short, 1975), *Working Models of Success* (1973)

Movies (editor): *Illusions* (short, 1982), *Diary of an African Nun* (1977), *Four Women* (short, 1975)

Television (producer): *American Masters*: "Zora Neale Hurston: Jump at the Sun" (2008)

Television (writer): *SUBWAYStories: Tales from the Underground*

(TV movie segment, 1997), *Women: Stories of Passion* (1997)

Television movies (director): *The Rosa Parks Story* (2002), *Love Song* (2000), *Incognito* (1999)

Television (director): *Queen Sugar* (2017), *SUBWAYStories: Tales from the Underground* (1997), *Women: Stories of Passion* (1997)

Ernest Dickerson (1951), director, cinematographer, screenwriter. It was at New York University that the Newark, New Jersey born Dickerson met one of his greatest collaborators, Spike Lee. His BA is in architecture from Howard University, advancing to an MFA from Tisch School of the Arts at New York University. Dickerson developed a deep appreciation for cinema at an early age, and after filming medical procedures while a young adult and teaching filmmaking, he decided to pursue a career in theatrical cinema by first enrolling in film school. His exquisite cinematography skills in films such as *Malcolm X* in 1992 gave way to his writing and direction of *Juice*, also a 1992 release. Dickerson has been on a fast television directorial track since 1990 with the critically acclaimed *The Wire* (2003–08), *Dexter* (2008–13), and *Treme* (2010–2013). His work is a reflection of being true to himself with the ability to appeal to mainstream.

Awards: Online Film & Television Association (2014), Image Award (2012, 2009), Daytime Emmy Award (2003), Austin Gay & Lesbian International Film Festival Award (1999), LA Outfest Award (1999), Gotham Award (1991), New York Film Critics Circle Award (1989)

Movie (writer): *Juice* (1992)

Movies (director): *Double Play* (2017), *Never Die Alone* (2004), *Bones* (2001), *Ambushed* (1998), *Blind Faith* (1998), *Tales from the Crypt: Demon Knight* (1995), *Bulletproof* (1996), *Surviving the Game* (1994), *Juice* (1992)

Movies (cinematographer): *Malcolm X* (1992), *Jungle Fever* (1991), *Mo' Better Blues* (1990), *Do the Right Thing* (1989), *School Daze* (1988), *Eddie Murphy Raw* (1987), *She's Gotta Have It* (1986), *Krush Groove* (1985), *The Brother from Another Planet* (1984), *Joe's Bed-Stuy Barbershop: We Cut Heads* (1983)

Television movies (director): *For One Night* (2006), *Good Fences* (2003), *Big Shot: Confessions of a Campus Bookie* (2002), *Monday Night Mayhem* (2002), *Our America* (2002), *Strange Justice* (1999), *Future*

Sport (1998), *Great Performances* (1990)

Television (director): *Bosch* (2015-18), *The Walking Dead* (2010–14), *Treme* (2010–13), *Dexter* (2008–13), *Lincoln Heights* (2007–09), *Burn Notice* (2009), *The Wire* (2003–08), *Weeds* (2007), *ER* (2005–06), *Heroes* (2006), *Night Visions* (2001)

Television (cinematographer): *Law & Order* (1990–91), *Tales from the Darkside* (1984–86)

Tracey Edmonds (1967), producer, music executive, business mogul. Destined for greatness, Edmonds's track record is a testament to the fact that she will exceed in any endeavor she puts her mind to. She produced the award-winning movie *Soul Food* in 1997 while in transition as founder of Yab Yum Entertainment, a rhythm-and-blues record label distributed by Sony Corporation. Prior to Yab Yum, right out of college, Edmonds was a real-estate broker who founded a mortgage company and real-estate office in Newport Beach, California. Born in Los Angeles, California, she graduated from Stanford University at age twenty with a degree in psychobiology, a major she created. While COO and president of Our Stories Films, the movie *Jumping the Broom* was released in 2011. Edmonds also serves as CEO and president of her own production company, Edmonds Entertainment. Edmonds is on the board of governors for the Producers Guild of America. She is involved with numerous humanitarian organizations, domestic and worldwide. Her many awards include the Turner Broadcasting System's Tower of Power Award, *Ebony* magazine's Outstanding Women in Marketing & Communications Entrepreneur Award, and the multicultural Prism Award.

Award: Daytime Emmy Award (2016)

Movies (producer): *Jumping the Broom* (2011), *New in Town* (2009), *Who's Your Caddy?* (2007), *Good Luck Chuck* (2007), *Josie and the Pussycats* (2001), *Punks* (2000), *Light It Up* (1999), *Hav Plenty* (1997), *Soul Food* (1997)

Television movie (producer): *With This Ring* (2015)

Television (producer): *Deion's Family Playbook* (2014-15), *Walk This Way* (2013), *College Hill: South Beach* (2009), *College Hill Atlanta* (2008), *College Hill: Interns* (2007), *College Hill* (2004–07), *DMX: Soul of a Man* (2006), *Lil Kim: Countdown to Lockdown* (2006), *Soul Food* (2000)

Jamaa Fanaka (1942–2012), director, writer, producer. His name in Swahili means "together we will find success." The scholarly Fanaka graduated from University of California, Los Angeles Film School with a BA and MFA summa cum laude. He was introduced to film study at community college then decided to do a stint in the United States Air Force. Born in Jackson, Mississippi, he was a member of the Los Angeles rebellion film movement (LA Rebellion), crusading for African American filmmaking acceptance that stretched beyond negative stereotypes. Three of his seven films, *Welcome Home Brother, Charles* (1975), *Emma Mae* (1976), and *Penitentiary* (1979), were made while still in film school. *Penitentiary* was the highest grossing independent film of 1979. At the time of his death, he was in postproduction for a documentary, *Hip Hop Hope*, focusing on underground hip-hop culture.

Movies (director, writer, producer): *Street Wars* (1992), *Penitentiary III* (1987), *Penitentiary II* (1982), *Penitentiary* (1979), *Emma Mae* (1976), *Welcome Home, Brother Charles* (1975), *A Day in the Life of Willie Faust, or Death on the Installment Plan* (short, 1972), *My Mic Sounds Nice: The Truth About Women in Hip Hop* (2010)

Reginald Hudlin (1961), producer, director, writer. Credited with introducing the hip-hop genre to film, Hudlin's Harvard University short film was later expanded to the big screen success *House Party* in 1990. A graduate of Harvard University Film School, he was born in Centreville, Illinois, the son of Warrington Sr. and Helen Hudlin. He has two brothers: Warrington Jr. is also a filmmaker, and Christopher, a businessman. After graduation, while establishing a career in cinema, Hudlin was guest lecturer in film at the University of Wisconsin in Milwaukee and worked as a copywriter at an advertising agency. One of the Producers of *Django Unchained* in 2012, Hudlin was the first president of entertainment for Black Entertainment Television. He is a member of the executive board at University of California, Los Angeles School of Theater, Film, and Television.

Awards: Chicago International Film Festival (2017), AFI Award (2013), Deep Ellum Film Festival Award (2001), CableACE Award (1995), Sundance Film Festival Award (1990)

Movie (producer, director) *Marshall* (2017)

Movies (producer): *Burning Sands* (2017), *Django Unchained* (2012), *Ride* (1998)

Movies (director and writer): *House Party* (1990), *House Party* (short, 1983)

Movies (director): *Serving Sara* (2002), *The Ladies Man* (2000), *The Great White Hype* (1996), *Boomerang* (1992)

Movies (writer): *House Party 3* (1994), *Bebe's Kids* (1992), *House Party 2* (1991)

Television specials (producer): *44th, 45th, 46th, 47th, 48th, 49th NAACP Image Awards* (2013-18), *The Oscars* (2016), *Richard Pryor: The Funniest Man Dead or Alive* (also director, 2005)

Television movie (director): *Untitled Burr and Hart Project* (2010), *Wifey* (2007), *Cosmic Slop* (1994)

Television (producer): *Showtime at the Apollo* (2017-18), *Black Panther* (also writer) (2010), *Bring That Year Back 2006: Laugh Now, Cry Later* (television movie) (2006), *The Boondocks* (2005–08), *The Bernie Mac Show* (2004–05)

Television (director): *Are We There Yet?* (2012), *The Bernie Mac Show* (2002–05)

Warrington Hudlin (1952), producer, director. Hudlin is highly acknowledged among contemporary filmmakers for his commitment to autonomous financing and providing visually praiseworthy films. He is a graduate of Yale University Film School. Hudlin is the older brother of sometimes collaborator, filmmaker Reginald Hudlin. Their great grandfather, Richard Hudlin, cofounded the Allmon-Hudlin Film Company, that he managed circa 1916. Warrington Hudlin is cofounder and president of the Black Filmmaker Foundation. Some of his most noted work is as a producer of *House Party*, *Boomerang*, and *Bebe's Kids*. Hudlin's DVRepublic, which he is founder and chief, is dedicated to multicultural, socially concerned, entertainment-driven digital films. He is a black-belt martial arts practitioner. His numerous awards include awards from African American Women in Cinema, the Revolution Award from ImageNation, and the Hip Hop Association.

Awards: Black Reel Award (2006), American Black Film Festival Award (2005), CableACE Award (1995)

Movies (producer): *Ride* (1998), *Bebe's Kids* (1992), *Boomerang* (1992), *House Party* (1990)

Television (producer): *Iron Ring* (2008), *Katrina* (TV movie, 2007), *Unstoppable: Conversation with Melvin Van Peeples, Gordon Parks, and Ossie Davis* (TV documentary, 2005)

Television (director): *Cosmic Slop* (TV movie, also writer, 1994), *Street Corner Stories* (1977), *Black at Yale* (documentary) (1974)

Cheryl Boone Isaacs, (1949), president of the Academy of Motion Picture Arts and Sciences. Isaacs was elected in 2013. The Whittier College political science major was born in Springfield, Massachusetts. The third woman and first African American to preside over the Academy of Motion Picture Arts and Sciences, the exuberant Isaacs, while at New Line Cinema, was also the first African American female to head a major studio marketing operation. As a mega-media executive, Isaacs is recognized for her global, innovative, and diverse perspective. In 2014, Isaacs was inducted into the NAACP Image Awards Hall of Fame. In 2013, she won the African American Film Critics Association's Special Achievement Award. In 2017 CinemaCon, USA recognized her as Pioneer of the Year.

George Jackson (1958–2000), producer, director, music executive. His life cut short at age forty-two; it's no telling how much more of an impact Jackson could have had on cinema than the huge influence he had while active. He brought hip-hop and rap to the big screen and initiated the neo-movie soundtrack era. With *Krush Groove* in 1995, *House Party 2*, and *House Party 3*, Jackson and collaborator Doug McHenry played an integral part ushering in the hip-hop and rap genre of film. In 1991, *New Jack City* dissected the inner workings and impact drugs have on urban communities. Born in Harlem, New York, Jackson graduated from Harvard University with a BA in sociology. A boundless talent, he was hired at one point as president of Motown to help rebuild the label in the late 1990s. Jackson's ultimate goal was to be a film mogul and head a studio. At the time of his death from a stroke, he was creating a series of websites called Urban Box Office Network.

Awards: NAACP Image Award, Black American Cinema Society

Award, Communications Excellence to Black Audiences Award

Movie (producer and director): *House Party 2* (1991)

Movie (producer and music supervisor): *New Jack City* (1991)

Movies (producer): *Body Count* (1998), *A Thin Line Between Love and Hate* (1996), *The Walking Dead* (1995), *Scenes for the Soul* (1995), *Jason's Lyric* (1994), *House Party 3* (1994), *Stalingrad* (1999), *Disorderlies* (1987), *Krush Groove* (1985)

Television movies (producer): *Mr. Murder* (1998), *Private Times* (1991), *Livin' Large* (1989)

Television (producer): *Malcolm & Eddie* (1997–2000)

T. D. Jakes (1957), bishop, author, producer. A man of the cloth determined to use media as a tool to carry a positive message, Bishop Jakes proves faith-based storytelling can attract a wide audience. Born in South Charleston, West Virginia, Jakes graduated from Friends University with a BA, MA, and Doctorate in Ministry. Aside from his ministry, he has been kept exceedingly busy in 2014 as a producer of the movie *Heaven Is for Real* and author of the book *Instinct: The Power to Unleash Your Inborn Drive*. He is a best-selling author of over two dozen major writings; some, like *Not Easily Broken* (2009) and *Woman Thou Art Loosed* (2004), have had movie box-office success. He produced and appeared in *Jumping the Broom* in 2011. In 2018 Bishop Jakes produced the television movie *Faith Under Fire,* staring Toni Braxton. A recipient of numerous honorary degrees and doctorates, Jakes has won multiple awards that include a Grammy and the President's Award presented by the NAACP Image Awards in 2004.

Movie (writer and producer): *Not Easily Broken* (*2009*)

Movies (producer): *Miracles from Heaven* (2016), *Heaven Is for Real* (2014), *Black Nativity* (2013), *Sparkle* (2012), *Woman Thou Art Loosed: On the 7th Day* (2012), *Jumping the Broom* (2011)

Television movie (producer): *Faith Under Fire* (2018)

Television (producer and host): *T.D. Jakes Presents: Mind, Body & Soul* (2013)

Television (host, Bishop): *The Potter's Touch* (2001–2018)

Woodie King Jr. (1937), director, producer, actor. King is the renowned founder and director of the New Federal Theatre in New York City. Founder of NFT in 1970 and the author of several books on the status of African American theater, King is considered a major contributor to the African American renaissance arts movement circa late 1960s and early 1970s. King has taken on acting roles in films that include *Serpico* in 1973 and *Men in Black 3* in 2012. NFT's alumni include Laurence Fishburne, Debbie Allen, Morgan Freeman, Lynn Whitfield, Robert Downey Jr., and Samuel Jackson to name a few. Born in Baldwin Springs, Alabama, son of Woodie and Ruby King, he graduated from Will-O-Way School of Theatre. Later in life, after major accomplishments, King returned to school and earned an MFA from Brooklyn College. His awards include the NAACP Image Award, the Obie Award for Sustained Achievement, and an honorary doctorate from Wayne State University. King showcased and introduced many playwrights such as Amiri Baraka, a.k.a. LeRoi Jones, and Ntozake Shange, who wrote *For Colored Girls Who Have Considered Suicide/When the Rainbow is Enuf*. King and Willie Mae King are the parents of Michelle, Woodie Geoffrey, and Michael.

Movie (producer): *The Minority* (2006)

Movie documentary (director, producer, writer): *Segregating the Greatest Generation* (2006)

Movies documentary (producer): *King of Stage: The Woodie King Jr. Story* (2017), *Black Theatre: The Making of a Movement* (also director,1978), *Right On!* (1970),

Movies (director): *The Torture of Mothers* (1980), *The Long Night* (1976)

Television movie (director, writer, and producer): *Death of a Prophet* (1981)

Television (writer): *Hot L Baltimore* (TV series episode,1975)

Movies (actor): *Men in Black 3* (2012), *The Long Night* (1976), *Serpico* (1973), *Together for Days* (1972), *Sweet Love, Bitter* (1967)

Television (actor): *Unforgettable* (2014)

Books (three selected from numerous published): Best Black Plays: *The Theodore Ward Prize for African American Playwriting* by Woodie King Jr., Leslie Lee, and Mark Clayton Crothers (2007), *The National Black Drama Anthology: Eleven Plays from America's Leading African-*

American Theaters by Woodie King Jr. and Hal Leonard Corp. (2000), *Black Poets and Prophets* by Woodie King Jr. and Earl Anthony (1972)

Spike Lee (1957), director, producer, screenwriter, actor. Lee is a twentieth-century cinematic game changer on many levels. He contributed greatly to the idea of women taking control of personal choices in the 1986 film *She's Gotta Have It*. The African American actors in the film were representative of a diverse type of human characters, not a specific ethnic group. He shed light on the African American caste system with *School Daze* in 1988. In 1992, Lee dissected aspects of opposing politics in the realm of different African American consciousness raising belief systems in the movie *Malcolm X*, based on the book by Alex Haley. Lee formed his production company, 40 Acres and a Mule, in 1986. Lee and his company had a major influence in opening doors in front of and behind the camera. His tireless campaign for equality in film is responsible for launching the careers of a substantial number of African Americans employed consistently in twentieth and twenty-first century cinema. The 1999 film *Summer of Sam* reflects many of Lee's projects to disprove the idea that African Americans are only bankable when directing a predominately African American cast. In the new millennium Lee hasn't missed a beat with highly praised *Inside Man* in 2006 and *Miracle at St. Anna* in 2008. His influence reined again with the movies *Chi-Raq* (2015) and *BlacKkKlansman* (2018) He stays true to his independent filmmaker roots as witnessed in his producing the groundbreaking film *Pariah* in 2011. Raised in Brooklyn, New York, Lee was born in Atlanta, Georgia, and received his BA from Morehouse College, third generation on his father's side. He received his MFA in film from New York University. "For his brilliance and unwavering courage in using film to challenge conventional thinking," he was the recipient of the 20th annual Dorothy and Lillian Gish Prize in 2013.

Awards (select): 20/20 Award (2018), Black Reel Award (2018, 2017, 2014, 2011, 2007, 2001), Cannes Film Festival (2018), Image Award (2007, 2003), Academy Award (2016), The Dorothy and Lillian Gish Prize (2013), Venice Film Festival Award (2012, 2006, 1990), Primetime Emmy Award (2007), Black Movie Award (2006), MTV Movie Award (2006). Atlanta Film Festival Award (2005), American Black

Film Festival Award (2004), Cesar Award, France (2003), Las Vegas Film Critics Society Award (2003), BAFTA Award (2002), Cinequest San Jose Film Festival Award (2001), Empire Award, UK (1999), Satellite Award (1998), Berlin International Film Award (1997), Chicago Film Critics Association Award (1993, 1990), Gotham Award (1992), Cannes Film Festival (1991, 1986), Los Angeles Film Critics Association Award (1989, 1986), Independent Spirit Award (1987), Locarno International Film Festival Award (1983), Student Academy Award (1983).

Movies (director, producer, writer, actor): *Red Hook Summer* (2012), *Summer of Sam* (1999), *Clockers* (1995), *Crooklyn* (1995), *Malcolm X* (1992), *Jungle Fever* (1991), *Mo' Better Blues* (1990), *Do the Right Thing* (1989), *School Daze* (1988), *She's Gotta Have It* (also editor, 1986)

Movies (producer, director, writer): *BlacKkKlansman* (2018), *Chi-Raq* (2015), *She Hate Me* (2004), *Bamboozled* (2000), *He Got Game* (1998, 1986), *Joe's Bed-Stuy Barbershop: We Cut Heads* (1983)

Movies (director, producer): *Pass Over* (2018), *Oldboy* (2013), *Miracle at St. Anna* (2008), *25th Hour* (2002), *Girl 6* (1996) Movies (producer): *The Girl Is in Trouble* (2012), *Pariah* (2011), *Dream Street* (2010), *Saint John of Las Vegas* (2009), *Love & Basketball* (2000), *The Best Man* (1999), *Tales from the Hood* (1995), *New Jersey Drive* (1995), *Drop Squad* (1994)

Movies (director): *Inside Man* (2006)

Movie documentaries (director and producer): *Bad 25* (2012), *4 Little Girls* (1997)

Documentary (director) *Michael Jackson's Journey from Motown to Off the Wall* (2016)

Television movies (director and producer): *Mike Tyson: Undisputed Truth* (2013), *Kobe Doin' Work* (2009), *Sucker Free City* (2004), *Jim Brown: All American* (2002)

Television movie (director): *A Huey P. Newton Story* (2001)

Television documentaries (director and producer): *If God Is Willing and the Creek Don't Rise* (2010), *When the Levees Broke: A Requiem in Four Acts* (2006)

Television (producer, director, writer): *She's Gotta Have It* (2017)

Television (producer, director): *Rodney King* (2017)

Television (director): *The Tonight Show Starring Jimmie Fallon* (2014)

Darnell Martin (1964), director, writer, producer. Acknowledged as being the first African American woman to write and direct a movie produced by a major studio, Martin persevered through some tough times to earn the title. *I Like It Like That* was released in 1994. She applied her writing and directing skills aptly to *Cadillac Records* released in 2008. Born in Bronx, New York, Martin graduated from Sarah Lawrence College where she studied theater and literature. During an academic break, while attempting to get into New York University to earn a Master's in Film, she worked in a film lab and freelanced doing assistant camera work. She eventually received her MA in Film from NYU.

Award: New York Film Critics Circle Award (1994)

Movies (director, writer, producer): *The Vicious Circle* (Spanish Language, 2003), *Prison Song* (2001)

Movies (director and writer): *Cadillac Records* (2008), *I Like It Like That* (1994)

Movie (director): *Wish You Well* (2013)

Television movies (director): *Firelight* (2012), *The Lost Valentine* (2011)

Television (director): *Big Dogs* (2018), *Lore* (2017), *Being Mary Jane* (2017), *Sleepy Hollow* (2017), *The Walking Dead* (2016), *Grimm* (2011–12), *Law & Order: Criminal Intent* (2002–10). *Law & Order* (2003–10), *Oz* (1997)

Doug McHenry (1952), producer, director, music supervisor. McHenry is able to guide herculean tasks through to completion. His professional resume includes being a music and movie executive at several studios before branching out on his own. He collaborated with producer George Jackson before Jackson's untimely passing in 2000. McHenry pioneered the introduction of hip-hop culture and music to film along with contemporary marketing of movie soundtracks. The neo soundtrack trend was evidenced with *House Party 2* in 1991 and *House Party 3* in 1994. *Jason's Lyric* was his homage to Romeo and Juliet. He graduated from Stanford University with a BA in economics and holds a JD/MBA from Harvard Law School and Business School. McHenry is the recipient of the ACE for Cable Programming Award and the NAACP Image Award. He also lectures on film finance.

Movies (producer and music supervisor): *A Thin Line Between Love and Hate* (1996), *New Jack City* (1991)

Movies (producer and director): *Jason's Lyric* (1994), *House Party 2* (1991)

Movies (producer): *Boogie Town* (2012), *Two Can Play That Game* (2001), *The Brothers* (2001), *Body Count* (1998), *Scenes for the Soul* (1995), *House Party 3* (1994), *Stalingrad* (1989), *Disorderlies* (1987), *Krush Groove* (1985)

Movie (director): *Kingdom Come* (2001)

Television movies (producer): *Mr. Murder* (1998), *Private Times* (1991) *Heart and Soul* (1988)

Television movie (director): *Keep the Faith, Baby* (2002)

Television (producer): *Malcolm & Eddie* (1996–2000)

Elvis Mitchell (1956), film critic, host, scholar, producer. A featured journalist of film review and critique for publications such as *The New York Times* and *LA Weekly*, Mitchell was host on *Under the Influence* for Turner Classic Movies. A lecturer in film at Harvard University and University of Nevada, Las Vegas, he is a graduate of Wayne State University with a BA in English. Documentaries produced by Mitchell include *The Black List: Volume One* in 2008, *The Black List: Volume Two* (TV documentary) in 2009, and *The Black List: Volume Three* in 2010. In the documentaries, influential African Americans opine on race identity and achievement. Mitchell was born in Highland Park, Michigan. He was appointed as curator in 2011 for the Los Angeles County Museum of Art's series, Film Independent. He served as a member of the dramatic jury at the Sundance Film Festival in 1999 and 2007. In 2009, he was the recipient of the Ashland Independent Film Festival Rogue Award.

Television (producer): *Black Lightening* (2018)

Television documentary (producer): *The Black List: Volume Three* (2010), *The Black List: Volume Two* (2009), *The Black List: Volume One* (2008)

Suzan-Lori Parks (1963), playwright, screenwriter, novelist. Encouraged to write plays by her mentor, novelist James Baldwin, Parks wrote the Pulitzer Prize–winning play *Topdog/Underdog*. Parks was the first African American woman to win the coveted prize in 2002 among numerous other awards for her mastery of the written word. She wrote the screenplay *Girl 6*, directed by Spike Lee, released in 1996. Parks adapted writer Zora Neal Hurston's *Their Eyes Are Watching God* into an award winning television movie that aired in 2005. From November 2002 to November 2003, she challenged herself by writing one complete short play a day for an entire year, culminating in a work titled *365 Days/365 Plays*. Born in Fort Knox, Kentucky, Parks graduated from Mount Holyoke College with a BA in English.

Movie (screenplay): *Girl 6* (1996)
Movie (adaptation): *Native Son* (2019)
Television movie (screenplay): *Their Eyes Are Watching God* (2005)
Documentaries (interviews): *The Black List: Volume One* (2008), *Stage on Screen: The Topdog Diaries* (TV) (2002)

Gina Prince-Bythewood (1969), writer, director, producer. Prince-Bythewood produced and wrote for the television network series *Felicity* in 1998–99. Before graduation from University of California, Los Angeles with honors, she ran competitive track. While working as part of a student film crew, she instantly knew she wanted to direct. As writer and director of the highly praised film *Love & Basketball* released in 2000, Prince-Blythewood's career soared. Prince-Blythewood maintained the high note directing the cable television presentation of *Disappearing Acts* in 2000. She wrote the screen adaptation and directed *Secret Life of Bees* released in 2008. In 2017 Prince-Blythewood produced, directed and wrote for the highly rated television series, *Shots Fired*.

Awards: Image Award (2018, 2009), Chicago International Film Festival (2014), Black Reel Award (2008, 2001), Independent Spirit Award (2001), Humanitas Prize (2000)

Movies (writer and director): *Beyond the Lights* (2014), *Blackbird* (2014), *The Secret Life of Bees* (2008), *Love & Basketball* (2000)
Movie (producer): *Biker Boyz* (2003)
Television (producer, director, writer): *Shots Fired* (2017)
Television (producer, director): *Cloak & Dagger* (2018)
Television (Producer): Felicity (1998–99), Courthouse (1995)
Television (writer): *Sweet Justice* (1994), *South Central* (1994), *A*

Different World (1992–93)
   Television: *Daddy's Girl* (documentary, producer) (2007), *Disappearing Acts* (TV movie, director) (2000)

John Ridley (1965), writer, producer, novelist. Ridley avoids the road well-traveled. At any given time, he can take on a different medium and totally excel in it. Born in Milwaukee, Wisconsin, he earned his degree in East Asian languages from New York University and spent a year in Japan after graduation. Upon his return to the United States, with an interest to enter the world of show business, he started out as a stand-up comic. After bookings on late-night television shows, Ridley transitioned to writing for television situation comedies. From 1993 to 1995, he wrote for situation comedies *Martin*, *The Fresh Prince of Bel-Air*, and *The John Larroquette Show*. While writing for television, Ridley also wrote novels.
He has written seven novels and three graphic novels. He adapted his novel *Stray Dogs* into a screenplay renamed *U Turn*, which was released in 1997. Ridley wrote the screenplay for *Red Tails* released in 2012 and *12 Years a Slave* in 2013. Honing his producing skills on television, Ridley produced the movie *U Turn* followed by *Three Kings* in 1999 and *Undercover Brother* in 2002 then *Bobby* in 2006. Ridley, a radio and television commentator, won an Emmy Award for news reporting in 2007.
Awards: Black Reel Award (2016, 2014), Image Award (2016, 2014), Academy Award (2014), Independent Spirit Award (2014), Southeastern Film Critics Association Award (2000) Urbanworld Film Festival Award (1997)
   Movie (writer, director, producer): *All Is by My Side* (2013)
   Movies (writer, producer): *Ben Hur* (2016), *12 Years a Slave* (2013), *Undercover Brother* (2002), *Three Kings* (1999), *U Turn* (1997)
   Movie (writer): *Red Tails* (2012)
   Movie (producer): *Bobby* (2006)
   Documentary (producer, writer, director): *Let It Fall: Los Angeles 1982-1992* (2017)
   Television mini-series (producer, director, writer): *Guerrilla* (2017)
   Television (producer, writer, director) *American Crime* (2015-17)
   Television (writer and producer): *The Wanda Sykes Show* (2009–10), *Barbershop* (2005), *Third Watch* (1999–2004), *Platinum* (2003), *The*

Show (1996), *The John Larroquette Show* (1995–96)

Malik Hassan Sayeed (1969), cinematographer. Sayeed knew early on he wanted to be behind the camera. He began his academic career at Howard University as a premed major then followed his true calling and graduated with a major in filmmaking. Sayeed was able to work his way through school as an electrician in theatrical venues such as the Kennedy Center, Wolf Trap Opera, and the Warner Theater with a focus on stage lighting. Born in New York City and raised in Los Angeles, Sayeed's talent as a director of photography can be seen in the Spike Lee production *Clockers*, his first major film in 1995. He also teamed up with writer and producer Hype Williams to direct the photography for the film *Belly* in 1998. Though Sayeed did not get accepted into a few graduate programs he applied to after his undergraduate degree, he was able to turn what could have been an adversity into an advantage. He had already been staging lights for entertainers on the road and decided to hit the ground running and focused on building a career based on real world experience.

    Award: MTV Video Music Award (2016)
    Movies: *Belly* (1998), *He Got Game* (1998), *The Players Club* (1998), *Cold Around the Heart* (1997), *Girl 6* (1996), *Clockers* (1995)
    Movie (documentary): *Cagefighter* (2012)
    Television special: *Beyonce': Formation* (2016)
    Television movies: *Da Brick* (2011), *Freak* (1998)
    Documentaries: *Cagefighter* (2012), *Life and Debt* (2001), *The Original Kings of Comedy* (2000)

John Singleton (1968), director, producer, writer. By the time Singleton was a sophomore at University of Southern California, he'd won three major writing awards and was signed to top tier, Creative Artists Agency. He followed through and graduated from USC School of Cinema and Television. His initial studio project was to write and direct the movie classic *Boyz in the Hood* in 1991, for which he was the youngest person ever to be nominated for an Academy Award in the category of writing and directing. He was born in Los Angeles, California. A keen sense for backing the right material, he came on board to produce *Black Snake Moan* in 2006 and *Hustle & Flow* in 2005. With the introduction of the phenomenal television series *Snowfall* in 2017, Singleton's all-inclusive talent was put to enormous use. In 2003, he was the recipient of a Star on the Walk of Fame.

Awards: Black Reel Award (2017), Image Award (2017, 2006), African-American Film Critics Association (2015), Acapulco Black Film Festival (2001), Locarno International Film Festival (2001), MTV Movie Award (1992), ShoWest Convention Award, USA (1992), Los Angeles Film Critics Association Award (1991), New York Film Critics Circle Award (1991)

Movies (director, producer, writer): *Baby Boy* (2001), *Shaft* (2000), *Higher Learning* (1995), *Poetic Justice* (1993)

Movie (director, producer): *Shaft* (2000)

Movie (director, writer): *Boyz in the Hood* (1991)

Movies (director): *Four Brothers* (2005), *2 Fast 2 Furious* (2003), *Rosewood* (1997)

Movie (producer): *Illegal Tender* (2007), *Black Snake Moan* (2006), *Hustle & Flow* (2005), *Woo* (1998)

Documentary (executive producer): *Through a Lens Darkly: Black Photographers and the Emergence of a People* (2014)

Television documentary (producer: *L.A. burning: The Riots 25 Years Later* (2017)

Television (producer, writer, director): *Snowfall* (2017-18)

Television (producer, director): *Rebel* (2017)

Tim Story (1970), director, producer. Affable, Story has managed to navigate the film industry directing box office hits such as *Barbershop* in 2002, *Fantastic Four* in 2005, and *Think Like a Man* in 2012. Though he was interested in film as a youth, he was also interested in music. As a teen, he set out to be a successful rapper until rival gang members shot and killed a member of his group. Story graduated from a three-year film program at University of Southern California and soon began directing music videos. Born in Los Angeles, California, he financed his first independent film, *One of Us Tripped*, in 1996.

Award: The Black Filmmakers Hall of Fame Festival Award (1996)

Movies (director): *Ride Along 2* (2016), *Think Like a Man Too* (2014), *Ride Along* (2014), *Think Like a Man* (2012), *Hurricane Season* (2009),

Fantastic Four: Rise of the Silver Surfer (2007), *Fantastic Four* (2005), *Taxi* (2004), *Barbershop* (2002), *The Firing Squad* (also writer) (1999), *One of Us Tripped* (1997)

Movie (producer): *First Sunday* (2008)

Television movie (producer, director): *What Goes Around Comes Around* (2016)

Television movie (producer): *The 12th Man* (2006)

Television (producer, director): *White Famous* (2017)

Television (producer): *Standoff* (2006–07)

George Tillman Jr. (1969), producer, director, writer. Film and television audiences have Tillman and his filmmaking partner, Robert Teitel, to thank for the groundbreaking family film *Soul Food* in 1997. Tillman wrote, directed, and produced, and Teitel was on board as producer. The movie *Notorious* in 2009 was directed by Tillman and produced by Teitel. Teitel wrote *Nothing Like the Holidays*, and they both coproduced the film in 2008. They met in college and have formed a film production company called State Street Pictures. A dynamic duo, Tillman and Teitel also successfully work projects independent of each other. Tillman directed the highly rated movies, *The Longest Ride* (2015) and *Men of Honor* (2000). He has consistently and successfully been involved in producing the *Barbershop* film franchise. Tillman graduated from Columbia College in Chicago, Illinois, a film and video major. While enrolled, he wrote and directed a thirty-minute award-winning short called *Paula* in 1992, which was a springboard for subsequent endeavors. *Paula* won the Student Academy Award and the Black Filmmakers Hall of Fame Award. Tillman was born in Milwaukee, Wisconsin. As a child, he was influenced by the use of his father's 8 mm camera.

Award: Black Reel Award for Television (2017)

Movies (producer and director): *The Hate U Give* (2018), *The Inevitable Defeat of Mister & Pete* (2013)

Movies (producer): *Mudbound* (2017), *Barbershop: The Next Cut* (2016) *Nothing Like the Holidays* (2008), *Roll Bounce* (2005), *Beauty Shop* (2005), *Barbershop 2: Back in Business* (2004), *Barbershop* (2002)

Movies (director and writer): *Soul Food* (1997), *Paula* (short) (1992), *Scenes for the Soul* (1995)

Movies (director) *The Longest Ride* (2015), *Men of Honor* (2000)
Television movie (producer): *The Brandon T. Jackson Show* (2006)
Television (director): *This Is Us* (2016-17), *Power* (2014-16)

Richard Wesley (1945), writer. Wesley holds dual honor for being a leading theatrical stage writer and screenwriter during the 1970s African American cultural arts renaissance. His work contributed to establishing a foundation for future writers and has continued to be produced in the twenty-first century. As a nineteen-year-old college sophomore, Wesley won praise and awards for his writing prowess. Soon after graduating with a BFA from Howard University, Wesley's stage play, a political drama, *Black Terror*, won the Drama Desk Award in 1971. Other wins followed, including the Broadway stage production of *The Mighty Gents* in 1978, which won the Audelco Award. Requested by Sidney Poitier, he wrote the screenplays for *Uptown Saturday Night*, released in 1974, and *Let's Do It Again* in 1975. Wesley's brilliant screen adaptation of *Native Son* by novelist Richard Wright was released in 1986. The 2003 television movie *Deacons for Defense*, cowritten with Frank Military, won a Black Reel Award in 2004. Born in Newark, New Jersey, he is associate professor in playwriting and screenwriting and chairman of the department of dramatic writing in the Tisch School of the Arts at New York University.

Award (television): Black Reel Award (2004)
Movies: *Native Son* (1986), *Fast Forward* (1985), *Let's Do It Again* (1975), *Uptown Saturday Night* (1974)
Television movies: *Deacons for the Defense* (2003), *Bojangles* (2001), *Mandela and de Klerk* (1997), *Murder Without Motive: The Edmund Perry Story* (1992), *House of Dies Drear* (1984)

Abdul Williams, screenwriter. Williams personifies persistence and patience, which defines an aspect of the movie-making process. A graduate of Ohio University majoring in communications with an English minor, Williams displayed his love of writing at age eight banging out a short story on an old typewriter. Fast forward and he is teamed with premier music video director Erik White to become the driving force behind the movie *Lottery Ticket* released in 2010. Williams was assured of his talent when he was employed in a range of positions from film development assistant to film executive, reading and recommending scripts for major agencies and producers. His scriptwriting skills were also applied to writing countless screen treatments and adapting novels. He was born in Cleveland, Ohio. Williams continues to write for film and television. Williams won the Image Award for his *New Edition Story* screenplay in 2018 and produced and wrote *The Bobby Brown Story* for television movie release that same year.

Award: Image Award (2018)
Movie (writer): *Lottery Ticket* (2010)
Television movies (writer, producer): *The Bobby Brown Story* (2018)
Television movies (writer): *The New Edition Story* (2017)

Oprah Winfrey (1954), media executive, talk show host, producer, actress, philanthropist. Winfrey is proof that for better or worse, with willpower, focus, and a goal, mega success can be within reach. One of the most influential people in the world, Winfrey was born into humble beginnings in Kosciusko, Mississippi. Winfrey's father was strict when it came to excelling in academics, and Winfrey rose to the task. She won a scholarship to major in speech communication and performing arts at Tennessee State University. While a student, she won beauty contests, Miss Black Nashville and Miss Tennessee. While a student, she was also offered a local evening co-anchor news job at CBS Broadcasting Inc. She was persuaded by a speech teacher to take a break from school and accept the once-in-a-lifetime opportunity. Winfrey would return twelve years later while in an admirable place in her career and finish the credits to earn her BA in speech and drama. In addition to hosting *A.M. Chicago*, Winfrey was cast in her first film role in 1985 as Sophia in *The Color Purple*. It was not long before she would add the titles *actress* and *producer* to her resume. *The Oprah Winfrey Show*, which aired from 1986 to 2011, was the catalyst for Winfrey's stratospheric success. The year 1986 was also when her company, Harpo Productions Inc., was established. Having conquered film, television, and publishing with the hugely successful *O, The Oprah Winfrey Magazine*, Winfrey has undisputedly earned the title of media mogul. She is also recognized for her extreme generosity to charitable causes in the United States and abroad. In 2011, Winfrey founded the Oprah Winfrey Network (OWN), and in 2014, she produced and acted in the movie, *Selma*. Major film award wins for her in 2018 was the Black Reel Award for Lifetime Achievement and the Golden Globe, Cecil B. Demille Award. For Winfrey, there is no limit.

Awards (select): Golden Globes, USA (2018), Black Reel Award (2018, 2015), Santa Barbara International Film Festival (2014), Academy Award (2011), Daytime Emmy Award (2011, 1998, 1997, 1996, 1995, 1994, 1993, 1992, 1991, 1989, 1987), Television Critics Association Award (2011), Image Award (2005, 1991), International Emmy Award (2005), Peabody Award (1996), People's Choice Award (2004, 1998, 1997, 1988), Primetime Emmy Award (2002, 2000)

Movies (producer, actress): *Selma* (2014), *Beloved* (1998)

Movies (producer): *The Hundred Foot Journey* (2014), *Precious* (2009), *The Great Debaters* (2007)

Movies (actress): *A Wrinkle in Time* (2018), *The Star* (2017), *Native Son* (1986), *The Color Purple* (1985)

Television movie (producer, actress): *The Immortal Life of Henrietta Lacks* (2017), *Before Women Had Wings* (1997), *The Women of Brewster Place* (1989)

Television movie (producer): *The Oprah Winfrey Oscar Special* (2007), *Their Eyes Are Watching God* (2005), *Amy & Isabelle* (2001), *Tuesdays with Morrie* (1999), *David and Lisa* (1998), *The Wedding* (1998), *Overexposed* (1992)

Television (producer/host): *Super Soul Sunday* (2014-16), *The Oprah Winfrey Show* (1989–2011)

Television mini-series (producer): *Central Park Five* (2019)

Television series documentary (producer): *Oprah's Master Class* (2012-18)

Television (producer): *Queen Sugar* (2016-18)

Television (producer, actress): *Greenleaf* (2016-18)

THE INDEPENDENT FILMMAKERS

Independent films are professional feature film productions usually produced on a minimal budget outside of the major film studio system.

Charles Burnett (1944), director, writer, cinematographer. Burnett exemplifies the independent filmmaker. Born in Vicksburg, Mississippi, his southern roots and being raised in the Watts section of Los Angeles had a profound influence on his film subjects. His cinematic focus is social commentary, slice of life. Though he was interested in the arts, due to economic pressure, he began his academic career majoring in electronics at a city college with the idea of becoming an electrician. While in junior college, exposure to creative writing convinced him to answer his calling. He transferred to University of California, Los Angeles where he graduated with a BA in Writing and Languages and, several years later, earned a Master's of Fine Art in film. His award-winning film *Killers of Sheep* was written for his master's thesis. In many instances, Burnett's film projects have benefited from prestigious grant awards. There has been involvement in studio-driven film projects such as *The Glass Shield* in 1994 and the television movie *Selma, Lord, Selma* in 1999. *To Sleep with Anger*, which many believe to be his finest work, was a grant award and private-investor funded.

Awards: Academy Award (2018), New York Film Critics Circle Award (2007), Sarasota Film Festival (2001), Arizona International Film Festival Award (2000), WorldFest Houston Award (2000), Nashville Film Award (1999), National Society of Film Critics Award (1998, 1991), American Film Institute Award (1991), Independent Spirit Award (1991), Los Angeles Film Critics Association Award (1990), Sundance Film Festival Award (1990), Berlin International Film Festival Award (1981) Movies (writer, director, cinematographer): *My Brother's Wedding* (1983), *Killer of Sheep* (also editor) (1979)

Movies (writer and director): *Namibia: The Struggle for Liberation*

(2010), *The Glass Shield* (1994), *To Sleep with Anger* (1990)

Movies (cinematographer): *Guests of the Hotel Astoria* (1989), *Bless Their Little Hearts* (1984), *Bush Mama* (1979)

Movies (writer): *America Becoming* (documentary, 1991), *Bless Their Little Hearts* (1984)

Movies (director): *The Annihilation of Fish* (1999), *Documenta X– Die Filme* (1997), *My Brother's Wedding* (1983), *America Becoming* (documentary) (1991)

Television documentary (director and writer): *Independent Lens*, "Nat Turner: A Troublesome Property" (2004), *The Blues*, "Warming the Devil's Fire" (2003), *For Reel* (2003)

Television movie documentary (director): *Power to Heal: Medicare and the Civil Rights Revolution* (2018)

Television movies (director): *Relative Stranger* (2009), *Finding Buck McHenry* (2000), *Selma, Lord, Selma* (1999), *The Wedding* (1998), *Nightjohn* (1996)

Television series (director): *American Family* (2002)

Zeinabu irene Davis (1961), director, producer, writer. Independent innovator, Davis is recognized for her diverse presentations of the African American female perspective. Her highly praised 1999 film *Compensation* is a love story that deals with the struggle to overcome racism, disability (deafness), and discrimination. Davis captures the intent of the group of filmmakers that make up the LA Rebellion in her 2011 film documentary *Spirits of Rebellion: Black Film at UCLA*. Davis began her academic career at Brown University majoring in international relations with the goal of becoming an attorney. Not satisfied with the major and after working as a student intern at a local Public Broadcasting Station (PBS), she created her own major and graduated with a BA in Mass images of Third-World Peoples. At the University of California, Los Angeles, Davis earned a Master's in African Studies with a major in African cinema and minor in folklore. Then she proceeded to earn another Master's in Fine Arts in motion picture and television production from UCLA. She was born in Philadelphia, Pennsylvania. Having taught at several colleges and universities, Davis is now an associate professor at University of California, San Diego. She was inducted into the Black Filmmakers Hall of Fame for her 1989 film short *Cycles*.

Awards: San Diego Film Festival Award (2017), African Movie Academy Award (2016)

Movies (producer and director): *Compensation* (1999), *A Powerful Thang* (1991), *Trumpetistcally, Clora Bryant* (short, 1989)

Documentary (producer, director, writer): *Spirits of Rebellion: Black Cinema at UCLA* (2016)

Documentary (director): *Spirit of Rebellion: Black Film at UCLA* (documentary, 2011), *Cycles* (short,1989), *Re-creating Black Women's Media Image* (documentary short,1983)

Ava DuVernay (1972), writer, producer, director, independent film distributor. In the vanguard of a new wave of twenty-first century independent filmmakers, DuVernay is the first African American female to win the Sundance Film Festival Best Director prize for the feature film *Middle of Nowhere* released in 2012. A graduate of University of California, Los Angeles, she majored in English and African American studies and began her career as a film marketer and publicist. DuVernay's award-winning firm, DVA Media + Marketing, provided strategy and execution for a vast array of film and television campaigns. She was born in Long Beach, California. Positive female representations that include the televised *My Mic Sounds Nice: The Truth About Women in Hip Hop* in 2010 and *Black Girls Rock!* in 2011 are included in her directing and producing body of work. DuVernay is founder of AFFRM, the African American Film Festival Releasing Movement. As the producer and director of the Academy Award–winning movie *Selma*, released in 2014, DuVernay has made a spectacular transition to mainstream cinema and television. She is a masterful cinematic, television and documentary storyteller/informer. Television's *Queen Sugar* has a most progressive storyline.

Awards (select): Image Award (2018, 2017), Primetime Emmy Award (2017), African American Film Critics Association (AAFCA) (2017, 2015, 2012, 2011), Black Reel Award (2017, 2015, 2013), Humanitas Prize (2017), Women in Film Crystal Award (2015), Independent Spirit Award (2013), Hollywood Black Film Festival (2008), Sundance Film Festival Award (2012), Los Angeles Pan African Film Festival (2008),

Toronto Reel World Film Festival Award (2008)

    Movie (producer and director): *Selma* (2014)

    Movies (writer, producer, and director): *Middle of Nowhere* (2012), *I Will Follow* (2011), *This Is the Life* (documentary) (2008)

    Movie (documentary producer): *99%: The Occupy Wall Street Collaborative Film* (2013)

    Television musicals (producer): *Hello Beautiful: Interludes with John Legend* (2013)

    Television (writer and director): *Essence Presents: Faith in 2010* (2010), *TV One Night Only: Live from the Essence Music Festival* (2010)

    Television documentary (producer and director): *Nine for IX* (2013)

Haile Gerima (1946), filmmaker, director, producer, screenwriter, educator, and businessman. Gerima is an alumnus of the LA Rebellion, also known as the Los Angeles School of Black Filmmakers. Born in Gondar, Ethiopia, he was heavily influenced by his father, who was a teacher for the Ministry of Education, dramatist, and playwright. Gerima graduated from University of California, Los Angeles with a BA and an MFA in Film. His most recognized film to date is *Sankofa* released in 1993. An international award-winner, *Sankofa* chronicled an African woman's trek back in time to African resistance during slavery. His 1976 film, *Bush Mama*, was the antithesis of the Blaxploitation film offerings of the era. *Bush Mama* addressed the everyday issues faced as a result of institutionalized racism.

    Awards: Ouagadougou Panafrican Film and Television Festival (2009), Rotterdam International Film Festival Award (2009), Thessaloniki Film Festival Award (2008), Washington, DC Independent Film Festival Award (2003), Berlin International Film Festival Award (1983), Locarno International Film Festival Award (1976)

    Movies (director, producer, writer, editor): *Teza* (2008), *Sankofa* (1993), *Bush Mama* (1979)

    Movie (director, producer, writer): *Ashes and Embers* (1982)

    Movie documentary segment (director, producer, and writer): *Venice 70: Future Reloaded* (2013)

    Movies (director, writer): *Harvest: 3,000 Years* (1976)

    Movie (director, producer, editor): *Hour Glass* (short, also

cinematographer) (2011), *Adwa* (1999)
    Documentary (Producer, Editor): *Footprints of Pan Africanism* (2018), *Through The Door of No Return*, (1997)
    Movie (producer): *Cutting Horse* (2002)
    Movie documentary (director): *After Winter: Sterling Brown* (1985), *Wilmington 10—U.S.A. 10,000* (1979), *Child of Resistance* (short, 1973)

Laurens Grant, documentary filmmaker. Grant brings insightful depth into the Pan African and Latin and South Asian cultural experience. She is a graduate of Northwestern University's Medill School of Journalism and was a foreign correspondent prior to filmmaking. The 2006 film *Hiding Divya*, which she produced, deals with the myths surrounding mental illness in the South Asian American community. Her more recognizable projects are through the medium of television. For the 2010 documentary *Freedom Riders*, she won a Primetime Emmy Award. In 2017 Grant's mainstream documentary success continued as a producer for CNN network series, *The Nineties*.
    Awards: News & Documentary Emmy Award (2013, 2006), Primetime Emmy Award (2011)
    Movie (producer): *Hiding Divya* (2006)
    Movie (writer and director): *Rokia: Voice of a New Generation* (documentary short, 2003)
    Television documentary (producer and director): *The American Experience*, "Jesse Owens" (2012)
    Television documentary (producer): *The Rape of Recy Taylor* (2017)
    Television documentary (director): *Stay Woke: The Black Lives Matter Movement* (2016)
    Television series documentary (producer): *The Nineties* (2017)
    Television (producer): *The American Experience*, "Freedom Riders" (2010), *Latin Music USA*, "The Chicano Wave" (2009), *Slavery and the Making of America*, "Seeds of Destruction" (2005), *The American Experience*, "The Murder of Emmet Till" (2003), *The Kennedys: The Curse of Power* (2000)

Shola Lynch (1969), documentary filmmaker, producer, director. A Texas Longhorn track-and-field star, Lynch was positioned for Olympic gold until sidetracked by a back injury. After her completion of a liberal arts degree with honors from the University of Texas at Austin, she earned a master's degree in history from the University of California, Riverside. With a combined interest in history and filmmaking, Lynch was able to secure a position as a researcher in New York City with renowned documentary filmmaker Ken Burns. In 2006, she won the Peabody Award for producing and directing *Chisholm '72: Unbought & Unbossed* based on the first female candidate, who was also African American, to run for president of the United States. Lynch received high praise in 2013 with the release of *Free Angela and All Political Prisoners*. She was born in Austin, Texas.

Movie documentary (producer and director): *Chisholm '72: Unbought & Unbossed* (2004)

Movie documentary (producer): *Frank Lloyd Wright* (1998)

Movie documentary (director): *The Talk: Race in America* (2017), *We The Economy: 20 Short Films You Can't Afford to Miss* (2014), *Free Angela and All Political Prisoners* (2012)

Television (producer): *Lessons from Little Rock: A National Report Card* (2008), *American Gangster* (two episodes) (2006, 2007), *Matters of Race* (2003), *Do You Believe in Miracles? The Story of the 1980 U.S. Hockey Team* (2001)

Television documentary (director): *Nine for IX*, "Runner" (2013)

Dee Rees (1977), writer, director, producer. In a bold move, Nashville, Tennessee–born Rees left her career in corporate marketing to pursue a passion for filmmaking. Already in possession of an MBA from Florida A&M University, Rees enrolled in the graduate film program at New York University. As part of her master's thesis, she wrote and directed the short film *Pariah* about an African American teen lesbian's search for identity. Out of submission to forty film festivals, the film won twenty-five awards. Mentored by filmmaker Spike Lee, Rees moved forward to make a full-length version of *Pariah* released in 2011 to exceedingly favorable reviews. Film industry stability followed the success of television movie *Bessie* (2015) and cinematic film, *Mudbound* (2017).

Awards: Film Independent Spirit Award (2018, 2012), Online Film & Television Association (2018), Black Film Critics Circle Award (2017),

Black Reel Award (2016), Directors Guild of America, USA (2016), Image Award (2016), Gotham Awards (2011), Sundance Film Festival Award (2011), Ashland Independent Film Festival Award (2008), Chicago Gay and Lesbian International Film Festival Award (2007), Los Angeles Film Festival Award (2007), Palm Springs International Short Fest (2007), San Francisco International Lesbian & Gay Film Festival (2007), Tribeca Film Festival Award (2007), Urbanworld Film Festival Award (2007)

Movie (producer, writer, director): *The Last Thing He Wanted* (2019), *Mudbound* (2017)

Documentary (producer, writer, director) *Eventual Salvation* (2008)

Movie (writer and director): *Pariah* (2011)

Television Movie (director, writer): *Bessie* (2015)

Cauleen Smith (1967), independent filmmaker, visual artist. Experimental in her approach to filmmaking, Smith is a proponent of the growing Afrofuturism movement. Afrofuturism bridges the connection between major historical events and celestial influence. Smith first gained notoriety as writer, producer, and director of the 1998 film *Drylongso*. Award-winning *Drylongso* is a study of a young woman balancing school, family, friends, and relationships. Born in Riverside, California, Smith received her BA in Cinema from San Francisco State University. Inspired by the legacy of LA Rebellion, she decided to pursue her MFA at University of California, Los Angeles. The musician Sun Ra, a creative influence for Smith, is quoted on a flyer that personifies her lectures stating, "You are all instruments. Everyone is supposed to be playing their part."

Awards: Independent Spirit Award (2000), Urbanworld Film Festival Award (2000), Hamptons International Film Festival Award (1998)

Movie (writer, director, producer): *Drylongso* (1998)

Movie shorts (director): *The Grid* (2011), *Remote Viewing* (2011), *I Want to See My Skirt* (2006), *The Changing Same* (2001), *Chronicles of a Lying Spirit* (1992)

Television movie (producer): *Don't Mess with Sketches* (2006)

Melvin Van Peebles (1932), actor, director, producer, screenwriter, playwright, book author. Van Peebles is looked upon as a pioneer of the

Blaxploitation film renaissance as a result of writing, directing, producing, starring, editing, and composing the soundtrack for the movie *Sweet Sweetback's Baadasssss Song* in 1971. He started making film shorts as early as 1957. Recognition at the San Francisco Film Festival for the independent film *The Story of a Three-Day Pass* in 1968 led to Van Peebles directing and composing a soundtrack for studio-driven film *Watermelon Man* in 1970. Though *Sweet Sweetback* was a mega success, contracts to do studio-driven films did not materialize, so Van Peebles turned to the Broadway stage. In 1972, he reaffirmed his writing talent with the productions of *Ain't Supposed to Die a Natural Death* and *Don't Play Us Cheap*. Born in Chicago, Illinois, he acquired his initial exposure to business working in his father's tailor shop. Prior to leading an exceedingly adventurous life, Van Peebles graduated from Ohio Wesleyan University with a BA in English Literature. Immediately after graduation, he served in the United States Air Force as a navigator bombardier. Upon completion of producing and acting in the television movie *The Sophisticated Gents* in 1981, Van Peebles took time to focus on Wall Street and became the first African American trader at the American stock exchange. He later wrote a how-to book, *Bold Money: A New Way to Play the Options Market*, and formed his own municipal-bonds firm.

Awards: African-American Film Critics Association (2010, 2008), Gotham Award (2008), Los Angeles Pan African Film Festival Award (2004), Acapulco Black Film Festival Award (2000), Chicago Underground Film Festival Award (1999), Daytime Emmy Award (1987), Humanitas Prize (1987)

Movies: *Confessionsofa Ex-Doofus-Itchyfooted Mutha* (director, writer, Producer, 2008), *Bellyful* (composer, director, writer, producer), *Panther* (writer, producer, actor,1995), *Identity Crisis* (director, writer, editor, actor, producer, 1989), *Don't Play Us Cheap* (composer, director, writer, editor, producer,1973), *Sweet Sweetback's Baadasssss Song* (1971), *Watermelon Man* (composer, director, Actor,1970), *The Story of a Three-Day Pass* (composer, director, Writer, 1968)

Movies (actor): *Peebles* (2013), *We the Party* (2012), *Redemption Road* (2010), *Blackout* (2007), *The Hebrew Hammer* (2003), *Posse* (1993), *Boomerang* (1992), *True Identity* (1991), *America* (1986)

Television: *Unstoppable: Conversation with Melvin Van Peebles,*

Gordon Parks, and Ossie Davis (TV documentary, composer, 2005), *Classified X* (documentary, writer, producer,1998), *Gang in Blue* (TV movie, director, producer, actor,1996), *Sonny Spoon* (TV series, actor, 1988), *The Sophisticated Gents* (TV movie, writer, producer, actor, 1981)

Kevin Willmott (1959), writer, director, producer, activist, educator. As a filmmaker, Willmott's approach is bold exposé. He first drew attention as the writer, director, producer, and actor in *Ninth Street* in 1999. He achieved critical acclaim for his feature *C.S.A.: The Confederate States of America* in 2004. He teamed with Spike Lee on a couple projects and achieved major film success for his screenplays *BlacKkKlansman* (2018) and *Chi-Raq* (2015). As a child who attended the movies every weekend, Blaxploitation and other film genres influenced Willmott. He graduated from Marymount College with a BA in Drama. He earned his MFA in Dramatic Writing from Tisch School of the Arts, New York University. Many of his films are shot in the midwestern United States, taking advantage of the best local talent. He has also written screenplays for Oliver Stone and NBC and had professional actors such as Isaac Hayes, Martin Sheen, and James McDaniel come on board to act in his independent films. Willmott is an associate professor of film studies at the University of Kansas. He grew up in Junction City, Kansas.

Awards: American Indian Film Festival (2009), Santa Fe Film Festival (2009), BendFilm Festival (2005)

Movie (producer, director, actor): *Destination Planet Negro* (2013)
Movie (director, writer): *Jayhawkers* (2014)
Movie (producer, director): *The Only Good Indian* (2009)
Movie (producer, writer, director): *The Battle for Bunker Hill* (2008)
Movie (writer, producer): *Chi-Raq* (2015)
Movie (writer): *BlacKkKlansman* (2018)
Movie (producer, writer, director, actor): *Ninth Street* (1999)
Television: *High Tech Lincoln* (TV documentary, producer, 2005), *The '70s* (writer, 2000)

Billy Woodberry (1950), independent filmmaker. An alumnus of the Los Angeles School of Black Filmmakers (a.k.a. LA Rebellion) at the University of California, Los Angeles, Woodberry is highly praised for his interpretation of slice-of-life urban drama. His award-winning 1984 film *Bless Their Little Hearts* continually premiers at film festivals, which pay homage to the best of the genre. Woodberry has participated in narration of the provocative documentaries *Spirits of Rebellion: Black Film at UCLA* in 2011 and *Red Hollywood* in 1996. His 2015 documentary, *And when I die, I won't stay dead* focuses on the life and work of beat poet, Bob Kaufman. Woodberry was born in Dallas, Texas, and graduated from University of California, Los Angeles film/television department with an MFA degree in production.

Awards: Doclisboa International Film Festival (2015), Berlin International Film Festival, (two categories, 1984), Amiens International film Festival (1983)

Movie (editor, producer, and director): *Bless Their Little Hearts* (1984)

Movie short (writer, editor, producer, and director): *The Pocketbook* (1980)

Movies (actor): *When It Rains* (short) (1995), *Ashes and Embers* (1982)

Documentary (producer, director): *And when I die, I won't stay dead* (2015)

LIST OF HONORABLE MENTIONS

Film, television enthusiasts and students may want to check the plethora of additional information available for those listed in 'honorable mentions' and those profiled in the book.

James Edwards (1918-1970) actor, screenwriter,
    MA in Drama, Northwestern University*
Tyler Perry, director, writer, producer, actor
Shonda Rhimes, producer, writer, director *
Danny Glover, actor, producer, activist
Jordan Peele, actor, writer, producer
Barry Jenkins, director, writer, producer*
Donald Glover, actor, soundtrack, writer*
Tarell Alvin McCraney, writer, actor, producer*
Will Packer, producer, actor*
Bradford Young, Cinematographer*
Tiffany Haddish, actress, writer, producer
Issa Rae, producer, actress, writer*
Sterling K. Brown, actor *
Mahershala Ali, actor *
Trevante Rhodes*
Joi McMillon, film editor*
Corey Hawkins, actor*
André Holland, actor*
*indicates who are college graduates

LIST OF HONORABLE MENTIONS: INTERNATIONAL

Abderrahmane Sissako, director, writer, producer
Adama Drabo, writer, director, producer
Ahmed Rachedi, director, writer, producer
Djibril Diop Mambéty, director, writer, actor
Flora Gomes, director, writer
Gavin Hood, actor, director, producer
Issa Serge Coelo, director, writer, editor, producer
Jean-Marie Téno, director, writer, producer, educator
Jean-Pierre Bekolo, director, writer, editor, educator
Jihan El-Tahri, director, producer, writer*
John Akomfrah, director, writer, educator*
Kwaw Ansah, directory, writer, producer*
Mahamat Saleh Haroun, director, writer, producer, cinematographer
Malika Zouhali-Worrall, director, writer, editor, producer*
Mama Keïta, director, writer, producer
Mansour Sora Wade, director, writer, producer*
Med Hondo, actor, director, writer
Mohammed Lakhdar-Hamina, director, writer, producer
Moussa Sène, director, writer, actor, producer, painter, music composer
Moussa Touré, director, writer, actor
Newton I. Aduaka, director, writer, producer
Ola Balogun, director, writer*
Ousmane Sembène, director, writer, producer
Paulin Vieyra, director, actor, production manager, writer, editor, producer*
Ramadan Suleman, producer, director, writer*
S. Pierre Yameogo, director, writer, producer
Souleymane Cissé, director, writer, producer
Tunde Kelani, director, producer, cinematographer*

Zézé Gamboa, sound department, director, writer
Zola Maseko, Director, writer, producer*
Tsitsi Dangarembga, writer director, producer, novelist
Yamina Benguigui, writer, director, producer, politician
Mati Diop, actress, director, cinematographer
Sarah Maldoror, director, writer
Abdoulaye Ascofare, director, writer, editor, poet*
John Kani, actor, writer, director
Dani Kouyaté, director, writer, actor*
Kollo Sanou, director, writer, producer
Peres Owino, actress, writer, producer
Frances Bodomo, writer, director*
Jim Chuchu, writer, director, editor
Rehad Desai, producer, director, writer*
Biyi Bandele, writer, director, producer, novelist

*indicates who are college graduates

BIBLIOGRAPHY
BOOKS

Bogle, Donald. *Toms, Coons, Mulattoes, Mammies, and Bucks: An Interpretive History of Blacks in American Films*. New York: the Continuum Publishing Company, 1989.

Bowser, Pearl and Louise Spence. *Writing Himself into History: Oscar Micheaux, His Silent Films, and His Audiences*. New Jersey: Rutgers University Press, 2000.

Bowser, Pearl, Jane Gaines, and Charles Musser, eds. *Oscar Micheaux and His Circle: African-American Filmmaking and Race Cinema of the Silent Era*. Bloomington, IN: Indiana University Press, 2001.

Field, Syd. *Screenplay: The Foundation of Screenwriting: A Step-by-Step Guide from Concept to Finished Script*. New York: Dell Publishing Co. Inc., 1984.

Green, Ronald. *With a Crooked Stick: The Films of Oscar Micheaux*. Bloomington, IN: Indiana University Press, 2004.

Hughes, Langston and Milton Meltzer. *Black Magic: A Pictorial History of the Negro in American Entertainment*. Englewood Cliffs, New Jersey: Prentice-Hall Inc., 1967.

Kisch, John and Edward Mapp. *A Separate Cinema: Fifty Years of Black-Cast Posters*. New York: Farrar, Straus, and Giroux, 1992.

McGilligan, Patrick. *Oscar Micheaux: The Great and Only: The Life of America's First Black Filmmaker*. New York: HarperCollins Publishers, 2007.

Patterson, Lindsay. *Black Films and Film-Makers: A Comprehensive Anthology from Stereotype to Superhero*. Cornwall, NY: Cornwall Press Inc., 1975.

Rhines, Jesse Algeron. *Black Film/White Money*. New Brunswick, New Jersey: Rutgers University, 1996.

Richards, Larry. *African American Films Through 1959: A Comprehensive, Illustrated Filmography*. Jefferson, NC: McFarland & Company Inc. Publishers, 2005.

Ross, Karen. *Black and White Media: Black Images in Popular Film and Television*. Cambridge, MA: Polity Press in association with Blackwell Publishers Ltd., 1996.

Berry, Torriano S. and Venise T. Berry. *Historical Dictionary of African American Cinema*. Lanham, MD: Scarecrow Press Inc., 2007.

WEBSITES

interactives.theroot.com/root-100-2017/
cineuropa.org/en/interview/334375/
Encyclopedia.com
achievement.org/autodoc/page/win0bio-1
africultures.com
answers.com.
askmen.com.
avaduvernay.com.
blackstuntmensassociation.com/members.html
blaxploitation.com/start.html
bloombergbusinessweek.com.
bombmagazine.org/article/5111/cauleen-smith
boris-world.com/
britannica.com.
charlesmicheaux.wordpress.com.
chickpeida.com.
cleveland.com/movies/.../east_cleveland_native_abdul_wi.html
culturebase.net
Dvrepublic.com
imdb.com.
in.com.
independent.co.uk/.
latimes.com.
lib.jmu.edu/smad/aadirectors.aspx. (African American Directors Guide, James Madison University Libraries & Educational Technologies).
lukeford.net/profiles/profiles/doug_mchenry.htm
mahoganycafe.com
maliksayeed.com/bio.

mts.lib.uchicago.edu/collections/findingaids/index. (Etta Moten profile)
newyorkdaileynews.com. (George Jackson, Producer)
newyorktimes.com
nicloeariparkeronline.com/
nndb.com.
ossieandruby.com/ (Ruby Dee)
parade.condenast.com/.../sunday-with-octavia-spencerthe-help-changed-my-life-and-my-perspective/
popsugar.com/Who-Lupita-Nyongo-33543323
shadowandact.com. (a.k.a. www.indiewire.com.)
shmoop.com.
showtimes.com.
shquilleoneal.com.
skillwho.com/Kevin+Willmot,+Alex+Heard+Interview
smu.edu/newsinfo/releases/01062.html (Regina Taylor).
spelman.edu
syrichardson.com/
tavissmiley.pbs.org.
thehistorymakers.com.
thehollywoodreporter.com (AderperoOduye)
thewashingtonpost.com. (Nate Parker)
tribute.ca.
usatoday.com/experience/.../vip-tatyanaali.../8076155/
wikipeidia.org.
yahoomovies.com.
*Websites researched June 2012–August 2018

Index

Actors

Ali, Tatyana	1
Allen, Debbie	2
Amos, John	3
Avery, Margaret	4
Aytes, Rochelle	5
Bassett, Angela	6
Beach, Michael	7
Beals, Jennifer	8
Bell, Darryl	9
Bellamy, Bill	9
Bledsoe, Tempest	10
Boseman, Chadwick	10
Braugher, Andre	11
Brooks, Golden	12
Browne, Roscoe Lee	12
Calloway, Vanessa Bell	13
Cedric The Entertainer	14
Charles, Gaius	15
Cheadle, Don	16
Chestnut, Morris	17
Cumbuka, Ji-Tu	18
Davis, Viola	19
Dee, Ruby	20
Devine, Loretta	22
Diggs, Taye	23
Dixon, Ivan	24
Dobson, Tamara	25
Duke, Bill	26
DuPois, Starletta	27
Dutton, Charles	28
Ealy, Michael	30

178

Elise, Kimberly 30
Fox, Vivica A. 31
Franklin, Carl. 32
Freeman Jr., Al 33
Givens, Robin 34
Gossett Jr, Louis. 35
Grier, David Alan 36
Gunn, Moses 38
Hall, Arsenio 39
Hall, Regina 39
Hamilton, Lisa Gay 40
Hardwick, Omari 41
Harewood, Dorian. 42
Harper, Hill. 42
Harris, Steve 44
Harris, Wood 44
Hayes, Reginald
"Reggie" C 45
Haysbert, Dennis 45
Henson, Taraji P 47
Hooks, Robert 48
Hudson, Ernie 49
Jackson, Samuel L. 50
James, Steve 51
Jenkins, Terrence "J". 52
Johnson, Anne-Mari 52
Johnson, Dwayne "The
Rock" Johnson 53
Jones, James Earl. 54
Jones, Rashida 56
Kelly, Paula 57
Kodjoe, Boris 58
La Salle, Eriq. 58
Lathan, Sanaa 59
Lennix, Harry 60
Lindo, Delroy 61

Little, Cleavon 62
Lumbly, Carl 62
Mackie, Anthony 63
Merkerson, S. Epatha 64
Moore, Melba 65
Moore, Shemar 66
Morton, Joe 67
Nicholas, Denise 67
Nunn, Bill 68
Oduyle, Adepero 69
Parker, Nate 69
Parker, Nicole Ari 70
Parker, Paula Jai 71
Patton, Paula 72
Peete, Holly Robinson 72
Poitier, Sydney Tamiia 73
Pulliam, Keshia Knight 74
Rashad, Phylicia 75
Reid, Daphne a.k.a Reid,
Daphne Maxwell 76
Reid, Tim 77
Rhames, Ving 78
Richardson, LaTanya 79
Richardson, Sy 80
Robinson, Wendy Raquel 81
Ross, Tracee Ellis 81
Rudolph, Maya 82
Sharp, Keesha 83
Simmons, Henry 83
Smith, Anna Deavere 84
Smith, Kellita 85
Smith, Roger Guenveur 86
Snipes, Wesley 87
Spencer, Octavia 87
Taylor, Regina 88

Thigpen, Lynne 89
Thomas, Sean Patrick 90
Torry, Guy 91
Torry, Joe 91
Toussaint, Lorraine, ... 92
Union, Gabrielle 93
Vance, Courtney B. 94
Van Peebles, Mario 95
Warren, Michael 96
Washington, Denzel 97
Washington, Kerry 98
Wayans, Kim 99
Whitaker, Forest 100
Whitfield, Lynn 102
Williams, Cynda 103
Williams, Vanessa L. 103
Woodard, Alfre 105
Wright, Jeffrey 106

Early Pioneers of Cinema

Hurston, Zora Neale 115
Moten, Etta 115
Norman, Maidie 116
Robeson, Paul 117
Whipper, Leigh 118

From Athlete to Cinema

Abdul-Jabbar, Kareem 109
Brown, Jim 110
Crews, Terry 111
O'Neal, Shaquille 111
Weathers, Carl 112
Williamson, Fred 113

The Independent Filmmakers

Burnett, Charles.. 161
Davis, Zeinabu 162
Du Vernay, Ava... 163
Gerima, Haile 164
Grant, Laurens... 165
Lynch, Shola.. 165
Rees, Dee.. 166
Smith, Cauleen 167
Van Peebles, Melvin.. 167
Willmott, Kevin... 169
Woodberry, Billy 169

International Talent Established In the United States and Indigenous African Cinema (Folk Life)

Akinnuoye-Agbaje Adewale.. 121
Faye, Safi.. 121
Sanaa Hamri 122
Harewood, David 123
Jean-Baptiste, Marianne 123
Kabore', Gaston 124
Gugu, Mbatha-Raw 125
McQueen III, Steve 125
Nacro, Fanta Regina... 126
Newton, Thandie 127
Nyong'o, Lupita.. 128
Ouedraogo, Idrissa 129
Oyelowo, David 130
Palcy, Euzhan 130
Pounder, CCH 131
Sinclair, Madge 132

Producers, Directors, Screenwriters, and Cinematographers

Akil, Mara Brock. 135
Akil, Salim 136
Allain, Stephanie 136
Bythewood, Reggie
"Rock"..137
Chase, Debra Martin 138
Coogler, Ryan..139
Cundieff, Rusty 139
Dash, Julie 140
Dickerson, Ernest 141
Edmonds, Tracey...142
Fanaka, Jamaa 143
Hudlin, Reginald 143
Hudlin, Warrington 144
Isaacs, Cheryl Boone...145
Jackson, George 145
Jakes, T.D...146
King, Jr., Woodie 147
Lee, Spike...148
Martin, Darnell 150
McHenry, Doug...150
Mitchell, Elvis..151
Parks, Suzan-Lori 151
Prince-Blythewood, Gina 152
Ridley, John..153
Sayeed, Malik Hassan 154
Singleton, John..154
Story, Tim...155
Tillman Jr., George 156
Wesley, Richard...157
Williams, Abdul...157
Winfrey, Oprah

Review Questions*

1. Name three film industry occupations.

2. Name three film genres.

3. Why is advanced education a great equalizer?

4. Name nine of your favorite profiles in the book and why.

5. List three types of undergraduate degrees.

6. List three types of graduate degrees.

7. Is a college degree necessary for everyone? Yes or No

8. Name a skilled training that can be lucrative while pursuing a solid foundation in the arts.

9. Name three of the book's profiles whose project you enjoyed that is not mentioned in the book and the name of the project.

www.ingramcontent.com/pod-product-compliance
Lightning Source LLC
Chambersburg PA
CBHW051432290426
44109CB00016B/1527